NO LONGER PROPERTY OF
FALVEY MEMORIAL LIBRARY

10

D1372012

# Language and
# Communication
# in the Elderly

# The Boston University
# Series in Gerontology

## Boston University Gerontology Center

The Gerontology Center is a multidisciplinary organization that integrates the biological, psychological, socioeconomic, medical, and humanistic concerns of aging and of the elderly.

*Public Policies for an Aging Population*
   edited by Elizabeth Markson and Gretchen Batra
*Language and Communication in the Elderly*
   edited by Loraine K. Obler and Martin L. Albert

# Language and Communication in the Elderly

## Clinical, Therapeutic, and Experimental Issues

Edited by
**Loraine K. Obler**
**Martin L. Albert**
Boston University
Medical School and
Boston Veterans Administration
Medical Center

**LexingtonBooks**
D.C. Heath and Company
Lexington, Massachusetts
Toronto

**Library of Congress Cataloging in Publication Data**

Main entry under title:
   Language and communication in the elderly.

   1. Language disorders—Age factors.   2. Communicative disorders—
Age factors.   3. Geriatrics.   I. Obler, Loraine K.   II. Albert, Martin L.
RC423.L33        618.97′6855        80-5348
ISBN 0-669-03868-7

*Copyright © 1980 by D.C. Heath and Company*

All rights reserved. No part of this publication may be reproduced or transmitted in any form or by any means, electronic or mechanical, including
photocopy, recording, or any information storage or retrieval system, without
permission in writing from the publisher.

Published simultaneously in Canada

Printed in the United States of America

International Standard Book Number: 0-669-03868-7

Library of Congress Catalog Card Number: 80-5348

RC
423
L33

To the memory of
*Clementina Allenby Dworsky and Philip Dworsky,
Augusta Wiener Obler and David Obler,
my grandparents—LKO*

*To Phyllis Cohen Albert—MLA*

11/24/81 YP 22.95

480313

# Contents

# Foreword

The frequently cited growth in the number and proportion of older persons and the projection of increases in this change in age demography have become commonplace. It is easy to overlook the implication of this fairly dramatic change in population. Older persons are at risk for a number of serious medical, psychiatric, and neurological disabilities, and also regarding social and economic privations. The need for a significant improvement in our data base concerning normal aging and concerning the changes that occur in dementing illnesses of later life is thus manifest.

Clinical care of the elderly patient is now assuming a major portion of all health services. The quality of care ranges from the superlative to the inadequate depending on a variety of factors, including the interest and availability of physicians and other health-care personnel, the concerns and support of the community, and the recognition on the part of older persons and their families of the need for help. What has been lacking, however, is a well-studied data base that will enable us to examine more critically the belief systems about the elderly.

The neurologist, psychiatrist, and psychologist find themselves in a very peculiar position regarding the elderly patient. A common belief in the lay community, shared all too often by clinicians, is that of an inevitable decline in a variety of capacities, including cognition, leading to "senility." Nevertheless, behavioral scientists and clinicians alike who have focused their attention on the normal elderly and the older patient have found that there is complexity when dealing with an older person partly because the mythology is just that—mythology—and partly because the complex, higher central nervous system processes in the elderly remain largely unstudied. To that end the activities of Obler and Albert are to be commended. Communication in the elderly is one of the most salient issues faced by the clinician. Several years ago I was able to demonstrate that hearing loss in older men was largely responsible for apparent drops in cognitive capabilities and the alleged appearance of psychopathology. Similar results had been shown with the young before and were replicated with middle-aged and older persons subsequent to my study. Clearly the impairment in communication between older patients and health and social-service clinicians, between older persons and their families, and among older persons themselves, can have not only direct manifest consequences but also indirect consequences in changing the nature of interpersonal and perhaps intrapersonal style.

In order to assess the state of the art, it is important to range in focus from the very basic experimental work to its manifest behavioral and clinical work. It is important to note that the editors of this book have proceeded very much along this line. A most distinguished group of scientists and clinicians was assembled to address the problems of change in the elderly and the reflection of this change in pathological conditions. Their focus has been not only on the obvious issues of aphasia and other aspects of language problems but also on key issues in clinical communication and the neurological aspects of these disorders.

Each chapter in this book addresses an important problem, and if more questions are raised than answered, we must remember that this reflects the state of the art. Language structure and performance clearly change with age; we can only speculate on the basis of this change at this time. Since language is so crucial a factor in interpersonal communication, it seems clear that it must become a high priority for study. We need to understand not only the neural substructures of language but also the semantic nature of human thought and its change in relation to anticipated change in the cognitive structure that occurs with age. I am pleased to recommend this book to all students, be they scientists or clinicians, in the field of aging. I think it is an important work that should lead to considerably more interest and concern with a problem that has traditionally been underaddressed by the professional and scientific community.

*Carl Eisdorfer Ph.D., M.D.*
Professor and Chairman
Department of Psychiatry and
Behavioral Sciences
University of Washington
Seattle

# Preface

During the last decade much work has gone into the study of language and brain development for language at the early end of the developmental scale—in children—but little work has gone into studies of language development in the elderly. Of the research that has been conducted on language in the elderly, only a small part has considered neurological-behavioral correlates. Our purpose in this book is to provide a multidisciplinary background for discussion of the medical aspects of language and communication in the elderly, with an emphasis on neurobehavioral correlates.

To produce a multidisciplinary book focused on a single theme is always a risky business. The greatest risk is that representatives of the several disciplines will provide information of use only to specialists in their own disciplines—that there will be little or no continuity from one chapter to the next. At the other extreme is the possibility that several contributors, working in overlapping areas, will say the same thing. With respect to these two problems, we, as editors, have been particularly fortunate. The distinguished contributors to this book are not speaking only to their closest colleagues or their students, nor is there unwarranted overlap.

The book is organized into two sections: experimental and clinical, with rehabilitation being handled as a separate section after clinical diagnosis. The experimental section complements the clinical, and the diagnostic and observational parts of the clinical section lead naturally to a discussion of rehabilitation. The experimental section (part I) is devoted to the interaction between language and cognition in the elderly, discourse style, comprehension and naming difficulties in the elderly, and language lateralization over the life span. Two introductory chapters not specifically related to language provide an essential background review of general experimental concerns relative to the neuropsychology of aging and verbal memory in the elderly.

The clinical section (parts II and III) is devoted to issues of medical and psychiatric communication with the elderly, language patterns in normal and dementing elderly, aural rehabilitation, and language rehabilitation in dementia and in aphasic elderly. As in part I, there are two introductory chapters, not specifically related to language, that provide the neuroanatomical background and a review of clinical approaches to the neuropsychology of aging. Concluding this section is a synthesis and overview of key clinical issues.

We have selected contributors who could explore aspects of the unifying theme—the neurological basis of language in the elderly, considered in its broadest sense to include neurology, psychiatry, gerontology, neuropsychology, neurolinguistics, neuroanatomy, and related areas of speech and language rehabilitation. We are specifically concerned with the possible relationship between changes in the brain and changes in natural language use associated with processes of aging. This book is intended to serve as an introduction to issues of language and communication over the life span. Rather than a definitive statement, we view it as a background for further work in a discipline of growing importance.

We take this opportunity to thank the people and institutions that have helped us in putting this book together. We are particularly grateful to the individual authors, who have responded promptly with the various drafts of their manuscripts. Our own thinking on the topic of language in aging has been enriched by discussions with our colleagues in the Department of Neurology, Aphasia Research Center of Boston University School of Medicine and the Boston Veterans Administration Medical Center. Both the Veterans Administration and the National Institutes of Health have supported our research. The conference titled "Language and Communication in the Elderly," which stimulated this work, was supported in part by a grant from the National Institute of Aging and was sponsored by the Department of Neurology and the Gerontology Center of Boston University School of Medicine, as well as by the American Geriatrics Society. Drs. Robert Feldman, Daniel Bernstein, and Knight Steel of Boston University Medical School were helpful in facilitating that conference, as was Donna Marcy, and they should be formally thanked at this time.

# Introduction

*Loraine K. Obler* and
*Martin L. Albert*

To maximize the human potential of our healthy aging population and to plan effectively for long-term management of elderly persons with mental deterioration, we must have a clear understanding of neurological and behavioral changes that elderly persons, normal or senile, undergo. Language behavior is critical to all aspects of human mental functioning. One goal of this book is to help provide a comprehensive picture of the language behavior of normal and senile elderly persons.

A parallel can be drawn between the clinical and experimental studies being reported in this book and studies of aphasia performed over the last century. Studies on aphasia have demonstrated that once we understood the patterns of language activity of aphasic subjects, we could understand more clearly the neurologic basis of language. When these neurologic aspects of language disturbances were elaborated, effective therapy programs for aphasic patients were developed. We believe a similar outcome will be found in our studies of language in the elderly. That is, if language patterns of normal and demented elderly people are understood, we will have a better appreciation of underlying neurological mechanisms, which when elaborated, will allow us to embark on programs of therapy and long-term management beneficial to both the individual and society.

Two contradictory positions on language skills in the elderly can be abstracted from a representative corpus of the literature. One stance holds that language functions may survive intact while other cognitive functions (memory, visuo-spatial abilities) deteriorate. This view is supported by Riegel (1968), whose studies show that vocabulary skills, specifically the range of new words learned, and association patterns, may improve throughout the life span. The peer-scale-correlation factors for the 1958 Wechsler Adult Intelligence Scale (WAIS) also highlight the relative stability of verbal scores; verbal scores must be compensated for by fewer points than performance scores in the oldest group.

The second position holds that linguistic skills deteriorate in the elderly. For example, elderly people themselves may notice that they are having more trouble finding words, or younger people around them may complain about rambling discourse. Moreover, a certain subgroup of the elderly, the demented elderly, are clinically observed to have impaired language and speech. Their output may be paraphasic and echolalic (Seglas, 1892) and anomic, with a limited range of vocabulary (Critchley, 1964). Irigaray (1967, 1973) demonstrated via a series of psycholinguistic tests that demented

1

patients, like children, let syntagmatic constraints dominate paradigmatic constraints (for example, they may associate *dog* with *bark* rather than *cat*); and Tissot and others (1967) observed that the speech of demented patients might be elliptical while also being redundant and elaborated. For example, in naming a cup the patient might say "a cup for drinking coffee." Tissot and his colleagues argued that anomalous utterances were more a cognitive than a language problem, but that linguistic impairments such as verbal paraphasias and neologisms were also a part of dementia. In the category of demented linguistic impairment they included a phonetic "disintegration" similar to that seen in Broca's aphasia, and a tendency toward neologistic and verbal paraphasias similar to that seen in Wernicke's aphasia.

This paradox, whereby elderly subjects have been shown to perform both well and poorly on language tests, may be partially resolved by considering that different subject populations have been tested and for different sorts of linguistic skills, as will become apparent throughout this book. Different interpretations of the same results may also yield different conclusions. We note, for instance, that studies of language in healthy elderly subjects are often framed in terms of the question: "Is there or is there not deterioration in a certain (lexical) skill with aging?" One might rather choose to ask: "Do strategies of language use change with aging? And if so, how?" The difference between the two approaches can be seen when we consider possible interpretations of the data collected by Botwinick and Storandt (1974). They tested 107 subjects aged 20 through 79 on the WAIS vocabulary test which was scored according to two methods: for correctness and for quality of response. Although correctness did not deteriorate with increased age, use of the "optimal" quality response, the superior synonym, declined; the elderly tended to use a good explanation of several words instead of a single-word synonym. One might argue that this strategy of providing a good explanation for a word stimulus that is to be defined is not worse but only different from finding a single synonym. Providing a definition of several words might also be seen as an adaptive strategy in response to the word-finding difficulty associated with aging.

Research literature specifically concerned with language use in the elderly has focused on two areas: the language produced by demented patients, and the lexical skills of healthy elderly people. Yet the broader question of communication with older persons involves many disciplines. For example, geropsychiatrists, such as Post (1965) and Epstein (see his chapter in this book), have emphasized the roles of loneliness, dependency, and isolation in contributing to communication problems in the elderly. Speech pathologists and audiologists have looked at hearing difficulties. Hearing loss is a common age-related problem in Western society; Stevenson (1975) has shown that it can lead to difficulty in discriminating phonemes. Yet even elderly patients whose hearing is relatively "normal" may be processing speech in a different way than younger people. This is suggested in a study by Obusek and Warren (1973) in which "well preserved" elderly people heard fewer verbal transformations in a recording that repeated the same sound many times than did young adults. Differences between elderly with normal hearing and younger adults were also seen in a study by Bergman et al. (1976) who found that although both groups responded equally well to control tapes of normal speech, the elderly showed worse comprehension when listening to tapes with various forms of degraded speech.

In this book we address a broad range of issues relating to language and communication in the elderly. We decided first to bring together at a conference clinicians and researchers working in several disciplines dealing with our topic, and from that conference to prepare this book. Both the conference and this book have focused on how and why language use changes in the elderly population; and how we may improve our own skills for effectively communicating with older people. Do changes in language use result from neurologically induced alterations in linguistic competence and/or performance? To what extent are deficiencies in language production or perception the result of factors related to cognition, emotion, physical health, and social expectation? Is a progressive language impairment necessarily linked to aging processes? To answer these questions we have assembled contributions from specialists in a variety of disciplines. One of the strengths of this book, we believe, is the diversity of attitude, approach, and opinion presented.

## References

Bergman, M., Blumenfeld, V.G., Cascardo, D., Dash, B., Levitt, H., and Margulies, M.R. Age-related decrement in hearing for speech. *Journal of Gerontology* 31: 533-38, 1976.

Botwinick, J., and Storandt, M. Vocabulary ability in later life. *Journal of Genetic Psychology* 125: 303-308, 1974.

Critchley, M. The neurology of psychotic speech. *British Journal of Psychiatry* 110: 353-64, 1964.

Irigaray, L. Approche psycho-linguistique du langage des déments. *Neuropsychologia* 5: 25-52, 1967.

———. *Le Langage des Déments*. The Hague: Mouton, 1973.

Obusek, C.J., and Warren, R.M. A comparison of speech perception in senile and well preserved aged by means of the verbal transformation effect. *Journal of Gerontology* 28: 184-88, 1973.

Post, F. *The Clinical Psychiatry of Late Life*. London: Pergamon Press, 1965.

Riegel, K.F. Changes in psycholinguistic performances with age. *Human Aging and Behavior*, edited by G. Talland, pp. 239-79. New York: Academic Press, 1968.

Séglas, J. *Des troubles du langage chez les aliénés*. Paris: Rueff, 1892.

Stevenson, P.W. Responses to speech audiometry and phonemic discrimination patterns in the elderly. *Audiology* 14: 185-231, 1975.

Tissot, R., Richard, J., Duval, F. and Ajuriaguerra, J. de. Quelques aspects du langage des démences dégénératives du grand age. *Acta Neurologica Psychiatrica Belgica* 67: 911-23, 1967.

Wechsler, D. *The Measurement and Appraisal of Adult Intelligence*. Baltimore: Williams and Wilkins, 1958.

# Part I
# Experimental Issues

# 1 Cognitive Development in Aging

*K. Warner Schaie*

The function of this chapter is threefold. First, I want to raise several methodological cautions that are needed to place into proper perspective some of the interesting findings and interpretations on language in aging presented elsewhere in this book. Second, I will present a broad overview of what seems to be the state of the art on cognitive development from adulthood into old age as seen from the psychometric point of view. Since both topics can best be related by examining a specific data base, I will draw heavily on the longitudinal-sequential work done by me and my associates. Third, I will try to relate my work more specifically to the narrower objectives of this book by examining in some detail the differential developmental course of two primary mental abilities: verbal meaning and word fluency. The former is a classical marker for crystallized ability and a well-accepted measure of recognition vocabulary; the latter's factorial place is not as clear, but it has a long history as a measure of vocabulary recall. My examination will therefore refer to the hierarchical model of adult development presented by crystallized-fluid theory as well as the possible relevance of our data to studies being done on memory for meaningful materials involving the reported differential age patterns for recognition and recall as retrieval paradigms.[1]

## Some Methodological Cautions

Although the study of age variables has been addressed time and again, unfortunately further repetition and explication is required because it still yields many surprises for the initiate and generates much misunderstanding and misuse for the new entrant to the field of gerontology. I am speaking of the status of age as an explanatory concept, the distinction between age changes and age differences, the kind of data that can allow inferences with respect to one or the other, and further the matter of how to define our target population, the elderly. I will also comment on the interpretation of test norms and other related concerns that arise when trying to obtain valid psychometric data on elderly clients or research participants.

*Age as an Explanatory Concept*

Let me begin by emphatically stating that chronological age per se cannot "cause" or be the direct antecedent condition for anything. A person's chronological age merely defines the time span from entry into the environment to the date of assessment. Nevertheless, age, like other index variables, may have some utility in defining the probability of occurrence of certain events that have an ordered incremental or decremental sequence at specific life stages. It is important here to distinguish between time-dependent variables, where the point of origin may be a date other than birth, and age-related variables, which seem generally to be ordered along the chronological time frame. In principle, however, other causal antecedents must always be substituted whenever an age change or age difference has been identified. In current research practice, it is common to identify variance that results from aging only after that which occurs because of differences in education, socioeconomic status, or health has been eliminated. Indeed, it has often been proposed that chronological age ought to be used as the dependent rather than independent variable, a notion prominent, for example, in discussions of functional age (Baltes and Willis, 1977; Schaie and Parr, 1980; Wohlwill, 1973).

*Age Changes and Age Differences*

Whether or not changes in cognitive behavior in adulthood can indeed be found in specific age ranges is often a matter of understanding the kind of information that can be obtained from different data sets. Most of the earlier studies involve the cross-sectional method where, at one point in time, individuals are compared from two or more age groups that, by definition, must belong to different birth cohorts and consequently will have had different life experiences. Longitudinal studies, by contrast, compare the same individuals over two or more points in time. The cross-sectional method confounds ontogenetic change with generational differences, whereas longitudinal studies compare ontogenetic change with the effects of sociocultural change occurring between times of measurement. These confounds are substantial for most behavioral variables. It is therefore unlikely that findings of cross-sectional age differences will agree fully with longitudinal age changes (Schaie, 1965, 1967, 1977). Many age differences reported in the literature could more parsimoniously be interpreted as generational differences, and results from single-cohort longitudinal studies of human behavior are primarily historical accounts of the life history of a particular generation (Schaie, 1972; Schaie and Gribbin, 1975).

Several alternative strategies, known as sequential methods, have been suggested to deal with these problems. Sequential methods make it possible to estimate the effects of age, cohort, and historical periods more precisely (see the references at the end of this chapter for more detail). Here I wish to reaffirm that results from studies which do not use methods appropriate to the question asked can only be generalized in a limited fashion. That is, cross-sectional studies are not likely to show how individuals have changed in the past, and simple longitudinal studies do not project accurately how people are likely to change in the future.

*Should We Study Aging or the Aged?*

Gerontologists seem to be divided among those whose primary interest is in the process of adult development and those whose major concern is the end product of such development, the elderly. One group of investigators, therefore, tends to be interested in changes occurring past a maturational asymptote, say in the early twenties, and pursues such changes until that stage, perhaps no later than the early seventies, where a substantial number of individuals can be found that are reasonably free from confounding pathology. The other group of investigators is more likely to begin the study with individuals who are in their fifties, and continue to an age level where subjects who are still assessable can be found. Botwinick (1977) has suggested that those who focus on the earlier "developmental" ages tend to believe there is no decline, whereas those who focus primarily on the later years generally argue that there is decline.

The major concern, however, is not simply whether decline can be demonstrated on some variables in some individuals; for it must be recognized that there may be some variables on which there is little or no decrement, and some individuals who may show little or no decrement on most variables into very old age (Baltes and Schaie, 1976; Schaie, 1974). What must be clearly in mind then is the question to be asked and the model subsumed (Schaie, 1973). Curiously, however, it is the basic age-function-oriented research which can surely rely on study of that part of the life span, say, beginning with the late fifties, where some reliable age changes can be found for at least some variables in many people, while it is the policy-oriented researcher, who must predict population changes in the future, who will be most concerned with the full adult age span in order to discover the generational differences of individuals in young adulthood and mid-life in order to predict the characteristics of the future.

Another related matter is sample selection. Just as experimental psychologists have often been accused of forging a science of the albino rat and the sophomore psychology student, so have gerontologists been accused of basing much of their knowledge on inhabitants of nursing homes and domiciliaries, frequenters of senior centers, and on catch-as-catch-can community-based samples. Clearly defined subpopulations with special characteristics are most useful, but they can only contribute much when compared against populations selected by a carefully stratified random sampling of a reasonably broad universe (Schaie, 1978). In work with the elderly there preferably should be knowledge of the research participants' health status. Only then can a knowledgeable decision be made as to whether one wishes to describe age changes in individuals with an incidence of pathology comparable to that found in the general population, or whether one wants to study a process in samples that are free from specified pathology (the well elderly), or to assess the influence of a particular disease entity or syndrome, such as cardiovascular disease.

## The Aging of Test Norms

Practitioners and researchers alike often call for the development of appropriate age norms on common marker variables of cognitive function. Such norms are clearly necessary and desirable, but the researcher must be aware that before the norms can be meaningful, it must first be established that the test is age appropriate. This matter has been studied for some time with respect to the early developmental stage, but only recently have there been some efforts to develop tests that will retain the construct validity of measures developed for the young while dealing with the response characteristics of the old. It should be stressed here, however, that there is no assurance a given test will remain appropriate for a particular age level. Because of changes in cultural content and context, tests do become obsolete rather quickly. However, they may retain their validity for a given population cohort throughout much of the lifespan, while being less appropriate for successive cohorts. Thus, the Wechsler-Bellevue I may be more appropriate for people now in their seventies (who were in the standardization age range for that test in their thirties) than would be the current revision of the WAIS. Also we have found that the 1949 edition of the Primary Mental Abilities (PMA) used in our work has greater validity for older adults than do more recent revisions.

Let me suggest further that the use of the age-corrected norms can be quite misleading when the objective is to obtain some absolute assessment as to the level of function, whether in an age-neutral in- or out-selection procedure or for the definition of pathology that may be prevalent in old age but is not really consequent to time-dependent processes. For the latter purposes, it may be better to use comparisons with a target population thought to be at an optimal level or meeting minimally acceptable criteria (Schaie, 1979; Schaie and Parr, 1980).

## Cognitive Development from Adulthood to Old Age

There has been a good deal of recent controversy on the issue of whether and when intellectual abilities decline during the course of young adulthood to old age (Botwinick, 1977; Baltes and Schaie, 1976; Horn and Donaldson, 1976; Schaie and Baltes, 1977). Actually this controversy merely sharpens discussions that have been going on for some time and that depend heavily on the data base used for one's interpretation.

## State of the Art

Intelligence in adulthood does not follow a single course. Reliable decrement for all abilities or all individuals cannot be found until very old age (the late eighties). Beginning in mid-life, most individuals show minor decrement in those abilities which involve speed of response. Where measurement is particularly sensitive to relatively modest impairment of the peripheral nervous system, modest decrement will be seen by the early sixties. Decrement also is likely to be found in most abililties for individuals with severe cardiovascular disease at any age, and for those living in undifferentiated or socially deprived environments by their late fifties and early sixties.

Longitudinal and repeated-measurement sequential studies accurately estimate age changes for individuals in above-average health who live in favorable environmental conditions, but overestimate maintenance of performance levels for those living under less favorable conditions and in less-than-average health. Also, cross-sectional or independent samples sequential studies tend to exaggerate "normal" age decrements because they include individuals who perform at lowered levels, not because of age, but because of ability-related disease or life-style variables. Moreover, although age changes in cognitive functions within individuals are small compared to generational differences until the mid-sixties, from then on there is a mix of cohort and age effects, with age affects assuming increasing importance as the eighties are reached. Also, in healthy, well-educated populations many older individuals perform within the middle (average) range of young adults. Some adults show decrement in some abilities quite early in life, but others maintain their function well into advanced old age. Finally, it must be kept in mind that much of what is known about adult intelligence has been learned by studying older individuals with measures developed for the young. The complex interaction between intellectual ability and situational competence in advanced age, therefore, still remains to be explored within an ecologically valid framework.

## A Brief Review of the Literature

An early finding of interest to students of adult cognitive development comes from Yerkes's 1921 study of World War I soldiers. He reported that the apparent average level of mental function for young adults was only at about thirteen years of age. Terman's original standardization of the Binet Intelligence Test for American Use also assumed that intellectual development peaked at age sixteen and then remained constant (Terman, 1916). However, Jones and Conrad (1933), on the basis of cross-sectional studies in a New England community, showed substantial age differences across adulthood on some subtests of the Army Alpha Intelligence Test, but few differences on others.

Similar findings were obtained in the standardization studies connected with the development of the Wechsler-Bellevue Intelligence Test. Wechsler (1939) emphasized that growth of intelligence does not end in early adolescence, that peak ages are not the same for different aspects of intellectual functioning, and that age differences are not uniform across the full spectrum of abilities tapped by most of the major batteries measuring intellectual development. Matters were complicated further by the studies of Bayley and Oden (1955) and Owens (1953, 1959) showing that when individuals are followed longitudinally, growth or stability of intelligence continues into mid-life.

Much of the cognitive appraisal of older adults in clinical settings has been conducted with one or another version of the WAIS. Normative data for older persons on this test are therefore of considerable interest. The Wechsler tests first appeared in 1939, although normative data for individuals beyond age sixty were not published until 1955 (Doppelt and Wallace, 1955). Tables 1-1 lists age differences from early adulthood to late middle age. These age differences are consistent but not particularly remarkable considering that the mean of the standardization group is ten and its standard deviation three. Those differences which approach significance involve measures that are speeded, suggesting that constant time intervals become less and less adequate for the equitable assessment of psychological constructs in successive age groups. No significant age differences occur over the entire mid-life period for each of the power tests—information, comprehension, arithmetic, similarities, and vocabulary. Until age sixty or so, there is virtually no drop on the verbal scale but quite a sharp drop prevails on the performance scale.

Norms for the WAIS for ages sixty-five and older have been reported by Doppelt and Wallace (1955). These norms do show significant drop, even for the verbal scales, past the age of seventy. Substantial drop is most noteworthy again for the performance (speed-implicated) measures. The verbal-performance discrepancy seems well replicated and has been found across the sexes, racial groups, and different socioeconomic levels (Eisdorfer, Busse, and Cohen, 1959), and a greater-than-average drop in performance IQ has been implicated as a predictor of survival (Hall et al., 1972).

Although cross-sectional age comparisons of the WAIS imply speed-related age decrements beyond the fifties, it has generally been maintained

**Table 1-1**
**Subtest Performance on the Wechsler Adult Intelligence Test during Mid-Adulthood.**
(*Mean scores*)

| | Ages | | | | |
|---|---|---|---|---|---|
| Subtest | 20-24 | 25-34 | 35-44 | 45-54 | 55-64 |
| Verbal Scale | | | | | |
| Information | 9.8 | 10.3 | 10.3 | 9.9 | 9.9 |
| Comprehension | 10.0 | 10.2 | 10.2 | 9.9 | 9.6 |
| Arithmetic | 10.0 | 10.1 | 10.2 | 9.8 | 9.4 |
| Similarities | 10.2 | 10.1 | 9.2 | 9.0 | 9.0 |
| Digit span | 9.9 | 10.0 | 9.6 | 9.0 | 8.4 |
| Vocabulary | 9.6 | 10.3 | 10.4 | 10.1 | 10.1 |
| Performance Scale | | | | | |
| Digit symbol | 10.1 | 9.9 | 8.5 | 7.5 | 6.3 |
| Picture completion | 10.1 | 10.0 | 9.8 | 8.6 | 8.0 |
| Block design | 9.9 | 10.0 | 9.4 | 8.5 | 7.7 |
| Picture arrangement | 10.5 | 9.7 | 9.1 | 8.0 | 7.3 |
| Object assembly | 10.1 | 10.0 | 9.3 | 8.5 | 7.8 |

Source: Adapted from table 12.11 in Matarazzo (1972, p. 354).
Note: Each mean is based on N = 200.

that verbal performance on the WAIS continues unimpaired into old age. Botwinick and Storandt (1974) recently challenged this notion by giving the WAIS vocabulary test to individuals ranging in age from sixty-two to eighty-three years who were matched in quantitative scores on that test. Qualitative scoring revealed that the younger subjects excelled in superior synonyms (the only scoring category yielding an age difference). In a later study the authors nevertheless concluded that qualitative and quantitative age differences in vocabulary performance did not differ except for nuances of fine meaning (Botwinick, West, and Storandt, 1975).

Longitudinal data on changes in WAIS scores during a ten-year period have been reported by Eisdorfer and Wilkie (1975) for persons in their sixties and seventies each tested four times. Only an average of 2 score points for the performance and 0.6 score points for the verbal scales were lost during the ten years between the sixties and seventies. The larger total loss of 7.3 score points from the seventies to the eighties was about equally divided between the verbal and performance scales. Declines from the mid-sixties into the eighties have also been reported in a twenty-year study by Blum, Fosshage, and Jarvik (1972). By contrast, other studies on highly selected groups report little or no drop in the vocabulary score even into very advanced age (Gilbert, 1973; Green, 1969). Further discussions of the Wechsler test and its limitations in older populations may be found in Botwinick (1977), Schaie (1980b), and Schaie and Schaie (1977).

The Wechsler subtests are factorially complex. A better picture may be obtained from age difference data for the more clearly defined primary mental abilities (Thurstone and Thurstone, 1949). Figure 1-1 presents results of the first parametric study for this test over the age range from early adulthood to early old age (Schaie, 1958). Five abilities were systematically assessed: *verbal meaning*, a measure of recognition vocabulary; *space*, the ability to visualize mentally the rotation of geometric objects; *reasoning*, a measure of the ability to identify rules and serial principles; *number*, a test of numerical skills; and *word fluency*, a measure of vocabulary recall. The data shown here come from a study of twenty-five men and twenty-five women randomly selected in each five-year interval from ages twenty to seventy from the membership of a large metropolitan health-care plan. Only insubstantial age differences occur until about age fifty for space, reasoning, and verbal meaning and until age sixty for number and word fluency. For the latter, even at seventy the drop from peak does not exceed one standard deviation. Note also that adult ability peaks appear to be located primarily in the thirty-one- to thirty-five-year old group. (For further discussioh of historical changes in adult ability peaks, see Schaie, 1970.)

As was noted earlier, cross-sectional studies confound age changes with generational differences. Therefore it is important to examine age trends determined by following samples of the same individuals over time supple-

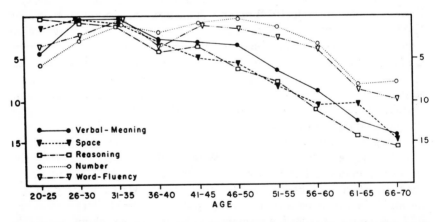

Source: K.W. Schaie, Rigidity-flexibility and intelligence: A cross-sectional study of the adult life span from 20 to 70. *Psychological Monographs* 72, no. 462 (1958). Copyright by the American Psychological Association. Reprinted by permission.

**Figure 1-1.** Mean Decrement in the Primary Mental Abilities from Mean Peak Level in T-Score Points from Cross-Sectional Data

mented by longitudinal studies based on independent samples, that is, successive samples drawn from the same birth cohort at different ages but each tested only once. Such data were obtained by retesting members of 1956 samples after seven, fourteen, and twenty-one years and obtaining new panels in 1963, 1970, and 1977 from the same population frame. The 1963 panel has been retested in 1970 and 1977, and the 1970 panel was retested in 1977.

From these data, let me first give you an example for the verbal meaning (recognition vocabulary) test for the initial fourteen years of our sequential study, based on the analysis of data for 300 persons followed from 1956 to 1963, 409 persons followed from 1963 to 1970, and 162 persons followed over the fourteen years from 1956 to 1970 (Schaie and Labouvie-Vief, 1974). Figure 1-2 plots the requisite data along a chronological age scale. The upper left quadrant of this figure shows the 1956 and 1963 cross-sectional studies as solid lines and the seven-year longitudinal studies as dotted lines. Note that there are gains for the younger cohorts up to age sixty, with some drop beyond that point. The lower left quadrant shows the replication of this study for the second sample followed from 1963 to 1979. The data are very similar except that drop does not occur before age sixty-

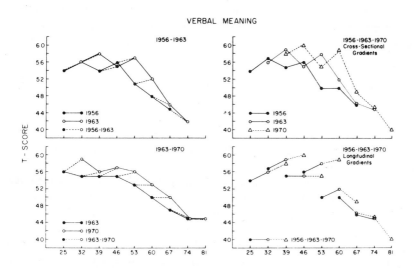

Source: From Schaie, K.W. and Labouvie-Vief, G. Generational versus ontogenetic components of change in adult cognitive behavior: A fourteen-year cross-sectional study. *Developmental Psychology* 10: 305-320 (1974). Copyright by the American Psychological Association. Reprinted by permission.

**Figure 1-2.** Mean Scores for Verbal Meaning from the Fourteen-Year Longitudinal Study

seven. The upper right quadrant shows the cross-sectional gradients for the three test occasions. These gradients lie on top of each other in orderly sequence, suggesting increments for younger cohorts at many ages. The lower left quadrant is perhaps the most interesting. The data shown there can be conceptualized as the simultaneous longitudinal study from 1956 to 1970 of seven cohorts, successively differing by seven years in average date of birth. The youngest cohort (average birth year, 1938) is followed from mean age twenty-five to thirty-nine; the oldest cohort (average birth year, 1889) is followed from age sixty-seven to age eighty-one, and so on. Note the prevalence of gain or stability until age sixty, modest decline until seventy-four, and steeper decline over the last seven-year period. Also note the obvious differences in cohort level, particularly the gap between the fourth and the fifth cohort.

Similar findings occurred for the other abilities studied. Statistically reliable decrement over a fourteen-year period was found for space and reasoning only for the oldest cohort from ages sixty-seven to eighty-one. No reliable fourteen-year change was found for number ability. Reliable age decrement for verbal meaning occurred for the two oldest cohorts beginning with age sixty. For word fluency, however, decrement was found for all but the two youngest cohorts, beginning from age thirty-nine to fifty-three. I will look at this discrepancy in development for the two vocabulary tests later in this chapter. Before doing so, however, I wish to call attention to the distinction between statistically reliable and practically significant age change.

*Cumulative Age Changes*

Although my work shows that statistically reliable age changes occur rather late, some critics have called attention to the possibility of the trend toward decrement starting earlier (Horn and Donaldson, 1976). I have tried to address this issue by computing cumulative age changes based on the average within subject changes from the 362 participants for whom fourteen-year data were available (Schaie and Hertzog, 1979). I have argued earlier that the practical implications of age change in cognitive function are best communicated when performance is charted at successive ages as a proportion of performance at a base age (Schaie, 1979; Schaie and Parham, 1977). In table 1-2, performance indexes are shown for ages thirty-two to eighty-one, where one hundred is the average performance level at age twenty-four. Note that by this criterion performance does not drop below the young adult level for verbal meaning until age eighty-one; for space, reasoning, and number until age seventy-four; but for word fluency it drops by age sixty.

Using average performance that remains at the young-adult average level as a criterion may be too severe for clinical use. A more lenient crite-

**Table 1-2**
**Estimated Performance Level as a Proportion of Performance at Age 25 Based on Cumulative Age Changes**
(*Decimals omitted; 100 = Average of 25-year-old comparison group*)

| Variable | 32 | 39 | 46 | 53 | 60 | 67 | 74 | 81 | 25th percentile at Age 25 |
|---|---|---|---|---|---|---|---|---|---|
| Verbal meaning | 108 | 110 | 112 | 112 | 113 | 108 | 102 | 85 | 86 |
| Space | 109 | 111 | 112 | 113 | 110 | 101 | 94 | 85 | 78 |
| Reasoning | 109 | 110 | 108 | 108 | 109 | 106 | 94 | 85 | 81 |
| Number | 116 | 111 | 114 | 107 | 108 | 100 | 93 | 70 | 74 |
| Word Fluency | 101 | 103 | 104 | 100 | 97 | 92 | 84 | 74 | 86 |

rion is suggested by psychometric tradition which assumes that performance within the middle 50 percent of the population is thought to be characteristic of average performance (Matarazzo, 1972, pp. 124-126). The lower boundary of this average range (twenty-fifth percentile) denotes the level below which an older group should fall before there has been sufficient decrement to conclude that the average member of the older group falls below the average range of the young comparison group. Table 1-2 indicates that a decrement of such magnitude is reached for word fluency at age seventy-four, for verbal meaning and number by age eighty-one, but that the average eighty-one-year-old is still within the average range of twenty-five-year-olds on space and inductive reasoning.

**Vocabulary Recognition and Recall**

The data and conclusions discussed in the previous section were restated to provide a general background on cognitive development in aging. In this last section, some new analyses are reported that relate directly to the issues addressed in this book. I have chosen to consider the very different developmental course of two of the variables systematically monitored over age and cohorts in our longitudinal study that seem to be most relevant to language behavior, namely, verbal meaning and word fluency.

There are several cogent reasons why one would expect diverging life courses for these abilities. But thus far in the empirical literature most of these premises have failed to receive proper attention because of the very different age patterns found in cross-sectional and longitudinal studies. First let me indicate the theoretical status of verbal meaning and word fluency within the context of current psychometric thinking.

*Verbal Meaning*

Within Guilford's (1967) structure of intellect model, this is defined as a prime example of cognitive semantic units. Within the crystallized-fluid model of Horn and Cattell (1966) it is an unambiguous marker of crystallized intelligence, *Gc* (Horn, 1978), although in earlier discussions some minor loading on a fluency factor (*F*) had been suggested (Horn, 1970). Further analysis suggests that the task of matching a stimulus word with a correct analogy from a set of multiple choices must also involve long-term memory for meaningful material as measured by a recognition paradigm. In this sense, developmental differences in performance would likely be affected by average cohort asymptotes in the acquisition of the vocabulary items contained in the test, but also by possible changes in the strength of the memory trace and in the operation of response bias (Kintsch, 1970). Since there is little evidence of age-related decrement in memory trace when a recognition task is involved (Craik, 1977), age differences on verbal meaning should primarily reflect cohort differences in vocabulary content (see also Gardner and Monge, 1977), whereas the small age changes are likely to be accountable as a function of difficulty with unfamiliar materials and cautiousness (Birkhill and Schaie, 1975).

*Word Fluency*

Within Guilford's schema this variable is designated as a marker for divergent-productive symbolic units. Earlier work by Horn and Cattell (1967) assigned word fluency to a simple fluency factor. More recently, however, Horn (1978) has elected to distinguish a verbal productive thinking factor (*VPT*) that seems quite similar to Guilford's description and seems to fit the salient characteristics of the word fluency task. It is important to mention here that whereas verbal meaning merely requires the matching of a stimulus to a limited number of alternatives, word fluency essentially requires minimally cued recall. According to Kintsch (1970) recall involves a search and retrieval process, the efficiency of which may depend on how well the material has been organized in memory. Since the task in word fluency is to list words beginning with a given letter of the alphabet, structural cues are quite limited. Younger individuals tend to superimpose search strategies, such as looking for numbers, names, or household objects that start with that letter, whereas older subjects are known to be less likely to use efficient classification strategies (for a detailed review of these issues see Schaie and Zelinski, 1980). It follows that adverse age changes in recall may be expected with increasing age, an observation supported by much of the literature on aging and memory (Craik, 1977), but such changes might not be clearly seen in cross-sectional studies because of concomitant adverse generation effects in educational practices that require memorization of verbal materials.

*Empirical Data*

To assess these predictions, I examined cross-sectional data on 2,810 people in the age range from twenty-two to eighty-four years arranged in subgroups by sex and age in seven-year intervals with mean ages from twenty-five to eighty-one years. These subjects were tested in the four waves of a longitudinal-sequential study from 1956 to 1977, and, of course, greater stability was obtained at the price of averaging at each age over four cohorts and times of measurement. Table 1-3 provides means and subsample sizes by sex and age for subjects combined across the sexes. Age differences behave as predicted, with overall differences between the youngest and oldest group amounting to approximately 1.7 standard deviations for verbal meaning, but only 1.1 standard deviations for word fluency. Women are slightly superior to men on both variables at all ages. Their range of age differences is similar to that of men for verbal meaning, but somewhat smaller for word fluency (standard deviation of 1.0 compared to 1.3).

The next step was to estimate comparable longitudinal age changes. This was done by relying on the most stable of the longitudinal samples, those 120 individuals on whom four assessment points were available. Age differences were averaged over all individuals available for a particular seven-year interval in order to average out cohort differences (see table 1-4).

**Table 1-3**
**Cross-Sectional Age Pattern for the Primary Mental Abilities of Verbal Meaning and Word Fluency**

| | Males | | | Females | | | Total | | |
|---|---|---|---|---|---|---|---|---|---|
| *Age* | *V* | *W* | *N* | *V* | *W* | *N* | *V* | *W* | *N* |
| 25 | 53.2 | 52.6 | 139 | 54.9 | 53.7 | 163 | 54.1 | 53.2 | 302 |
| 32 | 54.0 | 50.9 | 142 | 55.8 | 55.5 | 177 | 55.0 | 53.4 | 319 |
| 39 | 54.5 | 51.5 | 178 | 54.1 | 52.3 | 200 | 54.3 | 51.9 | 378 |
| 46 | 52.3 | 50.6 | 190 | 54.1 | 52.6 | 186 | 53.2 | 51.8 | 376 |
| 53 | 51.4 | 50.1 | 177 | 51.2 | 51.6 | 202 | 51.3 | 50.9 | 379 |
| 60 | 48.4 | 48.6 | 166 | 49.3 | 50.6 | 180 | 48.9 | 49.6 | 346 |
| 67 | 43.5 | 45.1 | 179 | 45.3 | 46.2 | 188 | 44.4 | 45.7 | 367 |
| 74 | 39.6 | 41.6 | 121 | 41.5 | 44.2 | 114 | 40.5 | 42.8 | 235 |
| 81 | 36.7 | 39.7 | 53 | 37.4 | 44.1 | 55 | 37.0 | 41.9 | 108 |

Scores scaled to a mean of 50 and standard deviation of 10 for the entire sample.
V = verbal meaning; W = word fluency; $N$ = sample size.

**Table 1-4**
**Longitudinal Age Pattern for the Primary Mental Abilities of Verbal Meaning and Word Fluency**

| | Males | | | Females | | | Total | | |
|---|---|---|---|---|---|---|---|---|---|
| Age | V | W | N | V | W | N | V | W | N |
| 25 | 52.0 | 51.6 | 8 | 57.2 | 53.4 | 9 | 54.8 | 52.6 | 17 |
| 32 | 54.4 | 52.3 | 15 | 58.3 | 50.6 | 19 | 56.5 | 52.1 | 34 |
| 39 | 55.8 | 50.5 | 24 | 60.5 | 47.9 | 31 | 58.2 | 48.8 | 55 |
| 46 | 56.5 | 47.8 | 39 | 59.1 | 47.9 | 44 | 57.8 | 47.7 | 83 |
| 53 | 57.1 | 47.1 | 41 | 59.6 | 45.5 | 48 | 58.4 | 46.9 | 89 |
| 60 | 57.9 | 45.3 | 36 | 59.7 | 44.1 | 45 | 58.8 | 44.9 | 81 |
| 67 | 54.1 | 46.0 | 30 | 57.1 | 42.0 | 35 | 55.6 | 44.0 | 65 |
| 74 | 52.2 | 43.6 | 15 | 55.2 | 40.0 | 22 | 53.7 | 41.9 | 37 |
| 81 | 48.0 | 41.1 | 5 | 54.2 | 37.2 | 9 | 51.6 | 39.2 | 14 |

V = verbal meaning; W = word fluency; N = sample size.

These results again are in line with our predictions. Verbal meaning appears to increase until age sixty, with some modest decrement occurring thereafter (perhaps a result of the slightly accelerated nature of this test). But the longitudinal change from the youngest to the oldest age is only a third of a standard deviation, and decline from adult peak is about two-thirds standard deviation. Word fluency, on the other hand, declines as much as 1.4 standard deviation, or twice as much. Interesting sex differences are also found: women at all ages perform better than men on verbal meaning, but women show greater loss than men in word fluency. Figure 1-3 illustrates these sex differences, showing the increasing divergence in performance on the active recall from the passive recognition vocabulary, a divergence that appears to be greater for women than for men. Figure 1-4 illustrates the importance of distinguishing the kinds of information to be obtained from longitudinal and cross-sectional data bases, showing the substantial divergence and crossover of results using the two approaches.

**Summary**

I have tried to call attention to some of the methodological problems that interfere with a clear understanding of results of studies on human cognition from young adulthood into old age. After reviewing some of the literature on age differences and changes in psychometric intelligence, I concluded that substantial generational differences, but few consequential ontogenetic changes, were to be found until age sixty. Beyond that age, however, progressive developmental change must be expected at least for

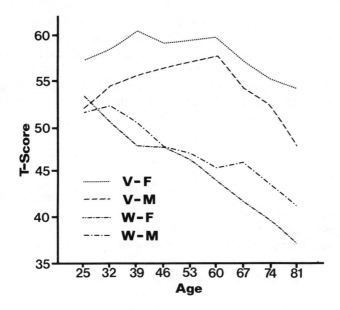

**Figure 1-3.** Cumulative Change with Age on Verbal Meaning and Word Fluency by Sex Estimated from Twenty-One-Year Longitudinal Data

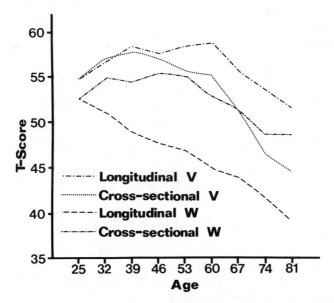

**Figure 1-4.** Comparison of Cross-Sectional and Longitudinal Data on Age Changes and Differences on Verbal Meaning and Word Fluency

some variables, although the cumulative magnitude and practical significance of such changes may still be quite modest. Finally, I examined some data on recognition and recall vocabulary, concluding that there were positive generational differences in the former but negative generational differences in the latter, and that age changes were minimal on recognition vocabulary but large on recall vocabulary, a difference more pronounced among women than men.

**Note**

1. The first two objectives have been covered more extensively elsewhere and involve the restatement of material in Schaie, 1973, 1977, 1978, 1979, 1980a, 1980b, and in Schaie and Willis, 1978, 1980. Data reported in this chapter were obtained in a project supported in part by research grant AG 00480 from the National Institute of Aging. The cooperation of the Group Health Cooperative of Puget Sound is gratefully acknowledged.

**References**

Baltes, P.B., and Schaie, K.W. On the plasticity of intelligence in adulthood and old age: where Horn and Donaldson fail. *American Psychologist* 31: 720-25, 1976.

Baltes, P.B., and Willis, S.L. Toward psychological theories of aging and development. In *Handbook of the Psychology of Aging*, edited by J.E. Birren and K.W. Schaie. New York: Van Nostrand Reinhold, 1977.

Bayley, N., and Oden, M.H. The maintenance of intellectual ability in gifted adults. *Journal of Gerontology* 10: 91-107, 1955.

Birkhill, W.R., and Schaie, K.W. The effect of differential reinforcement and intellectual performance of the elderly. *Journal of Gerontology* 30: 578-83, 1975.

Blum, J.E., Fosshage, J.L., and Jarvik, L.F. Intellectual changes and sex differences in octagenarians: a twenty-year longitudinal study of aging. *Developmental Psychology* 7: 178-87, 1972.

Botwinick, J. Intellectual abilities. In *Handbook of the Psychology of Aging*, edited by J.E. Birren and K.W. Schaie. New York: Van Nostrand Reinhold, 1977.

Botwinick, J., and Storandt, M. Vocabulary ability in later life. *Journal of Genetic Psychology* 125: 303-308, 1974.

Botwinick, J., West, R., and Storandt, M. Qualitative vocabulary test response and age. *Journal of Gerontology* 30: 574-77, 1975.

Craik, F.I.M. Age differences in human memory. In *Handbook of the*

*Psychology of Aging*, edited by J.E. Birren and K.W. Schaie. New York: Von Nostrand Reinhold, 1977.

Doppelt, J.E., and Wallace, W.L. Standardization of the Wechsler Adult Intelligence Scale for older persons. *Journal of Abnormal and Social Psychology* 51: 312-30, 1955.

Eisdorfer, C., Busse, E.W., and Cohen, L.D. The WAIS performance of an age sample: the relationship between verbal and performance IQ's. *Journal of Gerontology* 14: 197-201, 1959.

Eisdorfer, C., and Wilkie, F. Intellectual changes with advancing age. In *Intellectual Functioning in Adults*, edited by L.F. Jarvik, C. Eisdorfer, and J.E. Blum, pp. 21-29. New York: Springer, 1975.

Gardner, E.F., and Monge, R.H. Adult age differences in cognitive abilities and educational background. *Experimental Aging Research* 3: 337-83, 1977.

Gilbert, J.C. Thirty-five year follow-up study of intellectual functioning. *Journal of Gerontology* 28: 68-72, 1973.

Green, R.F. Age-intelligence relationship between ages sixteen and sixty-four: a rising trend. *Developmental Psychology* 1: 618-27, 1969.

Guilford, J.P. *The Nature of Human Intelligence*. New York: McGraw-Hill, 1967.

Hall, E.H., Savage, R.D., Bolton, N., Pidwell, D.N., and Blessed, G. Intellect, mental illness, and survival in the aged: a longitudinal investigation. *Journal of Gerontology* 27: 237-44, 1972.

Horn, J.L. Organization of data on life-span development in human abilities. In *Life-span Developmental Psychology: Research and Theory*, edited by L.R. Goulet and P.B. Baltes, pp. 424-67. New York: Academic Press, 1970.

_____. Human ability systems. In *Life-span Development and Behavior*, edited by P.B. Baltes, Vol. 1. New York: Wiley, 1978.

Horn, J.L., and Cattell, R.B. Refinement and test of the theory of fluid and crystallized intelligence. *Journal of Educational Psychology* 57: 223-70, 1966.

_____. Age differences in fluid and crystallized intelligence. *Acta Psychologica* 26: 107-129, 1967.

Horn, J.L., and Donaldson, G. On the myth of intellectual decline in adulthood. *American Psychologist* 31: 701-719, 1976.

Jones, H.E., and Conrad, H.S. The growth and decline of intelligence: a study of a homogenous group between the ages of ten and sixty. *Genetic Psychology Monographs* 13: 223-98, 1933.

Kintsch, W. *Learning, Memory, and Conceptual Processes*. New York: Wiley, 1970.

Matarazzo, J.D. *Wechsler's Measurement and Appraisal of Adult Intelligence*. Baltimore: Williams and Wilkins, 1972.

Owens, W.A., Jr. Age and mental abilities: a longitudinal study. *Genetic Psychology Monographs* 48: 3-54, 1953.

_____. Is age kinder to the initially more able? *Journal of Gerontology* 14: 334-37, 1959.

Schaie, K.W. Rigidity-flexibility and intelligence: a cross-sectional study of the adult life-span from 20 to 70. *Psychological Monographs* 72: No. 462 'whole No. 9', 1958.

_____. A general model for the study of developmental problems. *Psychological Bulletin* 64: 92-107, 1965.

_____. Age changes and age differences. *Gerontologist* 7: 128-32, 1967.

_____. A reinterpretation of age-related changes in cognitive structure and functioning. In *Life-span Developmental Psychology: Research and Theory*, edited by L.R. Goulet and P.B. Baltes. New York: Academic Press, 1970.

_____. Can the longitudinal method be applied to studies of human development? In *Determinants of Behavioral Development*, edited by F.Z. Moenks, W.W. Hartup, and J. DeWitt. New York: Academic Press, 1972.

_____. Methodological problems in descriptive developmental research on adulthood and aging. In *Life-span Developmental Psychology: Methodological Issues*, edited by J.R. Nesselroade and H.W. Resse. New York: Academic Press, 1973.

_____. Translations in gerontology—from lab to life: Intellectual functioning. *American Psychologist* 29: 802-7, 1974.

_____. Quasi-experimental designs in the psychology of aging. In *Handbook of the Psychology of Aging*, edited by J.E. Birren and K.W. Schaie. New York: Van Nostrand Reinhold, 1977.

_____. External validity in the assessment of intellectual development in adulthood. *Journal of Gerontology* 33: 695-701, 1978.

_____. The primary mental abilities in adulthood: an exploration in the development of psychometric intelligence. In *Lifespan Development and Behavior*, edited by P.B. Baltes and O.B. Brim, Jr., Vol. 2. New York: Academic Press, 1979.

_____. Intellectual development in adulthood. In *Intelligence and Aging*, edited by R.D. Sprott. New York: Van Nostrand Reinhold, 1980a, in press.

_____. Intelligence and problem solving. In *Handbook of Mental Health and Aging*, edited by J.E. Birren and R.B. Sloane. Englewood Cliffs, N.J: Prentice-Hall, 1980b, in press.

Schaie, K.W., and Baltes, P.B. Some faith helps to see the forest: a final comment on the Horn and Donaldson myth on the Baltes-Schaie position on adult intelligence. *American Psychologist* 32: 1118-20, 1977.

Schaie, K.W., and Gribbin, K. Adult development and aging. *Annual Review of Psychology* 26: 65-96, 1975.

Schaie, K.W., and Hertzog, C. Estimates of ontogenetic change in intelligence during adulthood: a 14-year cohort-sequential study. Unpublished manuscript, University of Southern California, 1979.

Schaie, K.W., and Labouvie-Vief, G.V. Generational versus ontogenetic components of change in adult cognitive behavior: a 14-year cross-sequential study. *Developmental Psychololgy* 10: 305-320, 1974.

Schaie, K.W., and Parham, I.A. Cohort-sequential analyses of adult intellectual development. *Develomental Psychology* 13: 649-53, 1977.

Schaie, K.W., and Parr, J. Concepts and criteria for functional age. In *Aging: A Challenge for Science and Social Policy*, edited by M. Marois. Oxford: Oxford University Press, 1980, in press.

Schaie, K.W., and Schaie, J.P. Clinical assessment and aging. In *Handbook of the Psychology of Aging*, edited by J.E. Birren and K.W. Schaie. New York: Van Nostrand Reinhold, 1977.

Schaie, K.W., and Willis, S.L. Life-span development: implications for education. *Review of Research in Education* 6: 120-56, 1978.

_____. Maintenance and decline of adult mental abilities: I. Empirical data and explanatory models. In *Western Washington University Ninth Symposium on Learning: Adult Learning and Development*, edited by F. Grote. Bellingham, Washington, 1980, in press.

Schaie, K.W., and Zelinski, E. Psychometric assessment of learning and memory dysfunctions in the elderly. In *Brain Function Changes in Normal and Abnormal Aging*, edited by F. Hofmeister. Essen, Germany: Bayer, 1980, in press.

Terman, L.M. *The Measurement of Intelligence*. Boston: Houghton, 1916.

Thurstone, L.L., and Thurstone, T.G. *Examiner Manual for the SRA Primary Mental Abilities Test*. Chicago: Science Research Associates, 1949.

Wechsler, D. *The Measurement of Adult Intelligence*. Baltimore: Williams and Wilkins, 1939.

Wohlwill, J.F. *The Study of Behavioral Development*. New York: Academic Press, 1973.

Yerkes, R.M. Psychological examining in the United States Army. *Memoirs of the National Academy of Sciences* 15: 1-890, 1921.

# 2  Verbal Memory in the Elderly

*Martha Storandt*

To review what is known about verbal memory in older adults, I will consider research within several conceptual frameworks that have been proposed for verbal memory. These include models from the fields of information processing and psycholinguistics. Tulving has provided a distinction between episodic and semantic memory. Episodic memory refers to perceptual events that occur to the individual and thus is autobiographical in nature. It "receives and stores information about temporally dated episodes or events and temporal-spatial relations among these events . . . Semantic memory is the memory necessary for the use of language. It is a mental thesaurus or lexicon" (Tulving, 1972, pp. 385-386). Most of the research on memory in the last twenty years has dealt with episodic memory and has classified it into three types—sensory, primary, and secondary. I will describe what is known of changes that occur in the normal older adult with respect to these types of episodic memory.

## Sensory Memory

Information is received from one of the senses and held for a very brief time (one-fourth to one-half second) in a specific sensory storage system. Visual information is held in a visual sensory store and is called iconic memory. Auditory information is held in an auditory sensory store and is called echoic memory. Iconic and echoic memory may operate in quite different ways. Some believe sensory memory represents the first step in acquisition of information. It is the system that allows a person to detect sensory stimuli. The information in sensory memory decays rapidly, or is "written over" by subsequent incoming information.

What happens to the capacity of sensory memory with increased age? Few studies have addressed this issue. An initial attempt to measure visual sensory memory in older adults failed when eight out of the ten older adults tested could not perform the task (Walsh, 1975). Later, Walsh and Thompson (1978) used a different task, one more similar to a critical flicker fusion procedure, and concluded that iconic or visual sensory memory lasted approximately 15 percent longer in young adults compared to older adults. However, Kline and Orme-Rogers (1978) examined age differences in the ability to recognize simple words that were presented in two parts, separated

27

by a time delay. Successful recognition of the word depended on retaining the first half of the word in sensory memory until it could be combined with the second half. Older adults performed better than young adults, suggesting that visual sensory memory persists longer in older adults, rather than for a shorter time as was suggested by Walsh and Thompson (1978).

Attempts to measure age differences in echoic or auditory sensory memory have largely involved studies of dichotic listening in which two brief series of digits, letters, or words are presented at the same time, one set to each ear. The individual is asked to report both sets, one at a time, the idea being that the set which is recalled second must be held in echoic memory during the waiting period while the first set is reported. Normal older adults generally perform at a level comparable to that of younger adults on the first-reported set, although they experience difficulties, in comparison to younger adults, on the second-reported set (Inglis and Caird, 1963). (This generalization is complicated by issues related to the order in which the right and left ear are reported.) However, a recent review by Craik (1977) has suggested that echoic memory may not be the ability measured in dichotic listening tasks and that performance on this procedure is related to the depth at which the material is processed. More will be said about depth of processing later, in this chapter.

It can be logically deduced then that older adults do have a sensory memory. If the information were not detected through sensory memory, nothing at all could be remembered. However, it is difficult to say at present just what age-related differences exist in this type of memory, although Horn (1979) recently concluded that sensory detector functions, if that is what sensory memory is, probably do decline with age.

**Primary Memory**

Primary memory represents items that are in conscious awareness; it is thought of as a temporary holding and organizing process rather than a structured memory store (Waugh and Norman, 1965). Primary memory appears to be able to deal with only two to four verbal items at a time. Items are maintained in primary memory by active rehearsal or attention and are rapidly displaced by subsequent incoming information unless they are processed sufficiently to become part of secondary memory.

Primary memory would appear to decline very little, if at all, with increased age. One set of evidence with respect to age differences in primary memory comes from experiments where the individual is asked to learn a list of words or items. Most people will remember the last few words very well and many will report the last word first. This recency effect may occur because the final items on the list are still in conscious awareness; they are being dealt with by primary memory. Older adults tend to show as strong a recency effect as do younger adults (Craik, 1968; Raymond, 1971) which seems to indicate that relatively little decline occurs in primary memory capacity with increasing age.

Other literature relating to primary memory comes from research on memory spans. Perhaps the most familiar task is the digit span from the Wechsler Adult Intelligence Scale or from the Wechsler Memory Scale. The individual is asked to listen to a list of digits and then repeat them. These spans are found to decrease only slightly with increasing age, if at all. The average twenty-five-year old can repeat a span of 7.1 numbers whereas the average seventy-five-year old can repeat a span of 5.9 (Botwinick and Storandt, 1974). The decline may be related to the secondary memory component of the task (Craik, 1977). That is, the primary memory system has a limited capacity—two to four items. Most individuals demonstrate digit or letter spans of greater length.

Thus, either some organizing of the material must be involved (grouping the digits or letters by twos or threes) or some of the items must be held in secondary memory. The rather small decline in memory span observed for people in their sixties and seventies may reflect poorer performance on that portion of the span which must be processed by secondary memory.

Older adults sometimes do have difficulty with tasks that seem to involve primary memory. These difficulties are usually revealed when the task involves organization, for example, in the backward digit span, where the person must repeat a string of digits in reverse order (Botwinick and Storandt, 1974). Thus, the digits have to be reorganized and the individual cannot just repeat what was heard. Also, age-related difficulties are observed in situations where the person must pay attention to two or more tasks at once, such as performing a letter cancellation task presented visually while listening for a repeated letter in an auditory series (Broadbent and Heron, 1962).

For example, we recently have had occasion to use an aphasia screening task called the token test (Spellacy and Spreen, 1969). This task is very similar to one that was used extensively with older adults and is called the following instructions task (Botwinick and Storandt, 1974). On the token test the individual is asked to act out the examiner's instructions by touching or rearranging colored plastic geometric shapes. At the beginning levels of the task the instructions are very simple, "Point to the white square," but they become more complex as the task progresses: "Put the small green circle between the large white square and the large blue triangle." Older adults who show no signs of aphasia sometimes fail these more difficult tasks which we suspect may exceed the individuals' ability to maintain conscious awareness of the entire set of instructions, thus requiring spill-over into secondary memory.

**Secondary Memory**

Secondary memory represents the permanent, large-capacity memory system. Many investigators would agree that older adults do have difficulty with secondary memory in comparison to younger adults (Craik, 1977). This has been demonstrated in several experiments. Now researchers are trying to determine the locus of the difficulty—does the deficit occur at acquisition or encoding into the memory system, during storage, or upon retrieval?

But before I discuss just where the difficulty in secondary memory arises, let me describe an alternative conceptualization of memory processes as proposed by Craik and Lockhart (1972). They prefer to think of memory as related to levels of perceptual processing. Memory is "viewed as a continuum from the transient products of sensory analysis to the highly durable products of semantic-associative operations" (Craik and Lockhart, 1972, p. 676), rather than as existing in discrete stages or stores. The durability of a memory "depends upon how 'deeply' the stimulus is processed . . . Depth in this sense refers to the number and qualitative nature of perceptual analyses carried out on input" (Craik, 1977, p. 391). Processing is generally considered to be of a semantic nature and may reflect the degree to which the person categorizes the information, forms associations, and uses mediators.

Craik and Lockhart divide the processes into two types. Type I processing involves repetition of a particular analysis of the information, and is thought to be characteristic of what is generally called primary memory; it involves "recirculating the information at one level or depth of processing" (Craik and Lockhart, 1972, p. 676). For example, when I am given a new lock for my locker, I read numbers off the card and then begin to work the combination, rehearsing the numbers over and over again as I turn the dial: 8-18-10, 8-18-10, 8-18-10. I am paying attention to, and am actively conscious of, the items to be remembered. If I stop paying attention, I will forget them, meaning that I have not analyzed them very deeply or formed any semantic associations with my more permanent cognitive structures.

However, suppose I try to form some associations with 8-18-10. The first number is 8 which is what I just did (ate) before I came here to use the locker. The second number is 18, which is 10 more than the first number, and the last number is the difference between the first and second numbers, again 10. I have applied a deeper level of analysis or stimulus elaboration. This is called Type II processing as opposed to Type I processing which merely involves recirculating or repeating the processing as I did when I read the numbers out loud from the card. The deeper analysis should lead to a more permanent memory.

Now back to the issue of where the difficulty arises in secondary memory for older adults. It appears that older adults do not process information as thoroughly or deeply upon acquisition or encoding as do younger adults. They do not spontaneously use mediators such as visual images or phrases related to the material to be recalled (Hulicka and Grossman, 1967), nor do they seem to organize the incoming information to the same extent as do younger people (Hultsch, 1969). Also, older adults may have difficulty ignoring irrelevant stimuli, so the amount of processing capability available for the item to be remembered is reduced (Kausler and Kleim, 1978). That is, they cannot spare as much effort for deeper analysis of the target stimulus. Since the material is less-deeply processed, it is less durable, less well remembered. The more cues available at retrieval, the better the retrieval. However, if the item to be remembered is not as elaborately connected to those retrieval cues, how can the cues help? This type of elaboration goes on at the time of encoding, or upon initial acquisition of the memory.

The storage system is another area where the material might be lost from permanent memory. Does the memory trace decay more rapidly in older adults? Are the elderly more susceptible to interference from competing information? Recent reviews tend to agree that information is not lost in storage among older adults any more rapidly than in younger adults (Kausler, 1970; Craik, 1977). In fact, one might speculate that the human being is like the fabled elephant that never forgets, if the information has been learned to begin with. I might not be able to remember something, but that does not mean the items are not stored in memory; rather I may be having trouble retrieving it.

This brings me to the third locus of possible age differences in secondary memory—retrieval. Several investigators suggest that older adults experience difficulty retrieving information from permanent memory (Schonfield and Robertson, 1966; Buschke, 1974). Most of the research compares tasks that require the subjects to recall the information with tasks that require them to recognize the information. In a recall task the subjects are asked to recall a list of words presented previously, whereas in a recognition task they are presented with a large set of words from which to select those heard earlier. In a recall task the subject has fewer cues to help retrieve information from memory. Recall tasks are differentially more difficult for older adults than are recognition tasks (Schonfield and Robertson, 1966). However, even recognition is sometimes hard for the older person, especially in difficult tasks (Erber, 1974).

Thus it would appear that older adults do not process information to be remembered as deeply at the time of acquisition or encoding and that they frequently have difficulty retrieving information (perhaps because it was less well encoded to begin with). However, there is little evidence to indicate that memory traces decay more rapidly in the elderly than they do in younger adults.

**Other Formulations of Memory Types**

The foregoing is a highly simplified version of what is known about verbal memory in later life. A great deal of disagreement exists regarding labels, what various experimental tasks and procedures actually measure, and the locus of memory deficits in later life. Further, not all researchers are satisfied with the three types of memory that have been described—sensory, primary, and secondary. Craik and Lockhart (1972) have recommended an alternative conceptualization that focuses on the depth of processing at the time of encoding, or the extent of perceptual analysis that is performed on the stimulus.

Most of the literature I have described to this point is derived from experimental psychology. Another perspective is represented by psychologists who focus on individual differences. A recent report on a program of research by Horn (1979) and his colleagues combines what has been called primary and secondary memory into one category of related memory processes that seem to involve short-term acquisition and retrieval and are related to the ability to maintain concentration. They define a second category of processes, called long-term storage and retrieval, and argue that processes in addition to those represented in measures of primary and secondary memory are involved in the storage and retrieval that occur over minutes, hours, days, weeks, and years. This long-term memory reflects the adequacy of organization that the individual applies to the to-be-remembered material and really represents learning. This position is not unrelated to Craik and Lockhart's (1972) depth-of-processing idea. However, Horn's work suggests that older adults have relatively little difficulty with long-term storage and retrieval.

Although we have not examined sensory memory, our own research supports the notion of distinct types of memory which could be called primary, secondary, and tertiary (Botwinick and Storandt, 1974). The first involves memory for things like digit and letter spans and appears to be related to attention or an ability to concentrate. This type of memory appears to decline somewhat with age, a conclusion similar to Horn's (1979). The second type involves more difficult memory tasks such as paired associates and serial recall and is also negatively related to age. This type of memory may involve deeper processing or organization as described by Craik and Lockhart (1972). The third type represents a very long-term memory that does not decline with age. I call this remote memory: it reflects how well people remember things they experienced long, long ago. It is possible that this information has been processed at a very deep level indeed.

Closely related to remote memory may be what is described as actualization of world knowledge or the effective use of permanent memory. At least three processes are required for actualization of world knowledge (Lachman and Lachman, 1979). First, the person must be able to locate and retrieve information from the permanent memory store. Second, the individual must employ inference, a process whereby gaps in knowledge can be filled in, such as when we automatically fill in or infer portions of linguistic messages that we have not really heard, or when we construct new pieces of information from other available information. Finally, there is metamemory, which describes the person's knowledge about his own memory processes or abilities. For example, my metamemory tells me whether or not I have a piece of information in my long-term memory—not precisely what it is, but rather whether it is in memory.

What happens to these three processes with increased age? Little is known yet about how inference may change with age, but a few studies examining age differences in retrieval from long-term store and differences in metamemory now exist.

With respect to very long-term memory, there appears to be some question as to whether or not there exist any age-related deficiencies. Studies by Schonfield (1972); Squire (1974); Bahrick, Bahrick, and Wittlinger (1975); Warrington and Silberstein (1970); and Warrington and Sanders (1971) seem to point to poorer retrieval of very old memories by the elderly. However, in addition to Perlmutter's work (1978) and my own (Botwinick and Storandt, 1974; Storandt, Grant, and Gordon, 1978), which indicate that older adults have good recall for very old memories, data from the laboratory of Janet and Roy Lachman (1979) indicate that there is little reason to believe that retrieval efficiency from very long-term memory declines as a function of age. Horn and his colleagues reached essentially the same conclusion regarding what they call permanent, long-term memory (Horn, 1979), and Eysenck (1975) found that older adults have no difficulty retrieving information from semantic memory. Perhaps these laboratory findings reflect the long-standing clinical observation that older adults seem to have little difficulty remembering things that happened long ago. Thus, although normal older adults seem to have difficulty remembering the type of things asked in laboratory tasks, many are capable of excellent retrieval of memories from their permanent storehouse of information and knowledge.

The age-related evidence on metamemory, or knowledge of one's own memory processes, comes primarily from the Lachmans (1979). This issue has been addressed in reaction-time studies and in studies that ask individuals to assess their degree of confidence about whether a specific piece of information is available in memory. Results to date indicate that young, middle-aged, and older adults are equally accurate in their metamemorial processes. That is, if a piece of information is in permanent memory, the older adult is as likely as the younger adult to know that it is there.

## Summary

Although numerous contradictions arise in the literature on verbal memory in the elderly, certain basic assertions can be made. First, it can logically be deduced that older adults do have a sensory memory. Although its efficiency in comparison to that of younger adults is not established, sensory memory must exist; otherwise, information could never get into the information processing system that leads to more permanent memories.

Second, older adults do attend to the information they are processing. That is, they can keep information in consciousness, pay attention to bits and pieces of information, and rehearse these items. One school of thought claims this is primary memory and that there are no age-related deficits in it. Another claims it is short-term acquisition and retrieval related to concentration, and that this is where older adults are especially vulnerable.

Third, there are probably a variety of "depths" at which information can be organized, analyzed, and processed as it is acquired at the time of encoding. The deeper the processing at the time of acquisition, the longer the memory lasts. Although some researchers suggest that older adults have difficulty retrieving material from permanent memory, it may well be that most of the observed memory deficits really represent acquisition difficulties. Older adults do not seem to process the typical tasks presented in the laboratory as deeply as do younger adults, probably for a variety of reasons. Therefore, the memory is less durable; the memory did not enter permanent memory with as much strength as it could have. However, material that is more closely related to world knowledge, material that may have been processed long ago when the individual was younger or material that may have been processed many times throughout a long life—these items are strongly embedded in permanent memory and are as available to the older person as those items equally well embedded in the younger adult. Thus, it may be that older adults do not have a problem remembering things once they have learned the material. Rather, the problem is with learning it well in the first place.

## References

Bahrick, H.P., Bahrick, P.O., and Wittlinger, R.P. Fifty years of memory for names and faces: a cross-sectional approach. *Journal of Experimental Psychology* 104: 54-75, 1975.

Botwinick, J., and Storandt, M. *Memory, Related Functions and Age.* Springfield, IL: Charles C. Thomas, 1974.

Broadbent, D.E., and Heron, A. Effects of a subsidiary task on performance involving immediate memory in younger and older men. *British Journal of Psychology* 53: 189-98, 1962.

Buschke, H. Two stages of learning by children and adults. *Bulletin of the Psychonomic Society* 2:392-94, 1974.

Craik, F.I.M. Two components in free recall. *Journal of Verbal Learning and Verbal Behavior* 7: 996-1004, 1968.

_____. Age differences in human memory. In *Handbook of the Psychology of Aging*, edited by J.E. Birren and K.W. Schaie. Van Nostrand Reinhold, New York, 1977.

Craik, F.I.M., and Lockhart, R.S. Levels of processing: a framework for memory research. *Journal of Verbal Learning and Verbal Behavior* 11: 671-84, 1972.

Erber, J.T. Age differences in recognition memory. *Journal of Gerontology* 29: 177-81, 1974.

Eysenck, M.W. Retrieval from semantic memory as a function of age. *Journal of Gerontology* 30: 174-80, 1975.

Horn, J.L. Concepts of intellect in relation to learning. Address given at the annual meeting of The American Educational Research Association, San Francisco, April 8-12, 1979.

Hulicka, I.M., and Grossman, J.L. Age group comparisons for the use of mediators in paired-associates learning. *Journal of Gerontology* 22: 46-51, 1967.

Hultsch, D.F. Adult age differences in the organization of free recall. *Developmental Psychology* 1: 673-78, 1969.

Inglis, J., and Caird, W.K. Age differences in successive responses to simultaneous stimulation. *Canadian Journal of Psychology* 17: 98-105, 1963.

Kausler, D.H. Retention-forgetting as a nomological network for developmental research. In *Life-span Developmental Psychology: Research and Theory*, edited by L.R. Goulet and P.B. Baltes. New York: Academic Press, 1970.

Kausler, D.H., and Kleim, D.M. Age differences in processing relevant versus irrelevant stimuli in multiple-item recognition learning. *Journal of Gerontology* 33: 87-93, 1978.

Kline, D.W., and Orme-Rogers, C. Examination of stimulus persistence as a basis for superior visual identification performance among older adults. *Journal of Gerontology* 33: 76-81, 1978.

Lachman, J.L., and Lachman, R. Age and the actualization of world knowledge. In *New Directions in Memory and Aging: Proceedings of the George Talland Memorial Conference*, edited by L.W. Poon, J.L. Fozard, L.S. Dermak, D. Arenberg, and L.W. Thompson. Hillsdale, NJ: Lawrence Erlbaum Associates, 1979.

Perlmutter, M. What is memory aging the aging of? *Developmental Psychology* 14: 330-45, 1978.

Raymond, B. Free recall among the aged. *Psychological Reports* 29: 1179-82, 1971.

Schonfield, D. Theoretical nuances and practical old questions: the psychology of aging. *Canadian Psychologist* 13: 252-66, 1972.

Schonfield, D., and Robertson, E.A. Memory storage and aging. *Canadian Journal of Psychology* 20: 228-36, 1966.

Spellacy, F., and Spreen, O. A short form of the Token Test. *Cortex* 5: 390-97, 1969.

Squire, L. Remote memory as affected by aging. *Neuropsychologia* 12: 429-35, 1974.

Storandt, M., Grant, E.A., and Gordon, B.C. Remote memory as a function of age and sex. *Experimental Aging Research* 4: 365-75, 1978.

Tulving, E. Episodic and semantic memory. In *Organization of Memory*, edited by E. Tulving and W. Donaldson. New York: Academic Press, 1972.

Walsh, D.A. Age differences in learning and memory. In *Aging: Scientific Perspectives and Social Issues*, edited by D.S. Woodruff and J.E. Birren. New York: Van Nostrand, 1975.

Walsh, D.A., and Thompson, L.W. Age differences in visual sensory memory. *Journal of Gerontology* 33: 383-87, 1978.

Warrington, E.K., and Sanders, H.I. The fate of old memories. *Quarterly Journal of Experimental Psychology* 23: 432-42, 1971.

Warrington, E.K., and Silberstein, M. A questionnaire technique for investigating very long term memory. *Quarterly Journal of Experimental Psychology* 22: 508-512, 1970.

Waugh, N.C., and Norman, D.A. Primary memory. *Psychological Review* 72: 89-104, 1965.

# 3 Naming Disorders in Aphasia and Aging

*Harold Goodglass*

The cerebral mechanism by which a verbal configuration is associated to a concept, stored, and retrieved is still a mystery. Research in verbal learning and lexical-semantics has taught us a great deal about the development and mental structure of verbal concepts, but has not contributed materially to our understanding of how storage, retrieval, and utterance come about. Some model of the production mechanism is essential if we are ultimately to relate a particular form of deficit in naming to a stage in a storage and retrieval model that has gone wrong. Obviously we cannot work with a simplistic computer model.

We turn to aphasia for help, because the symptoms of this disorder produce selective dissociations within language performance, which seem to give us some leads as to how speech is put together in the head and consequently, as to where the process may go astray in an individual who has a naming failure of any type. For example, an aphasic may show the phenomenon of partial retrieval of the acoustic and articulatory form of a target word, with the primary block being the recall of the articulatory movements. These may be dramatically released by a cue of the first sound of the word. In other instances the assistance of the examiner is of no avail, as the patient may be persistently incapable of putting the right sounds in the right order, as in the case of one man who could name a drawing of the zodiac perfectly clearly as *Zokiad* but could not rearrange the sounds with any amount of help. Some patients speak with facile grammar and articulation but use much circumlocution for every specific noun or verb because they are totally unable to bring them to mind—sometimes unable to recognize them when they are offered by the examiner. Other patients substitute wrong words, related either by sound or by meaning to the intended word, for example they may say *knife* for *scissors* or *sluff* for *cuff*.

In a certain sense we can present aphasia as a language disorder of the elderly. Certainly the older person is more at risk to develop a stroke and concomitant aphasia than the younger person. In most cases, aphasia results from a well-defined injury to the language area of the left hemisphere, commonly produced by a stroke, sometimes by brain tumor, often by head trauma. It may also result from degenerative disease or presenile dementia, such as Alzheimer's disease, where cortical atrophy extends into the language areas.

37

Thus it makes sense to review some of the approaches to the analysis of naming disturbances in patients who are clearly aphasic, because the questions we ask here are precisely the same as those asked in the case of anyone who experiences failures in word retrieval.

One question we (Goodglass et al., 1976) asked was, what implicit knowledge of a word did the patient have when he failed to name it? Did types of aphasic differ in this regard? Could some patients regularly show that the word was at the tip of their tongue while others had no idea of its structure? We probed for this tacit knowledge by asking the patient to do two things after failing to name an object—to show how many syllables it had and to show what the first letter was; a method based on the work of Brown and McNeill (1966) and Barton (1971). Of four patient groups only one—the conduction aphasics—were clearly superior to the others, demonstrating partial knowledge of the target word in 30 percent of the cases. Two groups—anomic and Wernicke's aphasics—had virtually no success in identifying letters or syllables, even though they missed naming no more words than the conduction aphasics. Thus, naming disorders in aphasics seem to fall into two groups—one in which words are either retrieved fully or at a subthreshold level of partial knowledge and another in which words are either retrieved fully or not at all. The latter mode is characteristic for Wernicke's and anomic aphasics. We can ask the same question for the elderly.

Another variable that seems to tell us something about the mechanism of naming failure is whether a cue provided by the examiner aids in retrieving the target word. Luria (1970) claims that this feature distinguishes between patients whose failure is at the level of motor expression and those whose breakdown is prior to the recovery of an acoustic model of the word, the latter being unable to benefit from priming with the first sound of the word.

Pease and I (1978) carried out an experiment where we compared three aphasic groups with respect to their ability to improve with a cue after they had failed to name a pictured object. Six types of cues were provided for six different sets of pictures matched in difficulty. They consisted of the first sound of the word, the superordinate class, a reference to the situational context or location, a rhyming word, a reference to the function, and a phrase-completion stimulus. Figure 3-1 shows that providing the first sound is by far the most effective aid for all three aphasic subgroups: Broca's, Wernicke's, and anomic patients. Sentence completion stimuli are second in effectiveness for Broca's and anomic aphasics, but Wernicke's aphasics derive little benefit from any cue other than the initial sound. These results could also be interpreted to mean that the more severe the naming disorder the more the resistance to aid by a cue, because the Wernicke's aphasics were the most impaired in naming. However, Stuss and I (in press) have since obtained data that support Luria's view, that is, the advantage of

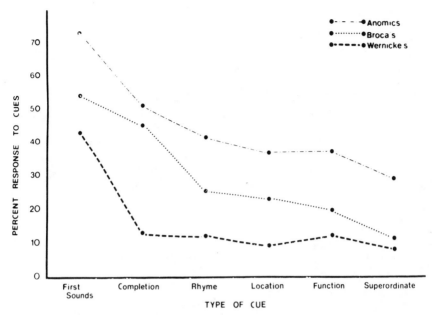

Source: D. Pease and H. Goodglass. *Cartex* 14: 178-189, 1978. Reprinted with permission.

**Figure 3-1**. Percent Correct Response to Each Cue Category for Subjects in Three Diagnostic Groups

Broca's over Wernicke's aphasics in benefiting from phonemic cuing greatly outweighs the difference in naming ability between these groups. We have included a test of responsiveness to cuing in elderly subjects which I review here.

In our continuing studies of naming, which have involved some aging subjects as well as aphasics and children, we have used a new instrument, the Boston Naming Test (Kaplan, Goodglass, and Weintraub, 1978), a series of eighty-five line-drawn pictures graded in difficulty. Figure 3-2 illustrates four of the items. Since a common complaint of aging people is a problem recalling proper names, we have added a test of twenty famous faces. As a control task we have also used a numerical facts test of twenty items, on the grounds that this taps the store of long-term memory for facts—but of a type that does not involve linguistic retrieval.

First let us look at the expected distribution of scores across the age range. Figure 3-3 shows that by age ten and a half, children are well into the range of normal adult naming, and that once over sixty, some people have naming scores that fall to very low levels.

Scores attained by ten ostensibly normal nursing-home elderly women in their eighties and an equal number of elderly in the community (see figure 3-4) showed that the community-based group averaged the same score of sixty-three that was obtained for the people over age seventy in our norma-

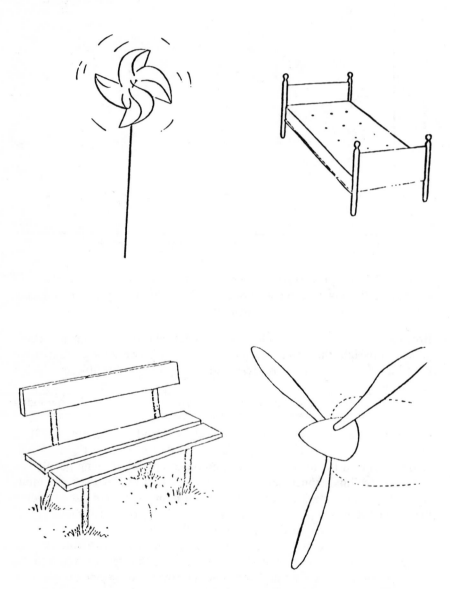

**Figure 3-2.** Samples of Picture Stimuli from Boston Naming Test

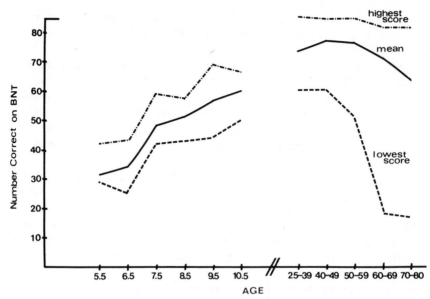

**Figure 3-3.** Scores of Various Age Groups on Boston Naming Test

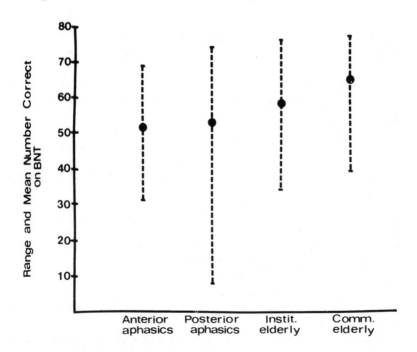

**Figure 3-4.** Range and Mean Number Correct for Four Subject Groups on Boston Naming Test

tive sample, but the nursing-home subjects were four points lower and just above the level of anterior and posterior aphasics shown in the two left-hand columns.

What happens when elderly patients miss a word and are supplied with the first sound? In figure 3-5 we see that both groups of elderly, like Broca's (or anterior) aphasics, had a successful response rate of 60 percent of these instances, distinguishing their underlying naming process from Wernicke's (posterior) aphasics whose cuing rate was only 23 percent. For the most part, then, we can be sure that they are not suffering from a profound dissociation between word and concept.

Figure 3-6 shows that both groups of elderly are on a par with the aphasics in the retrieval of proper names. Recalling that they were superior to aphasics in object naming, we have evidence that suggests they indeed have a selective deficit for people's names. The shorter column represents those who gave correct responses when aided by the initials; we see the same pattern of response to cuing for objects as in figure 3-5.

Finally, our most extensive analysis is based on a comprehensive categorization of all wrong responses. In figure 3-7 we see a comparison of the four groups on six of the error categories. We note the following:

1. *Phonologically based errors.* Both groups of elderly were clearly unlike the aphasics in that they made few errors based primarily on the change of a sound element. Not shown in figure 3-7 are secondary scores where a sound *resemblance* contributed secondarily to an ill-chosen word. Although the elderly made several errors of this type in their choice of response word, the aphasics exceeded them by far in this respect.

2. *In-class associates.* Both groups of elderly were much more prone than aphasics to err by naming a close associate of the target word—usually another object of the same category (70 percent).

3. *Other associates.* The elderly gave remotely associated words as often as aphasics, in proportion to total errors.

4. *Misperceptions.* Aphasics had no trouble indentifying the drawings, but nursing-home elderly misinterpreted the pictures, accounting for one-fifth of their errors. Even the community elderly showed a tendency in this direction, with a higher error rate than aphasics.

5. *Circumlocution.* The second most frequent error strategy was to tell something about the object when the name was lacking, seen in both groups of elderly. Here they exceeded even the Wernicke's aphasics, who are noted for this device.

6. *Negation.* Typical of the Broca's patients but no other group was the tendency to reject their errors, a sign of self-criticism lacking in both fluent aphasics and elderly.

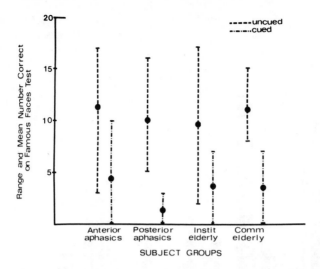

**Figure 3-5.** Percent of Correct Responses by Four Subject Groups When Primed Phonemically on Words Initially Failed

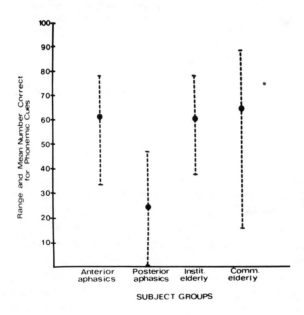

**Figure 3-6.** Mean Number and Range in Score of Twenty Famous Faces Named by Patients in Four Groups; Cued Responses Involved Supplying Initials after Prior Failure to Name

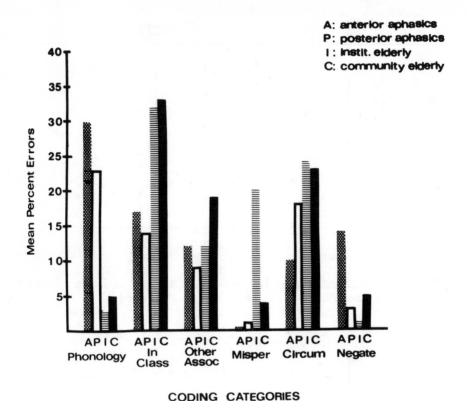

**Figure 3-7.** Distribution of Six Types of Naming Errors by Four Subject Groups

We tried to use some of the known features of aphasic naming disorders when looking at the age spectrum. Aphasics split into groups on the basis of whether their target words were usually close to being accessible through cuing or so dissociated that they could not be helped to retrieve them by means of a cue. Naming vocabulary rapidly approaches the adult range in mid-childhood and that the elderly showed a very wide scatter, with numbers of ostensibly normal individuals falling in the defective range.

Examining the character of errors in some detail we found that elderly do not make the characteristically aphasic errors of sound substitution. Their errors are primarily semantic—their substitutions are generally more often closely related to the target word, but not infrequently only peripherally related to it. Even the community-living elderly misperceived drawings more than aphasics, and misperception is a major source of errors in the older institutionalized group. Most important, all elderly had a high degree of responsiveness to priming with the first sound, unlike fluent aphasics in this respect. The relative deficit of the elderly in naming famous faces is hard to interpret. If we assume their perception and recognition are intact, we may be dealing with a special kind of long-term memory deficiency that is different from lexical retrieval of other vocabulary.

## References

Barton, M.I. Recall of generic properties of words in aphasic patients. *Cortex* 7: 73-82, 1971.

Brown, R., and McNeill, D. The "tip-of-the-tongue" phenomenon. *Journal of Verbal Learning and Verbal Behavior* 5: 325-27, 1966.

Goodglass, H., Kaplan, E., Weintraub, S., and Ackerman, N. The tip-of-the-tongue phenomenon in aphasia. *Cortex* 12: 145-53, 1976.

Goodglass, H. and Struss, D.T. Naming to picture versus description in three aphasic subtypes. *Cortex* (in press).

Kaplan, E., Goodglass, H., and Weintraub, S. *The Boston Naming Test.* (Experimental edition), Boston, 1978.

Luria, A.R. *Traumatic Aphasia.* The Hague: Mouton, 1970.

Pease, D.M., and Goodglass, H. The effects of cuing on picture naming in aphasia. *Cortex* 4: 178-89, 1978.

# 4 Semantic and Episodic Memory Impairment in Normal and Cognitively Impaired Elderly Adults

*Elisabeth O. Clark*

Elderly subjects complain of a range of memory difficulties. In this chapter two facets of memory will be examined as a function of both normal aging and cognitive impairment. The first type might be termed *dictionary memory*, or the store of words used in daily communication, which is measured by the amount of time necessary to access that store. Word-finding difficulties that the elderly experience may stem from a slowdown of the search in dictionary memory. Impairment of this store was determined experimentally by the increased time necessary to decide whether a string of letters was an English word. There also may be a lower activation level for words used by the elderly in conversation, making it more difficult to retrieve them from the store for repeated use.

The second type of memory tested was episodic memory, which was measured by the ability to recognize whether words had been presented on an earlier study list. Vocabulary is considered to be intact, but there has been some debate whether memory tested by recognition, as opposed to recall methods, is impaired in elderly subjects. The theoretical implications of this debate are not trivial, for the discrepancies between recognition and recall performance may indicate the stage or stages of memory processing that are impaired in elderly subjects. (See Glanzer and Clark, 1979, for a discussion on stages of memory.)

It is generally agreed that elderly subjects perform more poorly than young controls when tested by recall methods, but there is disagreement whether recognition performance is similarly impaired in aging. (See Craik, 1977, for a review of recall and recognition test results for young and elderly subjects.) In brief, a current argument holds that successful recall of information requires intact functioning of encoding, storage, and retrieval stages of memory, and that the retrieval stage is largely bypassed in recognition by providing a stimulus match. Thus, if recall performance differs but recognition performance is equivalent for young and old subject groups, the group with poorer recall suffers a retrieval deficit. Equivalent performance by both groups on a recognition task further indicates that encoding and storage stages are normal and that the recall difficulty for the one group lies solely in the retrieval stage of memory. If, however, this group is impaired on a recognition task as well, encoding and storage stages of memory are also implicated. Using recognition tests, some researchers have found no differences between old and young groups whereas others have shown impairment for elderly subjects. Therefore, it is unclear whether elderly people have memory deficits other than those at the retrieval stage of memory processing.

In a recent review, Craik (1977) concludes that recognition memory does not decline with aging but that the encoding processes normally used by the elderly are less efficient, leading to poorer recall and recognition. This is the case when young and older subjects are tested for memory using traditional intentional-learning paradigms. When subjects are instructed to study stimuli for later memory testing, intentional learning occurs. During intentional study older subjects apparently process information less deeply than do young subjects, which leads to poorer encoding and consequently poorer recognition.

In an attempt to equate encoding processes used by young and elderly groups, several researchers have recently employed an incidental-learning paradigm prior to memory testing by either recall or recognition methods. Incidental learning occurs when subjects are given a task to perform on stimuli and do not anticipate later memory testing. The task may be to count the number of vowels in the words on a list, find a rhyme for each word, or categorize them. Craik presents evidence that when simply incidental-learning paradigms are used, subsequent recognition performance is equivalent for young and old subjects (1977, pp. 412-413). These data support the view that encoding processes can function at young normal levels when elderly subjects are required to employ a given strategy during an incidental task. Left to their own devices, however, older subjects employ inefficient encoding strategies during intentional learning. The episodic-memory task described in this chapter used an incidental task to examine the encoding stage of memory for young and normal elderly subjects as well as for elderly subjects with cognitive empairment.

Elderly outpatient volunteers presented themselves at the New York University Medical Center Geriatric Study and Treatment Program with complaints of impaired memory. When asked for specific examples, they gave as one of the most frequent complaints—besides misplaced objects and missed appointments—difficulty in finding known words. A subject may say, "I'll be talking with someone and suddenly I can't find the word I need. It's gotten worse and is most embarrassing." This is not an aphasic patient nor is he impaired in describing the problem. One man told of an incident during which he was attempting to describe a material he wanted to purchase. He "knew" its name—it was a plastic substance, tough and easily cleaned, used for table tops and kitchen counters. He struggled to no avail, but a couple days later the word *formica* appeared in consciousness, unbidden and unsought. People of all ages occasionally experience this type of difficulty, but it is generally easy enough to circumlocute and choose an easier, less precise word or phrase. However, such complaints of word-finding difficulties are frequent enough among aged subjects to prompt the question: in the elderly, who may or may not have other memory impairments, what is happening to the use of the internal dictionary?

The dictionary memory or lexicon is part of the semantic memory system, one of the two systems proposed by Tulving (1972). The semantic memory system contains stored information about the language and about how to deal with this information. Semantic memory consists of the lexicon or internal dictionary, a grammar with rules for operating on the lexicon for sentence production and the like, and some type of decoder to enable the user to interpret incoming verbal information.

Episodic memory is the other memory system designated by Tulving; it deals with memory for events that are encoded with respect to time and place of occurence. This system is concerned with storage and retrieval of personally experienced events or episodes and the temporal-spatial relations among these events. Semantic memory contains the information that Boston is a city located in the northeastern United States, whereas episodic memory encodes a trip being made to Boston for a conference.

It is not surprising that the semantic memory system is taken for granted, and that most clinical references to memory are concerned with episodic memory. Standard clinical testing of elderly subjects with memory complaints examines the episodic system for deficits. Indeed, it is assumed that the semantic memory system functions normally in memory-impaired subjects to the point that vocabulary scores, based on the ability to define words, are often used as a gauge of presenile intelligence and memory ability. Thus, evaluation of memory impairment is based on comparing episodic-memory scores with a vocabulary score. Yet elderly people feel they are having difficulty with the semantic system, specifically with the lexicon. It is true that the vocabulary scores are often quite high for these people, yet on a vocabulary test the subject is given the word and needs only to enter the lexicon, search for a match to the item, and read out a definition. However, in everyday use the reverse process is required; it is retrieval from the lexicon that is important. Given a specific context, the speaker must produce words that fit the situation. One is not given the necessary words for conversation as in a vocabulary test, but must search for them.

In addition to being used for producing and comprehending verbal material, the semantic system is presumably tapped to aid in storage of memories for events in the episodic system. If retrieval from lexical memory is difficult and greatly slowed down in aging, it would indirectly affect episodic memory processes as well. This study examines performance of several elderly groups on both a semantic and an episodic memory task to assay the locus of word-finding difficulty and its effect on episodic storage.

The elderly volunteers who entered our program were initially screened using the WAIS vocabulary test of forty items and the Guild Memory Test,

Form A, a short half-hour battery developed by Gilbert (Gilbert, Levee, and Catalano, 1968; Gilbert and Levee, 1971). The vocabulary score was used as a presenile memory standard against which scores on the Guild were compared. The Guild consisted of several short subtests that evaluated aspects of learning and memory. The degree of impairment on the various subtests was assessed by comparing the scores with norms for ages sixty and over geared to a particular vocabulary level (Gilbert and Levee, 1971). Subjects were given a Global Deterioration Scale (GDS) rating on the basis of results from a screening battery and a mental status questionnaire. A rating of GDS-1 was normal, and higher ratings indicated increasingly greater episodic-memory impairment.

There were three sets of elderly subjects (age sixty to eighty-five) who participated in the two experiments: a normal elderly control group with GDS ratings of 1, a mildly impaired GDS-2 group, and moderately impaired GDS-3 and GDS-4 groups. College students (age eighteen to twenty-six) represented a young control group.

The experimental session was divided into two segments and lasted approximately fifteen minutes. The equipment consisted of a projector and screen. The subjects sat approximately fifteen to eighteen inches from the screen with their fingers on two buttons labeled "yes" and "no." The buttons were connected to a timer and a digital printer in a separate room that measured and printed the response type and the reaction time in milliseconds for each response. A standard reaction time, free of decision process, was checked for both right and left hands of each subject.

**Experiment One**

The first half of the testing session consisted of a lexical-decision task, during which the subject indicated by pressing the "yes" or "no" button whether items presented on slides were words. Subjects were given a series of twelve practice trials to familiarize them with the task. The instructions stressed speed of response and accuracy. Subjects were told that errors were unlikely and that the time to make each decision was being measured. They were told that the task was analogous to looking up the string of letters on each slide in the internal dictionary and deciding whether it was an entry. Each string consisted of three to seven letters. There were eighty slides, each bearing a single string of letters. Forty of the strings were English words, such as *cat*, and the other forty were nonwords, such as *gatch*. Of the forty words, half were high-frequency, common English words, for example, *table* and *job*, which have a Kucera-Francis (1967) occurrence of $\geq 100/$ million. The other twenty were rare, low-frequency words, such as *rift* and *fluke*, with a Kucera-Francis occurrence of $\leq 1/$million. Each slide appeared on the screen for approximately four seconds (less a brief pause for shutter opening) and the letter string remained on for study even after the decision was made. This insured equal study time for stimulus-encoding by all subjects.

Subjects in all groups made very few errors on this task. The most cognitively impaired subjects, a few GDS-4s bordering on 5s, missed no more than three to five of the low-frequency words, performing about the same as some of the college students. This indicated that the lexicon is essentially intact in these elderly subjects despite great cognitive and even functional impairment. However, the reaction-time data presented in figure 4-1 distinguished among the groups. The standard lexical-decision results were found for the young control group. High-frequency words took an average of 585 milliseconds to identify, low-frequency words required 748 milliseconds, and nonwords took longer still (776 milliseconds) to correctly reject. Although the other groups were as accurate in their decisions as the young group, they were slower at every point. This slowdown was far greater than the normal slowdown in simple or disjunctive reaction time that occurs with age. Mean reaction times (in milliseconds) on a simple "go-no go" task were 333 for the young control group, 395 for normal elderly subjects, 411 for the mildly impaired group, and 476 for the moderately impaired group. It is clear from figure 4-1 that the differences among the groups in lexical-decision reaction times were far greater than the control reaction-time differences.

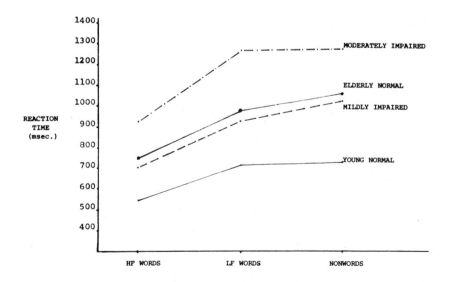

**Figure 4-1.** Performance on Lexical Decision Task

In terms of time to access lexical memory, it was obvious that the mildly impaired subjects were virtually identical to the elderly normal subjects in using the lexicon and in the decision process. Both these groups fell midway between the young normal and the moderately impaired groups. The difference between groups was statistically significant beyond the .0001 level.

The moderately impaired group had tremendous difficulty, over and above a simple motor slowing, in the time necessary to access the lexicon as a function of word frequency. Relative to the other groups, the moderately impaired subjects required more time to search for and find low-frequency words. This indicated that as task difficulty increased from high-to low-frequency word identification, there was impairment in reaction-time performance as a function of both age and cognitive impairment.

**Experiment Two**

A word-recognition test followed the lexical-decision task. The subject again saw a series of eighty slides, but this time all stimuli were words. Half were the words seen earlier during the lexical-decision task, mixed randomly with forty words seen for the first time. None of the nonwords were repeated. Again half of the repeated words were high frequency, and half were low frequency. The same was true for the new words. Again the slides were exposed for four seconds each. Subjects were asked to respond "yes" if the word had been seen before, and "no" if not, using the same buttons. They were told that about half the words were old and half were new. In terms of the dictionary analogy given earlier, subjects were told that they were either returning to the same entry and checking for a tag, or recent marker (which would serve as a clue that they had been there recently), or looking up a new word in which case there would be no recent time tag. Subjects were encouraged to make a decision as quickly as possible for each item, even if it seemed like a guess. To allay any feeling that deception had been employed, the concept of incidental memory was described.

The $d'$ statistic from signal-detection theory was employed to assess recognition memory. This measure is based on the proportion of hits, or correctly identified old words, and the proportion of false alarms, or erroneously recognized new words. It provides a more sensitive correction for guessing than older methods and reflects a subject's ability to detect a signal from noise regardless of response criterion used (Banks, 1970). The more successful a subject is in distinguishing the signal (hear an old word) from the noise (hear a new word) the larger the $d'$ measure will be.

Figure 4-2 gives the average $d'$ for high-and low-frequency word-recognition memory for each of the four subject groups. Again, the young subjects were better at recognizing words seen earlier in the lexical-decision task. The difference between groups was significant beyond the .001 level.

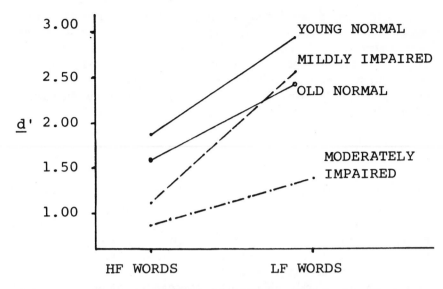

**Figure 4-2.** Performance on Recognition Memory Task for Low-Frequency (LF) and High-Frequency (HF) Words

The classic recognition-memory pattern was also found for all groups. That is, a low-frequency word was easier to recognize when encountered again than was a high-frequency word. For the young group the mean $d'$ for high-frequency words was 1.85; for low-frequency words, 3.07. The normal elderly subjects had a similar pattern, but their $d'$ values were lower, with a mean $d'$ of 1.59 for high-frequency words and 2.41 for low-frequency words. This indicated that episodic memory, as measured on a recognition-memory task, was impaired in normal elderly subjects.

As would be expected, the moderately impaired group performed very poorly on this task. Although they had been able to identify words correctly, albeit slowly, in the earlier task, they were greatly impaired in marking those words with episodic-memory tags for later recognition. In fact, two subjects in this group performed at chance level or below on the recognition-memory task, although they had both made accurate decisions on the lexical-decision task.

An interesting shift is evident in the data for the midly impaired group. In addition to the highly significant differences among the groups, there was also a large interaction. It was produced by the recognition-memory performance for the mildly impaired group. Although the mildly impaired subjects' performance was like that of the elderly control group on the lexical-decision task, their pattern was notably different on the recognition-memory task. They still resembled the normal elderly in recognizing low-frequency words, but they were quite impaired in recognizing high-frequency words. In fact, their performance was almost as poor as that of the moderately impaired group. As mentioned earlier, it is much easier to recognize a low-frequency word than a high-frequency word. As one subject expressed, "Those odd words sort of 'stick out' in your mind." Thus, as the task became more difficult, the mildly impaired group, who functioned at the normal elderly level on the easier lexical-decision task and on recognition of low-frequency words, demonstrated an episodic-memory impairment in poorer recognition of high-frequency words.

**Discussion**

The results of the two experiments indicate that memory decline among the elderly is not limited to the episodic system but is more general, affecting both semantic and episodic memory. The lexical-decision task in experiment one taps the semantic memory system and requires semantic processing. On this task all elderly groups were significantly slower than young controls, indicating that processing in the semantic system is less efficient. Moreover, the impairment of elderly subjects in word recognition found in experiment two demonstrates episodic-memory decline. Finding such an impairment after an incidental-learning task supports the hypothesis that more than the retrieval stage of memory is affected in aging subjects. A recognition-memory test largely bypasses the retrieval stage of episodic memory by providing the strongest retrieval cue possible, unlike a recall test which requires that subjects independently retrieve correct responses. Most researchers would agree that recognition is an easier task, requiring less retrieval. That a deficit in elderly memory scores persists with recognition testing, when encoding requirements have been equated during the study, implicates encoding and storage stages of memory.

It is proposed that normal encoding and storage in episodic memory require fairly rapid interaction with the semantic memory system. In other words, semantic knowledge is used to set episodic traces. The impairment in access to the lexicon of the semantic network, apparent in the data for normal and mildly impaired elderly groups in the first experiment, is still more marked for the elderly group with a moderate degree of clinically defined episodic-memory loss. Impaired use of the semantic system may exacerbate existing difficulties in the encoding and storage stages of episodic memory. Therefore, as clinically-diagnosed memory decline becomes more marked, there is additional decline in performance on both experiment one, a semantic-memory task, and experiment two, an episodic-memory task. As both memory systems become increasingly inefficient, later recall or recognition of poorly encoded information becomes more difficult. Thus, decrements traditionally found among normal elderly groups with either recall or recognition tests of episodic memory may be partly a result of the slowdown of semantic-memory processing. A greater degree of slower processing would lead to a correspondingly greater degree of episodic-memory impairment.

It is of interest that the incidental-learning task employed in this study failed to equate subsequent recognition performance in the young and elderly normal subjects, unlike data reported in other studies (Craik, 1977; Eysenck, 1974). The lexical-decision task, which served as an incidental-learning task, required semantic processing of each stimulus during lexical search. It appears that in most cases cited by Craik (1977) the incidental-learning conditions that have led to equivalent recall or recognition performance by young and old groups of subjects do not require semantic processing. Determining whether a word is printed in upper- or lower-case letters (White, in Craik, 1977) or counting the number of letters or vowels in each word (Eysenck, 1974) are structural and orthographic tasks. Likewise, determining whether a word rhymes with another (White, in Craik, 1977) or producing such a rhyme (Eysenck, 1974) are phonemic tasks. In terms of depth of processing (Craik and Lockhart, 1972) these tasks require only shallow processing; they are not semantic tasks which require lexical access. If the processing-deficit hypothesis proposed by Eysenck refers to semantic-memory processing, then incidental tasks that do not require semantic processing would not be expected to distinguish between old and young groups. Furthermore, recall and recognition performance following these shallow-processing tasks are abysmally low for both old and young subjects, lending credence to a hypothesis that semantic processing at some depth or level is required for successful verbal memory encoding in subjects of all ages.

Incidental tasks that require access to semantic information generally distinguish between old and young subject groups given subsequent memory tasks. In the present study the incidental-task requirement was to decide whether each stimulus was a word, which produced large age differences when subjects were tested for later recognition of the words. In Eysenck's study the incidental-semantic tasks required subjects to find adjectives appropriate for each stimulus word or to image the words. These tasks involve the use of semantic information. On recall testing his elderly subjects performed much more poorly, but on incidental tasks requiring no semantic processing the groups did not differ. Eysenck has interpreted his findings as support to a processing-deficit hypothesis. That is, elderly people are more handicapped when a task requires deeper, more elaborate processing of information. I would designate his more shallow tasks as non-semantic and conclude that the elderly are at a disadvantage whenever processing or encoding for a learning task requires the use of the semantic system. Slower processing in the semantic system leads to inefficient, ineffective encoding in the episodic system. The results from experiment two of this study and those from Eysenck's two semantic tasks support a processing-deficit hypothesis. This deficit is conceived here as broad-based, affecting search in the semantic system, which in turn results in loss of efficiency in episodic-memory encoding and improper coordination of the two memory systems.

In conclusion, therefore, I wish to stress the importance of the interrelationship rather than the separation of the two memory systems proposed by Tulving (1972). Information stored in the semantic system must have entered the system during some period of episodic learning. That is, the semantic system is initially built from episodic learning. Conversely, episodic memories are built from information in semantic memory. A trip to Boston can only be encoded and stored in episodic memory if the semantic system contains the name *Boston* and other concepts having to do with travel and the like. If access to semantic information is slowed, it is more difficult to encode appropriate information in the episodic store. This semantic slowing may partly explain why elderly people have difficulty with episodic memory. The slower search rate hinders episodic processes of encoding and storage. Cognitively impaired elderly with poorer access to semantic information are even more impaired at episodic processing and have correspondingly more difficulty with memory tasks.

**References**

Banks, W.P. Signal detection theory and human memory. *Psychological Bulletin* 74: 81-89, 1970.

Craik, F.I.M. Age differences in human memory. In *Handbook of the Psychology of Aging*, edited by J.E. Birren and K.W. Schaie. New York: Van Nostrand Reinhold, 1977.

Craik, F.I.M., and Lockhart, R.S. Levels of processing: a framework for memory research. *Journal of Verbal Learning and Verbal Behavior* 11: 671-84, 1972.

Eysenck, M.W. Age differences in incidental learning. *Developmental Psychology* 10: 936-41, 1974.

Gilbert, J.G., Levee, R.F., and Catalano, F.L. A preliminary report on a new memory scale. *Perception and Motor Skills* 27: 277-78, 1968.

Gilbert, J.G., and Levee, R.F. Patterns of declining memory. *Journal of Gerontology* 26: 70-75, 1971.

Glanzer, M., and Clark, E.O. Cerebral mechanisms of information storage: the problem of memory. In *Handbook of Behavioral Neurobiology*, edited by M.S. Gazzaniga, vol. 2. New York: Plenum, 1979.

Kucera, H., and Francis, W.N. *Computational Analysis of Present-Day American English*. Providence, RI: Brown University Press, 1967.

Tulving, E. Episodic and semantic memory. In *Organization of Memory*, edited by E. Tulving and W. Donaldson. New York: Academic Press, 1972.

Tulving, E., and Thomson, D.M. Retrieval processes in recognition memory: effects of associative context. *Journal of Verbal Learning and Verbal Behavior* 87: 116-124, 1971.

# 5

# A Pragmatic Evaluation of Discourse Communication in Normal and Senile Elderly in a Nursing Home

*John M. Hutchinson* and
*Mary Jensen*

Several years ago an intriguing concept was introduced that has the potential for providing a unifying conceptual framework for discussions of social interaction across an individual's life span. Piaget (1966) accorded this concept a central place in his theories of cognitive maturation in children. Later, Looft (1972) extended the impact of this idea to interpretations of social behavior in adolescents, adults, and the elderly. The concept has been termed *egocentrism* and it refers not to selfishness or narcissism, but rather to an exclusive reference to one's own point of view. In this rather primitive state of conscious development, people seem unable to evaluate their actions or the actions of others within a perspective other than their own.

Generally, patterns of egocentric behavior change as a child grows and may even disappear in adulthood. This maturation process was termed *decentration* by Piaget (1966). With respect to social interaction, decentration is characterized by anticipation of the reactions that others will exhibit toward an individual's behavior. As Looft (1972) has pointed out, such anticipation requires the ability to see an intended behavior from the viewpoint of another person. Therefore, effective social interaction is engendered by simultaneous attention to different perspectives, a skill in which most adults are quite accomplished. Why does decentration—and therefore a decrease in childhood egocentrism—occur? Ironically, perhaps one of the most satisfactory explanations is the process of social interaction itself. Verbal exchanges provide the opportunity for conflict and reinforcement in a child's belief structure. The presence of dissonant information generally forces children to reexamine their ideas, thereby leading to greater cognitive maturity. Flavell has stated, "It is social interaction which gives the ultimate *coup de grace* to childhood egocentrism" (1963, p. 157).

If social interaction is crucial to the recession of egocentrism, then it follows that reduced or deficient social interaction might be associated with the reappearance of this more primitive cognitive state. As one surveys the typical human life span in Western society there emerges one phase where deficient social interaction is an ubiquitous feature: old age. Senescence is often a time of decreased social interaction for many reasons. First, the general process of aging is associated with reductions in hearing that render social exchange considerably more difficult (Schow et al., 1978). Second, the elderly have reduced social networks partly because of the death of friends and the dispersion of family, but also because of societal alienation of and prejudice against the elderly (Schwartz and Proppe, 1970; Butler and Lewis, 1977). Third, there is the controversial phenomenon known as disengagement which is characterized by withdrawal from social involvement and increased preoccupation with the self (Bell, 1978). Fourth, inevitable biological changes may prompt the elderly to conserve energy by reducing social contact (Rosow, 1967; Botwinick, 1973).

Unfortunately, the typical reduction in social interaction among the elderly is exacerbated in many by the insidious appearance of senile dementia. Those affected by this problem often evidence impoverished cognitive abilities and also personality changes that are seldom to the patient's benefit. These clinical manifestations could naturally be expected to lead to serious disturbances in social interaction. The disturbances are frequently serious enough to warrant institutionalization and there is mounting evidence that institutionalization itself causes even further reductions in socialization (Rosow, 1967; Hulicka, 1972; Abdo et al., 1973; Miller, 1977).

One could conclude, then, that reduced social interaction may lead to greater egocentrism among the elderly. This reappearing egocentrism would be particularly evident in the institutionalized elderly who have symptoms of senile dementia. Accordingly, research involving senile patients in nursing homes should be quite helpful in analyses of egocentric behaviors.

An implicit assumption underlying this research is that social interaction is largely accomplished through oral language. Further, the nature of such social exchanges depends heavily on the content and structure of the linguistic message. But it must also be recognized that language is conditioned by the social context in which it appears. If the social context is altered physically (through variances in physical surroundings, such as institutionalization) or conceptually (through variations in cognitive structure, such as may occur with senile dementia) then one must expect changes in language as well. The study of language formulation should be a sensitive indicator of the nature of social interaction and therefore a potential measure of the reemergence of egocentrism in advancing age.

One of the most avant-garde strategies being used by psycholinguists today in their study of language function is pragmatics. Pragmatics may be defined as "the rules governing the use of language in context" (Bates, 1976, p. 420). This approach has received considerable attention in the study of childhood language and the results of these research efforts have provided insight regarding cognitive development. It is not unreasonable to assume that the extension of such evaluative strategies to the language of the senile elderly could provide considerable insight regarding cognitive functioning in this population, particularly as it relates to reemerging egocentrism.

**Method**

*Subjects*

The subjects for this investigation were ten elderly female patients residing in a county nursing home in southeast Idaho. There was a control group of five subjects who had normal intellectual functioning for their age and an experimental group of five who exhibited symptoms of senile dementia. Since there is some evidence that social community has an influence on language (Coulthard, 1977), the experimenters decided to select a control group from the same nursing home. Presumably, this would permit greater precision in interpreting the data obtained, since one potential source of contamination—the place of residence—would be controlled.

Determination of the presence of senile dementia was based on four sources of information. (1) Medical records were searched for the diagnosis of senility, senile dementia, organic brain syndrome, and so on. (2) A questionnaire was prepared and distributed to informed staff members and nurses. This questionnaire was developed by combining lists of common symptoms of senile dementia, as stated by Katzman and Karasu (1975), Miller (1977), and Butler and Lewis (1977). The questions focused on memory difficulties; problems in orientation to person, time, and place; evidence of confusion or incoherence in utterance; self-help problems; and alterations in personality. Coblentz et al., (1973) discovered that confirmed cases of senile dementia exhibit noticeable problems with memory and orientation. Therefore, we included as senile subjects only those for whom memory and orientation problems were reported on the questionnaires. (3) An earlier questionnaire was examined, the *Questionnaire for the Determination of Mental Status* developed by Kahn et al., (1960). It was arbitrarily decided that at least four incorrect responses to the ten simple questions were required to be included in the experimental group. (4) Finally, the experimenters talked with the patients to evaluate subjectively the mental status of these cases and to insure their ability to engage in conversational discourse.

Occupational and educational history of the subjects was controlled only to the extent that no significant discrepancies existed between groups. All participants had at least a high school education and there were professionals in both groups. The age range was 65 to 95, with the mean age for the control and experimental groups being 83.6 and 83.4 respectively. All subjects had resided in the nursing home at least six months.

The medications of each patient were reviewed by a qualified pharmacologist, and although some of the patients occationally took drugs that could cause depression of the central nervous system (chiefly tranquilizers), none were on such medication at the time of the experimental sessions.

### Experimental Procedure

For the experimental recordings, each subject was individually engaged in conversation by an assistant to the experimenters. The recordings were made in a quiet room in the nursing home, usually the patient's room. Three fifteen-minute conversation sessions were recorded for each subject. The sessions took place on three different days but at approximately the same time to minimize potential effects of the time of day on mental status. Prior to the initial recordings, an instructional session was held with each subject to introduce the assistant and to familiarize the patient with the recording equipment. The assistant began each recording session with a predetermined topic that was constant for all participants. However, no attempt was made to control or limit the natural conversational process beyond that point.

All sessions were tape recorded using a high-quality recorder and microphone. The initial recording sessions were also videotaped, but inspection of these visual records revealed little or no additional information, so the video taping was discontinued.

### Discourse-Evaluation Strategy

Since this study represents an initial foray into the nature of discourse among the normal elderly and among those with senile dementia, frequency tabulations of rather broad discourse features were deemed appropriate. The first analysis involved calculating the number of utterances accumulated by each subject during the forty-five minutes of conversation. The operational definition of *utterance* was twofold: (1) A separate linguistic unit demarcated by pauses or terminal intonation contours whether or not the units were completed thoughts or sentences, and (2) one complete (or incomplete) sentence followed by another if no pause were taken, or with a pause if the second sentence were an elliptical thought completion of the first. For example, "I used to go to eat [pause] you know, to the cafe." The conversation samples were then analyzed by the number of turns. A *turn* was defined as one or more consecutive utterances by a given speaker.

The second general procedure for evaluating discourse was to categorize utterances according to the type of speech act. The term *speech act* was derived from the philosophical work of Austin (1962) and Searle (1965,

1969). Analyzing speech acts involves describing the intent of the speaker without referring to syntactic structure. For example, in a cold room a person may say, "It's awfully cold in here." Structurally that sentence appears as a statement of fact but it may really have been uttered with the intent of directing someone to close the window. Quite frequently that intent can only be discerned by evaluating social context and the previous conversational progress. For this study, four of the speech acts cataloged by Searle (1975) were used:

1. *Representatives* convey the belief that some proposition is true. Usually representatives take the form of assertions or hypotheses.
2. *Directives* to get the listener(s) to do something. Requests and questions are directives.
3. *Expressives* convey information about the speaker's psychological state. Common expressive forms are statements about how one feels, apologies, and thanks.
4. *Commissives* commit the speaker to some future course of action. Promises, pledges, vows, and guarantees would generally be commissive acts.

The third evaluative procedure was related to topic-control characteristics. A *topic* was considered to be a series of utterances by one or more speakers related to the same general theme. That is, the utterances were semantically consistent. Four strategies for maintaining topical coherence were examined: (1) the number of times the subject initiated a new topic, (2) the number of utterances in which the subject continued her own topic, (3) the number of times the patient continued her partner's (experimental assistant's) topic, and (4) the number of times no discernible topic was recorded.

For analyses of all these discourse features, measures of intra- and interjudge reliability were obtained in identification and classification of a hundred randomly selected utterances. These reliabilities exceeded .85 in both cases. Appropriate parametric statistical procedures (*t*-tests and analyses of variance) were used to test the significance of differences between the control and experimental groups.

## Results and Discussion

### Frequency of Utterances and Turns

The frequency of utterances and turns, and the average number of utterances per turn for the control and experimental groups are displayed in table 5-1. Inspection of this table reveals that the patients with senile dementia generally exhibited fewer utterances and more turns with the

**Table 5-1**

**Frequency of Utterances, Turns, and Utterances per Turn in Conversational Discourse of Normal Subjects and Patients with Senile Dementia.**

|  | Number of Utterances | Number of Turns | Average Utterances per Turn |
|---|---|---|---|
| Normal | 1979 | 1,070 | 1.85 |
| Senile | 1878 | 1,433 | 1.31 |

result of noticeably fewer utterances per turn. Statistical analysis of these results using $t$-tests for uncorrelated data revealed that the groups were not significantly differentiated for total number of utterances ($t = 1.17$, $d.f. = 28$, $p > .05$). However, group differences for number of turns ($t = 3.89$, $d.f. = 28$, $p \leq 01$) and average number of utterances per turn ($t = 3.77$, $d.f. = 28$, $p \leq .01$) were statistically significant. The appearance of fewer utterances per turn by those in the experimental group suggests that the patients' elaboration on various discourse topics was reduced. The presence of more turns among the experimental group lends credence to this hypothesis of minimized elaboration. Indeed, some support for this view was provided by Halpern, Darley, and Brown (1973) who offered a rather comprehensive experimental overview of language functioning in patients with aphasia, apraxia, confusion, and generalized intellectual impairments. One typical characteristic of patients in the last group was less elaboration in answering questions.

Of course, the obvious explanation for reduced elaboration is the presence of cognitive deterioration resulting from a reduction in the number of functional neurons in the central nervous system, a potential increase in random neural activity that acts as noise in the brain, and a decrease in arousal levels (Welford, 1965). The immediate impact of cognitive deterioration would be a reduction in the complexity of verbal messages produced with complications from problems in word-finding and loss of memory for past events.

The concept of egocentrism may also help explain some of the noted changes in discourse among senile patients. Egocentrism, as an explanation for these changes, is not antithetical to but rather quite compatible with the view on cognitive deterioration previously mentioned. Perhaps as a result of changes in cognitive capacity, senile individuals adopt the strategy of limited elaboration because they assume their words convey much more meaning than they actually do. Looft (1972) describes this point with respect to young children and claims that this assumption of inflated informational load is evidence of egocentrism. Looft argues that children are often unable to differentiate their points of view from those of others and, therefore, see no need to expand or elaborate their utterances.

Piaget (1926) offered another explanation concerning egocentric language by claiming that children frequently exhibit centration in their interactions by an unwillingness to communicate socially. That is, many of their speech efforts seem to lack any communicative intention to inform or direct the listener. As a result, elaboration and attempts to repair misunderstandings by the listener are seen as unnecessary. It is quite conceivable that senile dementia also involves the lack of a social will to communicate.

This may be related to Bernstein's (1966) distinction between restricted and elaborated codes. One feature of restricted codes is the extensive use of elliptical references to knowledge presumably shared between speaker and listener. Elaborated codes involve much more explicit expressions, without extensive presuppositions regarding shared knowledge. It was our impression that patients with senile dementia used inappropriately restricted coding much more often than their normal peers.

*Speech Acts*

The distribution of speech acts in discourse samples for the control and experimental groups is presented in table 5-2. Both groups used substantially more representatives than any other speech act. This suggests that the majority of utterances in these conversations were statements of belief or assertions. Both groups used a small but roughly equal number of expressives and commissives. One might conclude that the type of discourse in which the subjects were engaged did not provide the opportunity or require substantial use of expressions of feeling, promises, and the like. However, the groups were statistically differentiated with respect to directives ($F = 9.10$; $d.f. = 1,164$; $p \leq .01$). The senile patients exhibited roughly twice as many utterances aimed at directing the listener to do something. It is not immediately apparent why this result was obtained. Although no formal quantification was undertaken, a review of the transcripts revealed that most of the directives used by the senile elderly were requests for confirmation, identification, and explanation. Interestingly, many of these requests were predicated on objects or events that were completely irrelevant and tangential to the conversation. For example, the patients often made sudden shifts in attention from the progress of the discourse to an object in the room or a fellow patient walking down the hall, and asked for information about this new focus.

We can relate this to the three cognitive components identified by Bloom, Rocissano, and Hood (1976) in their discussions of adult-child discourse. During message generation and reception they noted that memory, the scheme for linguistic processing, and immediate consciousness interact. They observed that in the child's early states of cognitive development, that which is in immediate consciousness is that which is in immediate environ-

**Table 5-2**
**Distribution of Speech Acts in Conversational Discourse of Normal Subjects and Patients with Senile Dementia.**

|  | Repre-sentatives | Directives | Expressives | Commissives | Fillers | Unclassified | Total |
|---|---|---|---|---|---|---|---|
| **Normal** | | | | | | | |
| Number | 1,467 | 189 | 193 | 4 | 126 | 0 | 1,979 |
| Percentage | 74 | 10 | 10 | — | 6 | — | 100 |
| **Senile** | | | | | | | |
| Number | 1,140 | 376 | 176 | 6 | 96 | 84 | 1,878 |
| Percentage | 61 | 20 | 9 | — | 5 | 5 | 100 |

ment. The children understand and speak in the here and now (p. 545). With increasing cognitive maturity, however, messages can be encoded and decoded without references to the immediate environment. That is, the immediate consciousness need not be directly tuned to salient perceptual events. This cognitive maturation is fundamental evidence of decentration and is obvious in language formulation. As Hunt has noted, "The new independence of thought from perceptual and egocentric focus permits the child to sustain a topic . . . Only thus can a communicative interchange take place in which there is a progressive unfolding of a topic, the chief thing missing in egocentric speech" (1961, p. 218).

If this line of reasoning is applied to the senile elderly, it is clear that many of the directives were encoded with reference to events or objects that transitorily entered the immediate consciousness. A large percentage of these directives violated the progression of discourse and prevented the unfolding of the topic at hand. In that sense, these directive intents may have been reflective of egocentric behavior.

Two other categories are depicted in table 5-2. The term *fillers* was reserved for extraneous vocalizations ("um," "uh," "oh," and so on) for which no intent could be discerned from context. The control and experimental groups were not differentiated with respect to fillers. However, the experimental group did evidence more well-formed utterances for which no intent could be determined and these were labeled as *unclassified*. This may constitute additional evidence of egocentrism in that the senile elderly violated a basic rule of conversation—that one should be relevant and perspicuous in contributions to discourse (Grice, 1975). The senile patients may have presupposed that the listeners understood what was being said when, in fact, they did not. Of course, unclassifiable utterances could also reflect inadequacies in Searle's system (Rees, 1978), cognitive disturbances and memory constraints confounded by the choice of inappropriate lexical items that obscure the intent of the utterance, or the absence of any communicative intent. This last view might be consistent with the Piagetian idea about a lack of will to communicate.

## Topic Controls

The final area of investigation regarding discourse characteristics was the use of various topic-control techniques, shown in table 5-3. These data reveal:

1. The senile patients initiated new topics much more frequently than did those in control group ($F = 7.17$; $d.f. = 1,8$; $p \leq .01$). This difference between groups was particularly dramatic in the case of violations of conversational rules for initiating new topics.
2. With respect to continuation of one's own topic the groups were not observed to differ significantly ($F = 2.28$; $d.f. = 1,8$; $p > .10$). However, a significant interaction between the groups and the normal/violation category ($F = 15.12$; $d.f. = 1,8$; $p \leq .01$) would suggest that the senile patients exhibited significantly more violations of rules for the continuation of one's own topic.
3. Similar findings may be reported for instances where the subject continued her partner's topic. Though the groups did not differ in a statistical sense ($F = .04$; $d.f. = 1,8$; $p > .10$), a significant interaction ($F = 6.07$; $d.f. = 1,8$; $p \leq .05$) would imply that the normal elderly violated conversational rules much less frequently than those with senile dementia.
4. No formal statistical tests were completed for instances when no topic could be discerned, but inspection of the data reveals that the senile patients manifested these obscure utterances much more frequently.
5. By combining the frequency of violations in each category with the number of "no topic" assignments, nearly 30 percent of the utterances of the senile elderly were deemed inappropriate to the conversational context in which they were spoken.

When these differences in topic-control behaviors are examined with reference to known rules for discourse communication, several interesting interpretations of cognitive functioning in the senile are possible. Grice (1975) has argued that any conversation should proceed in accordance with what he termed the *cooperative principle*. In essence, this principle requires participants to make appropriate contributions to discourse, at the appropriate time, and by the accepted purpose or direction of the conversation. Failure to do so implies a purposeful violation of the integrity of the discourse or an unwitting disregard for the maxim. We contend that unwitting

**Table 5-3**
**Topic-Control Characteristics in Conversational Discourse of Normal Subjects and Patients with Senile Dementia.**

| | Initiation of New Topic | | Continuation of Own Topic | | Continuation of Partner's Topic | | No Topic | No Response | Total |
|---|---|---|---|---|---|---|---|---|---|
| | Normal | Violation | Normal | Violation | Normal | Violation | | | |
| **Normal** | | | | | | | | | |
| Number | 56 | 2 | 794 | 6 | 1,099 | 9 | 13 | 0 | 1,979 |
| Percentage | 3 | — | 40 | — | 56 | — | 1 | — | 100 |
| **Senile** | | | | | | | | | |
| Number | 63 | 100 | 335 | 174 | 933 | 144 | 122 | 7 | 1,878 |
| Percentage | 3 | 5 | 18 | 9 | 50 | 8 | 7 | — | 100 |

disregard is a result of the more primitive cognitive state that attends the presence of egocentrism. The following lines of reasoning may be used as support for this contention.

With respect to the intitiation of new topics, Coulthard (1977) suggests that violations will occur unless a proper closing to the previous topic has occurred. Proper closings include a summarizing comment (often proverbial), the failure of one speaker to add new information over several turns, and a preclosing statement indicating the desire to bound a conversation. In this study, the senile elderly frequently introduced new topics in the absence of appropriate closings of previous topics. A typical example follows.

Subject (#78)   And she was my horse and I would harness her and hitch her up.

(#79)   I would always pat her and smooth her hair and pet her so she'd like me.

(#80)   I didn't want her to be afraid that I'd hurt her, but I never did.

(#81)   I never did whip her.

(#82)   She was a nice horse.

(#83)   We liked her.

Experimenter   Did you train her?

Subject (#84)   Well, my flowers you folks brought me today . . . Aren't they beautiful?

The subject inappropriately introduced the topic of flowers in utterance #84 when the topic of horses had not been closed. The experimenter provided a clear directive for new information regarding the horse, which was ignored. Thus, the senile patient disregarded her partner's desire for additional information and changed to a new topic—totally from her own perspective.

As any topic unfolds over several turns, each participant has some responsibility for making contributions that are relevant to and clearly understood in light of previous contributions. If this responsibility is not exercised, the utterances become semantically unclear and the topic may dissolve. In other words, all contributions to the topic must be made with reference to what the listener knows about the context and the topic. If the talker is to be understood, she or he must learn when not to presuppose or take for granted that the listener is aware of appropriate background information. To do so is a violation of the cooperative principle and is egocentric. In this regard, Bates argues:

> The development of presuppositions is tied to the decline of egocentrism in early childhood. As the child learns to distinguish between his own viewpoint and that of his listeners . . . he will gradually realize that his own pre-

suppositions may not be readily available to his listeners. Hence, he will learn to rearrange and expand his utterances, so that *both* the asserted and presupposed information are clear to others (1976, p. 445).

In our study, there were several examples of inappropriate continuations of partner's or one's own topic by the senile subjects. In many cases, the background of the utterance was not clear and the patient may have presupposed that the experimenter grasped the context of the utterance. An example of a violation in the continuation of the partner's topic is as follows:

Experimenter   Did you have to go to Boise to be in the senate?
Subject (#102)   Yes, yes, yes, we make laws down there to help . . . how much you have to go to school, who the teachers are, and how they're paid.
   (#103)   Some of them will be teachers after a while.

Utterance #102 fulfills the experimenter's directive, but utterance #103, though tangentially related to the issue of educational policy presented in #102, is obscure. The experimenter does not know to whom the patient refers and why the issue of the time necessary to become a teacher is of any consequence. One cannot assume that #103 is necessarily an extraneous and irrelevant comment. It is quite possible that this is evidence of information presented without reference to the listener's perspective.

Another example of such a violation, in this case during the continuation of one's own topic, is illustrated in the following:

Subject (#16)   When will that little girl come back that wears the cap?
Experimenter   She's going to come and get you in a little while.
Subject (#18)   How soon?
Experimenter   She's talking to some other people right now.

[Experimenter, 24 utterances; patient, 22 utterances]

Experimenter   What do you do when she comes to visit?
Subject (#40)   Just visit.
Experimenter   Just visit?
Subject (#41)   Where's that girl with the little cap?

Here the patient asks about the "little girl with the cap" and four turns are devoted to that topic. The conversation ultimately drifts to an exchange regarding the upcoming visit by the patient's daughter. The experimenter responds to utterance #40 by indicating the desire for more information. To this directive the patient replies, "Where's that girl with the little cap?"

One might be tempted to equate this utterance with the example of an inappropriate initiation of a new topic described earlier. However, within the total conversation, it was not a new topic; it had been discussed some twenty utterances earlier. This is an example of what Coulthard (1977) calls *skip-connecting*. Chafe (1974) discusses it in relation to egocentrism, reasoning that the speaker cannot be ignorant of the material or themes in the listener's consciousness. If the transmission of information is to be efficient, "What a speaker shares with his addressee must be a part of what is in the speaker's consciousness at the time" (p. 112). However, a rather important characteristic of anyone's consciousness is its limited capacity. A theme cannot be expected to remain there indefinitely. Therefore as more and more utterances and topics intervene between a particular conversational theme and its reintroduction, the less likely the theme will be contained in the listener's consciousness. To reintroduce a theme without reference to what might be in the listener's immediate consciousness is an act of inappropriate presupposition. This, according to Chafe, is egocentric. In such circumstances, the speaker operates exclusively from a personal point of view by "extrapolating into the hearer's mind something that is really only in his own mind" (p. 130).

**Conclusion—To What End?**

In our introductory comments we suggested that the process of aging and the presence of senility might be associated with the reemergence of a cognitive pattern known as egocentrism. The term *reemergence* was used because egocentrism is an obvious characteristic of early childhood. However, a disclaimer is warranted at this point. We do not contend that reemergence implies regression. Cognitive capabilities are diminished in both childhood and senility because of decreases in cortical capacity, but the presence of egocentrism at those times in life may be traced to quite different processes. In one case the cortex is immature but of normal potential; in the other, the cortex is degenerated and not of normal potential. In addition, such factors as experience and environment are quite different for the two extremes of one's life. Therefore it would be tenuous to assert that egocentrism in senility is evidence of wholesale regression to childhood patterns of cognition, even though similarities in behavior are often apparent.

It has been assumed here that egocentrism, if it is a feature of senility, should be discernible in the pragmatic aspect of conversational discourse. This is indeed the case, but one might ask, "So what? Of what significance is that?" Aside from the insight gained regarding cognitive patterns, these data may provide an initial drop in a data pool from which therapeutic strategies for senility might emerge. The nihilistic approach to therapy for such patients is no longer accepted by responsible health professionals. Speech and language pathologists have the potential to help these people retain a higher quality of life for as long as possible. However, our knowledge of language patterns in senility is so embryonic that therapeutic efforts are generally inefficient and misdirected. That is why interdisciplinary research and clinical cooperation are so desperately needed.

## References

Abdo, E., Dills, J., Schectman, H., and Yanish, M. Elderly women in institutions versus those in public housing: comparisons of personal and social adjustments. *Journal of the American Geriatrics Society* 21: 81-87, 1973.

Austin, J.L. *How to Do Things with Words.* Cambridge: Harvard University Press, 1962.

Bates, E. Pragmatics and sociolinguistics in child language. In *Normal and Deficient Child Language*, edited by D. Morehead and A. Morehead. Baltimore: University Park Press, 1976.

Bell, J.Z. Disengagement vs. engagement—a need for greater expectations. *Journal of the American Geriatrics Society* 26: 89-95, 1978.

Bernstein, B. Elaborated and restricted codes: their social origins and some consequences. In *Comunication and Culture*, edited by A.G. Smith. New York: Holt, Rinehart, and Winston, 1966.

Bloom, L., Rocissano, L., and Hood, L. Adult-child discourse: developmental interaction between information processing and linguistic knowledge. *Cognitive Psychology* 8: 521-52, 1976.

Botwinick, J. *Aging and Behavior.* New York: Springer, 1973.

Butler, R.N., and Lewis, M.I. *Aging and Mental Health.* St. Louis: C.V. Mosby, 1977.

Chafe, W.L. Language and consciousness. *Language* 50: 111-33, 1974.

Coblentz, J.M., Mattis, S., Zingesser, L.H., Kasoff, S.S., Wisnieski, H. M., and Katzman, R. Presenile dementia. *Neurology* 29: 299-308, 1973.

Coulthard, M. *An Introduction to Discourse Analysis.* London: Longman, 1977.

Flavell, J.H. *The Developmental Psychology of Jean Piaget.* Princeton: Van Nostrand, 1963.

Grice, H.P. Logic and conversation. In *Syntax and Semantics* Speech Acts, edited by P. Cole and J.L. Morgan, vol. 3. New York: Academic Press, 1975.

Halpern, H., Darley, F.L., and Brown, J.R. Differential language and neurologic characteristics in cerebral involvement. *Journal of Speech Hearing Disorders* 38: 162-73, 1973.

Hulicka, I. Understanding our client, the geriatric patient. *Journal of the American Geriatrics Society* 20: 438-48, 1972.

Hunt, J. McV. *Intelligence and Experience.* New York: Ronald Press, 1961.

Kahn, R.L., Goldfarb, A.I., Pollack, M., and Peck, A. Brief objective measures for the determination of mental status in the aged. *American Journal of Psychiatry* 117: 326-30, 1960.

Katzman, R., and Karasu, T.B. Differential diagnosis of dementia. In *Neurological and Sensory Disorders in the Elderly,* edited by W.S. Fields. New York: Stratton, 1975.

Looft, W.R. Egocentrism and social interaction across the life span. *Psychological Bulletin* 78: 73-92, 1972.

Miller, E. *Abnormal Aging.* London: Wiley, 1977.

Piaget, J. *Language and Thought of the Child.* London: Routledge and Kegan Paul, 1926.

_____. *Psychology of Intelligence.* Totowa, N.J.: Littlefield, Adams, 1966.

Rees, N.S. Pragmatics of language. In *Bases of Language Intervention,* edited by R.L. Schiefelbusch. Baltimore: University Park Press, 1978.

Rosow, I. *Social Integration of the Aged.* New York: Free Press, 1967.

Searle, J.R. What is a speech act? In *Philosophy in America,* edited by M. Black. Cornell: Allen and Unwin, 1965.

_____. *Speech Acts.* London: Cambridge University Press, 1969.

_____. A taxonomy of illocutionary acts. In *Minnesota Studies in the Philosophy of Language,* edited by K. Gunderson. Minneapolis: University of Minnesota Press, 1975.

Schow, R., Christensen, J., Hutchinson, J., and Nerbonne, M. *Communication Disorders of the Aged: A Guide for Health Professionals.* Baltimore: University Park Press, 1978.

Schwartz, A.N., and Proppe, H.G. Toward person/environment transactional research in aging. *The Gerontologist* 10: 228-32, 1970.

Welford, A.T. Performance, biological mechanisms and age. In *Behavior, Aging, and the Nervous System,* edited by A.T. Welford and J.E. Birren. Springfield, IL: Charles C. Thomas, 1965.

# 6

## Narrative Discourse Style in the Elderly

### Loraine K. Obler

In an effort to determine precisely how language develops at the late end of the life span, one focus of our research has been narrative discourse. It is commonly maintained that elderly people "tend to run on," to ramble in their speech. Thus we hypothesized that patterns of narrative discourse might evidence language change even though other linguistic skills such as vocabulary or comprehension remain stable, as the WAIS and similar tests suggest.

Early attempts to elicit and analyze spontaneous discourse showed that the wide range of individual variation in narrative styles, when combined with the freedom of conversation, made it extremely difficult for us to draw conclusions about changes in narrative style across age groups. As a result we turned to more directed discourse tasks by which we could elicit narrative discourse units that would be comparable across subjects. Four studies will be discussed in this chapter, two dealing with written discourse and two with oral discourse. Although there are differences in style engendered by the differences between the two modalities (see Ulatowska, Hildebrand, and Haynes, 1978), our concern here is the parallel age-related developments in the two narrative modalities.

We tested both dementing and healthy elderly subjects in our research. A major goal has been to distinguish the language of dementing patients from that of both healthy peers and aphasics. In many instances, we have discovered, the language of the dementing patients appears to be an exaggerated form of the language of their healthy peers. That is, the characteristics that distinguish older healthy subjects from younger ones are more pronounced in the dementing patients. We may want to modify this statement, however, by considering the specific language features associated with the various dementing diseases. Also worth mentioning is that linguistic similarities (or differences) between the two groups cannot themselves resolve the medical debate as to whether the dementias are precipitous versions of healthy aging processes or distinct diseases.

Martin Albert and Edith Kaplan participated in designing and interpreting studies reported here. They are to be thanked, as are Harold Goodglass and Bracha Mildworf, for sharing data with me. I am grateful for the assistance of Tedd Judd, Amy Veroff, and Omar Othman in collecting data. Analyses of these data were performed with the help of Mary Hyde, Ken Albert, Michael Albert, Susanna Haberman, Campbell Leaper, Maude Salinger, Jennifer Sandson, and Mindy Schimmel.

**Written Discourse: Two Studies**

Subjects were shown the cookie-theft picture from the Boston Diagnostic Aphasia Examination (Goodglass and Kaplan, 1972) and asked to write what was going on in it. A standard four-point scale and additional qualitative and quantitative analyses were used to evaluate the responses. To verify the alleged loquaciousness of aging, we counted the number of words per response, and compared this to the number of themes represented. To investigate the nature of this loquaciousness, we explored sentence type (abbreviated versus full) and discourse connection type (conjoined versus embedded versus contiguous). We also determined the frequency of the various parts of speech (nouns, verbs, articles, and so on) since verb-to-noun ratio has been reported to distinguish among Broca's aphasics, Wernicke's aphasics, and matched controls (Gleason and others, 1978).

In the first study our subjects were eighteen male parkinsonian patients in their fifties and sixties and eighteen healthy controls matched as a group for age, sex, and education level (see table 6-1). The healthy controls were hospital patients with no neurological pathology above the neck. Due to the small sample size, statistical analyses have not been undertaken. The results which follow, then, reflect trends.

Using the standard scoring measure, we found no difference between either the parkinsonians and the healthy or between the fifty and sixty year olds. Yet two quite distinct styles stood out on this task—one we call abbreviated, the other elaborate, shown in items #1 and #2 respectively.

1. Healthy male aged 53, twelfth-grade education: Boy at cookie jar, passing them to girl, women drying dishes, sink overflowing, two cups and plate beside sink.
2. Healthy male aged 62, eighth-grade education: We have a lady washing dishes unaware the sink is running over, while behind, her little boy and girl are trying to help themselves to some cookies. Soon the little boy is going to take a fall.

The abbreviated style generally predominated in the younger group, the fifty year olds, and in the healthy as opposed to the parkinsonian group. This can be seen by counting the number of subjects in each group using the full-sentence strategy (table 6-2); the average number of full or partial sentences per subject (tables 6-3 and 6-4); and the average number of words produced on the task, where loquaciousness again becomes evident (table 6-5). If we disregard whether sentences were full or abbreviated, it becomes apparent that the older group and the parkinsonians used fewer sentences (table 6-6) yet they were doing more embedding of one sentence within another (table 6-7).

**Table 6-1**
**Written Discourse: Study 1**

| Subject Group | Median Age | | Average Number of Years of Education | |
|---|---|---|---|---|
| | Healthy | Parkinsonian | Healthy | Parkinsonian |
| Fifties, $N = 7$ (each group) | 56 | 56 | 11.6 | 10.4 |
| Sixties, $N = 11$ (each group) | 64 | 63 | 10.6 | 11.1 |

**Table 6-2**
**Subjects Using Full Sentences**
(*number/percent*)

| Subject Group | Parkinsonian | Healthy |
|---|---|---|
| Fifties, $N = 7$ (each group) | 4  57% | 2  28% |
| Sixties, $N = 11$ (each group) | 8  73% | 6  55% |

**Table 6-3**
**Average Number of Full Sentences per Subject**

| Subject Group | Parkinsonian | Healthy |
|---|---|---|
| Fifties, $N = 7$ (each group) | 1.3 | 1.1 |
| Sixties, $N = 11$ (each group) | 1.8 | 1.3 |

**Table 6-4**
**Average Number of Partial Sentences per Subject**

| Subject Group | Parkinsonian | Healthy |
|---|---|---|
| Fifties, $N = 7$ (each group) | 2.3 | 2.0 |
| Sixties, $N = 11$ (each group) | 1.0 | 1.2 |

**Table 6-5**
**Average Number of Words per Response**

| Subject Group | Parkinsonian | Healthy |
|---|---|---|
| Fifties, $N = 7$ (each group) | 27.0 | 20.3 |
| Sixties, $N = 11$ (each group) | 31.0 | 26.2 |

**Table 6-6**
**Average Number of Sentences (Abbreviated and Full)**

| Subject Group | Parkinsonian | Healthy |
|---|---|---|
| Fifties, $N = 7$ (each group) | 3.6 | 3.1 |
| Sixties, $N = 11$ (each group) | 2.8 | 2.5 |

**Table 6-7**
**Average Number of Embedded Sentences**

| Subject Group | Parkinsonian | Healthy |
|---|---|---|
| Fifties, $N = 7$ (each group) | 1.0 | 0.9 |
| Sixties, $N = 11$ (each group) | 1.5 | 1.1 |

We also considered data on the parts of speech used. In the abbreviated style of the younger and healthier groups, function words such as pronouns, articles, prepositions, and conjunctions were underrepresented (table 6-8). Yet verbs and nouns were pretty much equally represented in all groups (the young *and* healthy group having the fewest of both), and the $N$-to-$V$ ratio used for distinguishing between aphasic and normal groups on another discourse task (shown in Gleason, Goodglass, et al. 1978) is fairly consistent across groups. The trend is predictable, however, with the older people and parkinsonians showing fewer nouns per verb (table 6-9), as was true of the Wernicke's aphasics relative to normal controls in the Gleason study.

Finally, confirming the general loquacity of the older and parkinsonian subjects was the words per theme score; both evidenced a greater number of words per theme. However, the parkinsonian patients actually tended to report more themes than did the healthy controls (table 6-10).

**Table 6-8**
**Function Words**

| Subject Group | Pronouns | Articles | Prepositions | Con-junctions | Total |
|---|---|---|---|---|---|
| Parkinsonian | | | | | |
| Fifties, $N=7$ | 0.4 | 2.9 | 3.1 | 1.7 | 8.1 |
| Sixties, $N=11$ | 1.4 | 4.4 | 3.0 | 1.5 | 10.3 |
| Healthy | | | | | |
| Fifties, $N=7$ | 0.6 | 2.3 | 1.7 | 1.1 | 5.7 |
| Sixties, $N=11$ | 0.8 | 3.0 | 2.2 | 2.0 | 8.0 |

**Table 6-9**
**Nouns and Verbs**

| Subject Group | Nouns | Verbs | Noun per Verb |
|---|---|---|---|
| Parkinsonian | 9.0 | 7.4 | 1.2 |
| Fifties, $N=7$ | 8.9 | 7.7 | 1.2 |
| Sixties, $N=11$ | | | |
| Healthy | | | |
| Fifties, $N=7$ | 7.4 | 5.5 | 1.4 |
| Sixties, $N=11$ | 8.0 | 6.2 | 1.3 |

**Table 6-10**
**Words and Themes**

| Subject Group | Words | Themes | Words per Theme |
|---|---|---|---|
| Parkinsonian | 27.0 | 5.0 | 5.4 |
| Fifties, $N=7$ | 31.0 | 4.5 | 6.8 |
| Sixties, $N=11$ | | | |
| Healthy | | | |
| Fifties, $N=7$ | 20.3 | 4.3 | 4.7 |
| Sixties, $N=11$ | 26.2 | 4.4 | 5.8 |

In summary the sixty year olds as compared to the fifty year olds, and the parkinsonians as compared to the healthy, had more elaborate speech. This consisted of more total words in responses, especially function words, embodied in fewer but more complex sentences. Yet fewer themes were reported within this elaborate speech.

In the second study we performed the same analyses on cookie-theft data that Goodglass had collected from 106 healthy unhospitalized male subjects. In this group less education was associated with increased age (table 6-11).

To make sense of the data presented in table 6-12 we must first consider the three oldest decades studied, the fifties through seventies, where a pattern similar to that seen in the first study was obtained. We will then return to the data on the thirty and forty year olds, which did not conform in linear fashion to the hypothesis reached in the first study, that increased age (or dementia) concurs with more elaborate speech.

From the fifties through the seventies, there is again a greater tendency to use the full sentence rather than the abbreviated style.

As in the previous study, the number of functors used tends to increase across age from the forties through seventies, as do the number of words, although there is a slight dip from the fifties to the sixties.

On several counts it would appear that health actually increased with age in this population, unlike in the first study. The number of themes and sentences increases across the fifties and the seventies, and the number of words per theme actually decreases slightly. We must surmise that with age increasing from fifty through the seventies, a volunteer population self-selects for greater sharpness with age.

If we look at the younger decades, and particularly the highly educated thirties group, we see that in several of the tests they most resemble the seventy year olds. Thus a very high percentage select the full-sentence strategy—they use a large number of words, sentences, and functors. That is, discuss many themes in a fairly wordy way.

The most convincing interpretation we come up with for this U-shaped finding, whereby the oldest and youngest groups share many features, is that the two polar age extremes are producing similar language configurations for quite different reasons. The younger group, we would suggest, writes fluent and lengthy prose because it is easy for them to; they are comfortable with the task and expect to do well at it. In the older groups, how-

**Table 6-11**
**Study 2: Education**

| Subject Group (age) | N | Average Education |
|---|---|---|
| Thirties | 10 | 14.6 |
| Forties | 7 | 13.0 |
| Fifties | 25 | 12.8 |
| Sixties | 27 | 11.7 |
| Seventies | 18 | 11.3 |

**Table 6-12**
**Study 2: Healthy Population**

| Subject Group (age) | Percent Using Full-Sentence Strategy | Average Number of Sentences | Average Number of Words | Nouns | Verbs | Noun per Verb | Functors | Themes | Words per Theme |
|---|---|---|---|---|---|---|---|---|---|
| Thirties, $N=10$ | 80 | 3.9 | 46.5 | 12.5 | 11.5 | 1.1 | 18.1 | 7.4 | 6.5 |
| Forties, $N=7$ | 71 | 3.2 | 26.1 | 8.7 | 7.1 | 1.2 | 9.1 | 5.0 | 5.4 |
| Fifties, $N=25$ | 44 | 2.5 | 29.3 | 10.5 | 7.3 | 1.4 | 9.7 | 4.6 | 6.4 |
| Sixties, $N=27$ | 55 | 3.5 | 28.4 | 9.5 | 7.7 | 1.2 | 10.0 | 5.0 | 6.3 |
| Seventies, $N=18$ | 61 | 3.9 | 36.5 | 12.2 | 8.9 | 1.4 | 12.2 | 5.9 | 6.2 |

ever, the fluency of elaborate speech results less from comfort than necessity. The alleged necessity on the part of the elderly to use full language is borne out in the next study.

## Oral Narrative on a Memory Task: Two Studies

In this experiment comparable oral narratives were elicited from sizable populations by asking them to reproduce a story that was read to them. Talland (1965) had run a similar study on Korsakoff patients and normal controls, and observed several response types peculiar to the Korsakoff patients. In addition to giving shorter and sparser responses, the Korsakoff patients distorted responses by both generalizing and embellishing with comments and fabrications.

We undertook qualitative analyses of oral narrative responses that refined Talland's categories and added others, and measured the frequency of occurrence of the various phenomena observed by Talland and additional ones, such as paraphrasing, repetition, specification, and the use of indefinite terms like *something* or *anyone*. The target passage is a Wechsler Memory Passage:

> Dogs are trained to rescue the wounded in wartime. Police dogs are also trained to rescue drowning people. Instead of running down to the water and striking out, they are taught to make a flying leap by which they save many swimming strokes and valuable seconds of time. The European sheep dog makes the best police dog.

Several characteristic responses follow with standard point scores:
Male, age 68, 6 points (Note indefinites, additions)

> About the dogs. Talking about the, I didn't get. It's supposed to be shepherd dog and trying to save life. If there's anyone in the water. You referred to the dog instead of crawling to it would jump to save strokes—from the stream or pool—they were also used in the service in world wars. Most was used in the second world war. Most was used in the second world war in capturing the enemy, disarming his rifles. Till somebody came or he probably killed the prisoner. I guess they both about as good a dog as the other type you mentioned.

Female, age 68, 5.5 points (Note recency effect, indefinites, comments)

> The European dog makes the best police dog. Something about a German shepherd and something about going to water to rescue somebody drowning. That's all I can remember. I guess I'm not concentrating.

Female, age 84, 13.5 points (Note repetition, indefinites)

> Dogs are trained to rescue wounded in wartime. Dogs are trained to rescue drowning, people drowning. Something about trained to go to the water and make a flying leap. And something sheep dog make the best trained rescue dog.

Female, age 60, 2.5 points

> About a dog. Sheep dog rescues.

## Procedure

In the course of a screening battery of neuropsycholological tests, individual subjects were told they would hear a story passage and then be asked to "tell everything they remember." The tester then read the passage at a measured rate (probably louder and better articulated for subjects who had previously demonstrated or reported hardness of hearing), and upon conclusion said "OK, now tell me everything you remember." The subjects' responses were written down by the examiner with appropriate nods and encouragement. An interval of approximately ten minutes was filled with other testing. The experimenter then asked if the subject remembered that a story had been read before and to tell what was remembered. If the subject claimed not to remember anything (under both immediate and delayed recall conditions), the tester asked if she or he remembered that a story had been read, and noted the response.

## Material and Analysis

A logical memory passage from the Wechsler Memory Scale, Form II was selected since a standardized scoring procedure was available. An additional scoring system was developed in which thirty-five closed-class elements were identified as follows:

> Dogs are trained to rescue the wounded in war time. Police dogs are
>   1     2       3         4      5  6     7
> also trained to rescue drowning people. Instead of running down to the
>  8    9      10     11     12     13      14    15
> water and striking out, they are taught to make a flying leap by which
>   16       17    18     19     20     21  22
> they save many swimming strokes and valuable seconds of time. The
> 23 24  25    26     27       28     29      30
> European sheep dog makes the best police dog.
>    31       32      33     34     35

The tester wrote down all verbal responses to the task, but unstressed function words were not included in the analysis because the recording procedure precluded confidence in their accuracy. First a score was computed by Wechsler's standard system for each of the two recalls the subject made. Then each story was prepared for computer analysis by listing each element in order, providing information about its type (story, item number, comment, addition, question), and noting whether it occurred verbatim or in paraphrase. Certain paraphrases were employed so frequently that we decided to identify them with abbreviations. Among these items were *used* for *trained* in "dogs are trained to rescue the wounded," and *save lives* for *rescue drowning people* in "police dogs are also trained to rescue drowning people."

*Study 1*

Subjects were selected randomly from a larger sample in order to fill an eighteen-cell matrix of gender *x* age group *x* education level. There were 45 males and 45 females, equally distributed in the age groupings 55-64, 65-74, and above 74. One third of the subjects in each of the sex *x* age cells had had only primary education, one third had continued through high school, and one third had studied beyond high school. Effort was made to select only native speakers of English, but to complete the low-education group it was necessary to select seventeen nonnative speakers of English (eight females and nine males). Here again, our findings reflect trends rather than statistical "truths."

By the standard scoring system, subjects did worse with increased age, and performed somewhat worse in the delayed than in the immediate condition (table 6-13).

By our length measure, fewer items were employed with increasing age in both conditions (table 6-14). This finding appears to contradict those of the written narrative stories, but can probably be explained by the interaction of memory in this task.

Incidence of paraphrase and use of indefinite terms like *something* or *any* tended to increase with age. Comments and questions increased with

**Table 6-13**
**Standard Recall Score by Age Group**

| Type of Response | 55-64<br>(N = 30) | 65-74<br>(N = 30) | 75 +<br>(N = 30) |
|---|---|---|---|
| Immediate | 8.1 | 6.6 | 5.8 |
| Delayed | 7.0 | 5.4 | 4.2 |

**Table 6-14**
**Average Number of Items per Story**

| Type of Response | 55-64 (N = 30) | 65-74 (N = 30) | 75 + (N = 30) |
|---|---|---|---|
| Immediate | 17.0 | 15.4 | 14.6 |
| Delayed | 17.3 | 13.6 | 11.5 |

age in the immediate condition, but not in the delayed condition. The fact that all three age groups used much fewer comments and questions in the delayed condition suggests that all subjects were sensitive to the memory nature of the task. Those who did not expect to perform well felt obliged to fill out their speech in the immediate-recall condition (where they were expected to do well), but did not feel so obliged in the delayed-recall condition (table 6-15).

The use of comments, additions, and indefinites decreased with increasing education (table 6-16). Counter to our expectations, the contribution of repetition to the stories increased in the higher-education groups. This may simply reflect the lessened use of comments, additions, and indefinites, however. For both recall conditions the total amount of paraphrasing was *highest* in the high-education group, and lowest in the medium group. This may reflect a different understanding of the instructions given for the task.

**Table 6-15**
**Age and Item Information**

| Item | 55-64 (N = 30) Immediate | Delayed | 65-74 (N = 30) Immediate | Delayed | 75 + (N = 30) Immediate | Delayed |
|---|---|---|---|---|---|---|
| Words/story | 17.0 | 17.3 | 15.4 | 13.6 | 14.6 | 11.5 |
| Questions | 2 | 3 | 5 | 0 | 6 | 1 |
|  | .4% | .6% | 1.1% | 0% | 1.4% | .3% |
| Comments | 24 | 15 | 30 | 19 | 36 | 10 |
|  | 4.7% | 2.9% | 6.5% | 4.6% | 8.2% | 2.9% |
| Repetitions | 67 | 79 | 53 | 44 | 51 | 45 |
|  | 13.2% | 15.2% | 11.4% | 10.8% | 11.6% | 13.1% |
| Additions | 39 | 57 | 47 | 68 | 39 | 45 |
|  | 7.6% | 11.0% | 10.2% | 16.7% | 8.9% | 13.1% |
| Total paraphrases | 107 | 143 | 83 | 110 | 110 | 95 |
|  | 21.0% | 27.5% | 18.0% | 27.0% | 25.1% | 27.6% |
| Indefinites | 14 | 36 | 18 | 24 | 23 | 37 |
|  | 2.7% | 6.9% | 3.9% | 5.9% | 5.3% | 10.7% |

**Table 6-16**
**Education and Item Information**

| Item | Elementary Education | | High School | | More Than High School | |
|---|---|---|---|---|---|---|
| | Immediate | Delayed | Immediate | Delayed | Immediate | Delayed |
| Story score | 4.4 | 2.8 | 6.8 | 5.5 | 9.4 | 7.6 |
| Words/story | 10.8 | 8.2 | 14.7 | 14.2 | 21.4 | 19.9 |
| Questions | 0 | 0 | 6 | 3 | 7 | 1 |
| | 0% | 0% | 1.4% | .7% | 1.1% | .2% |
| Comments | 33 | 10 | 28 | 14 | 29 | 20 |
| | 10.2% | 4.0% | 6.3% | 3.3% | 4.5% | 3.3% |
| Repetitions | 30 | 26 | 61 | 58 | 81 | 77 |
| | 9.2% | 10.5% | 13.8% | 13.1% | 12.6% | 12.9% |
| Additions | 36 | 40 | 39 | 58 | 51 | 72 |
| | 10.3% | 16.2% | 8.8% | 13.1% | 7.9% | 12.0% |
| Total paraphrase | 82 | 70 | 82 | 109 | 137 | 195 |
| | 25.2% | 28.3% | 18.6% | 25.6% | 21.3% | 32.6% |
| Indefinites | 25 | 35 | 12 | 26 | 18 | 36 |
| | 7.7% | 14.2% | 2.7% | 6.1% | 2.8% | 6.0% |

In any case, this paraphrasing pattern was more a result of synonymous paraphrasing than inflectional paraphrasing, the rate of which hovered around 9 percent for all groups in both conditions.

Sex differences on this task were not as striking as the other differences; neverthless a few trends can be detected (table 6-17). While the men gave somewhat fewer items in both conditions than did the women, their story score was higher than that of the women in the delayed condition, but not in the immediate condition. With respect to repetitions and paraphrasing, the groups performed identically. The women seem to have increased their story length, then, by a much greater use of comments, particularly in the immediate-recall condition, and by a greater use of indefinites and questions. The men, on the other hand, made more additions to the stories than did the women, and were much more likely than the women to incorporate their own additions to the first recall into the second retelling.

We analyzed some of the factors discriminating the good (standard score greater than 12 from the poor scores (standard score below 5), as shown in table 6-18.

Those who scored high on the standard measure gave much longer responses than those who scored poorly. Less of the good stories consisted of comments, and much more consisted of repetitions. The good group used much more paraphrasing than did the poor group, but it constituted a smaller percentage of their stories. Likewise there were more actual additions made in the good stories but they represented a smaller percent of the good responses.

**Table 6-17**
**Sex and Item Information**

| Item | Women | | Men | |
|---|---|---|---|---|
| | Immediate | Delayed | Immediate | Delayed |
| Story score | 6.9 | 5.1 | 6.8 | 5.6 |
| Words/story | 16.3 | 14.4 | 15.0 | 13.8 |
| Questions | 9 | 3 | 4 | 1 |
| | 1.2% | .5% | .6% | .2% |
| Comments | 64 | 24 | 26 | 20 |
| | 8.7% | 3.7% | 3.8% | 3.2% |
| Repetitions | 197 | 215 | 179 | 200 |
| | 26.8% | 33.1% | 26.5% | 32.2% |
| Additions | 55 | 71 | 71 | 89 |
| | 7.5% | 10.9% | 10.5% | 14.3% |
| Total paraphrase | 154 | 176 | 147 | 162 |
| | 21.0% | 27.1% | 21.7% | 26.0% |
| Indefinites | 38 | 54 | 17 | 43 |
| | 5.2% | 8.3% | 2.5% | 6.9% |

**Table 6-18**
**Good versus Bad Stories**

| Item | Immediate | | Delayed | |
|---|---|---|---|---|
| | Bad | Good | Bad | Good |
| Questions | 0 | 5 | 1 | 3 |
| | 0% | .9% | .6% | .6% |
| Comments | 18 | 23 | 10 | 12 |
| | 10.9% | 4.3% | 6.5% | 2.2% |
| Repetitions | 29 | 151 | 34 | 191 |
| | 17.6% | 28.5% | 22.2% | 35.5% |
| Additions | 18 | 29 | 26 | 48 |
| | 10.9% | 5.5% | 17.0% | 9.0% |
| Total paraphrases | 45 | 94 | 52 | 141 |
| | 27.3% | 17.8% | 34.0% | 26.2% |

Paraphrasing aside, if we count the ten most frequent target items in the good and bad stories, a pattern emerges. The good stories emphasize the words that sum up most of the narrative: *dogs rescue people*. The poor stories show a recency effect; after *dogs*, the most frequent words are mostly from the final sentence: *European*, *Sheep dog*, *police*, and *best*. Indeed, the two words from the top ten of the poor group that do not make the top ten of the good group are from the final sentence: *European*, and *police dogs*. The good group includes two verbs that are used with much lower relative frequency by the poor group: *leap* (including its paraphrase, *jump*), and *save*.

*Study 2*

In the second study using the same Wechsler memory passage, two very different populations were selected. The first was a group of thirty-eight subjects selected out of six hundred people tested who were older than age fifty-five and had been adjudged demented on the rest of the neuropsychological battery. Matched to this group for sex, age (within two years), education, and native language were thirty-eight of the people whose performance was superior on the neuropsychological battery. (Dementing patients scored above 3.5 in the 6-point organic scale of Albert, Kaplan, and others; superior subjects scored below 1.5.) The resulting population consisted of 55 females and 22 males. There were 20 subjects age 55-64; 34 were age 65-74; and 23 were age 75 and over. Native English-speaking subjects numbered 28; native Italian, 27.

The dementing patients of course recalled very little on this test (table 6-19). When they did respond, they used more additions and indefinites than the superior subjects, who, in line with our findings of the previous study, made somewhat greater use of repetition.

These studies suggest that indefinite terms characterize the narrative speech of older and also dementing individuals. Comments and questions

**Table 6-19**
**Dementia Score**

|  | Exceptional Group | | Dementing Group | |
|---|---|---|---|---|
|  | *Immediate* | *Delayed* | *Immediate* | *Delayed* |
| Story score | 80.0 | 66.5 | 28.2 | 17.1 |
| Words | 18.0 | 17.6 | 8.1 | 5.3 |
| Comments | 8 | 2 | 4 | 0 |
|  | 1.1% | .3% | 1.3% | 0% |
| Repetitions | 207 | 218 | 76 | 51 |
|  | 29.3% | 31.6% | 24.8% | 25.1% |
| Additions | 56 | 74 | 26 | 29 |
|  | 7.9% | 10.7% | 8.5% | 14.3% |
| Indefinites | 33 | 55 | 28 | 23 |
|  | 4.7% | 8.0% | 9.2% | 11.3% |

may also fill their speech. Repetition, contrary to expectation, may characterize the more successful stories of these people.


## Storytelling

The third type of data which must be discussed in this context derives from a study that differs methodologically from those discussed previously. This study involved tale telling by fifteen individuals ranging in age from nineteen to eighty-three who live in a culture where storytelling is a respected skill (an Arab community outside Jerusalem). In our sample the three most renowned tale tellers were the oldest three, aged 65, 75, and 83. Structural analyses were performed comparing their stories with those of the less proficient tale tellers. The following characteristics were evident (Obler, 1978):

1. Master tale tellers had certain filler phrases, such as "as they say," which they used comfortably in the course of telling their tale.
2. Indefinite terms took on a role in distinguishing the world of the tale, for example, "once upon a time," "a woman with three or four daughters," and so on.
3. Asking questions and commenting served important rhetorical functions in storytelling.
4. Repetition served important functions at many levels in tale performance. Within a sentence or across sentences, literal repetition gave rhythm to a phrase; across the story it added coherence. Modified repetition (paraphrase), enriched the story at the word or phrase level, and may have actually provided the vehicle for the tale at the incident level.

An example that demonstrates these findings is the beginning of a tale told by the sixty-five-year-old woman.

> Once upon a time there was a woman who didn't conceive and didn't have children. She went up to the market of Bethlehem to shop. When she went up to shop, she saw some cheese. She saw some women selling the cheese (jibne), you know, the gypsies, selling cheese. She said, "Dear Lord give me a daughter as white as this cheese, and I'll call her Jabeyna." God fulfilled her prayers; she got pregnant and gave birth to a daughter and called her Jabeyna.

> So she called her Jabeyna, you hear, and she grew up; at first she was like this son of yours, but how beautiful she was, how white like cheese! She was astonishing. Time passed and Jabeyna grew and the village girls were jealous of her. [*Beautiful Jabeyna*, translated from the Arabic]

We are left with the question *why* language use becomes more elaborate with increased age. Is it primarily related to neurological changes in brain substrate? Does it result by way of compensation for loss of primary cognitive functions, like memory or attention? Does it represent cultural and/or educational differences between cohorts? Is it a result of different responses to test-taking situations? The latter seem unlikely (that differences in culture, education, or attitude toward testing account for the differences in narrative language we have reported between younger and older adults) since parallel results have obtained across cultures, in different sorts of testing situations, with illiterates as well as with groups controlled and matched for education.

It is tempting but probably premature at this point to link together the features of narrative language we have reported for the elderly with those seen less subtly in cortically dementing individuals and Wernicke's aphasics. Wernicke's aphasics, whose language is fluent though empty, as Albert mentions elsewhere in this book, tend to be a decade older than Broca's aphasics whose language is abbreviated telegraphically. Cortically dementing patients (in periods when they are not mute) tend to speak quite fluently, even though their discourse may not make sense. The difference between these two groups and our healthy elderly may not be so much one of style as of content: Wernicke's and cortically dementing individuals present fluent but empty or anomalous speech that therefore cannot be considered elaborate, whereas healthy elderly individuals develop an enriched, elaborate style.

### References

Gleason, J., Goodglass, H., Obler, L., Green, E., Hyde, M., and Weintraub, S. Narrative strategies of aphasic and normal subjects, presented at Academy of Aphasia, 1978.

Goodglass, H. and Kaplan, E. *The Assessment of Aphasia and Related Disorders.* Philadelphia: Lea and Febiger, 1972.

Obler, L. Tale-telling conventions of three elderly Palestinians, presented at Middle East Society of America, 1978.

Ulatowska, H., Hildebrand, B., and Haynes, S. A comparison of written and spoken language in aphasia. Unpublished manuscript, 1978.

# 7 Hemispheric Specialization and Development

*Joan C. Borod* and
*Harold Goodglass*

In the last few decades, investigations of hemispheric asymmetry in cognitive functioning have provided new conceptions of brain behavior relations and suggested possible underlying neurological mechanisms. Each of the two cerebral hemispheres in the human brain appears to be dominant for different materials and modes of processing. In right-handed people the left hemisphere is dominant for linguistic and mathematical reasoning functions, whereas the right hemisphere is superior for spatial relations, patterns, transformations, and for music (Sperry, 1974; Nebes, 1974; Milner, 1971; Gazzaniga, 1970). With respect to modes of processing, Sperry has contrasted the functions of the right hemisphere with those of the left. "They seem to be holistic and unitary rather than analytic and fragmentary, and orientational more than focal, and to involve concrete perceptual insight rather than abstract, symbolic, sequential reasoning" (1974, p. 11). Carmon (1969), in fact, suggests that the two hemispheres deal with two major dimensions of our world: the temporal and the spatial.

It has been taken for granted that the two cerebral hemispheres develop in such a way as to subserve different perceptual-cognitive mechanisms. Although these hemispheric differences have been reliably demonstrated in the visual, auditory, and tactual modalities, the percentage of people with right or left hemispheric dominance for language may vary with age, method of measurement and data analysis. To date, attention to the developmental course of hemispheric asymmetries has focused on childhood and young adulthood while virtually neglecting old age. However, there has been recent speculation about hemispheric specialization with age based on observations from aphasia and normal aging. Since we felt this issue required serious study, we decided to research it using a standard experimental index of brain laterality, the dichotic-listening procedure, with normal subjects from young adulthood into the eighth decade.

We are grateful to Edward A. Peck for generating the tapes, Mary Hyde and Errol Baker for assistance with data processing and analysis, Robert Sparks and Barbara Barresi for audiological screening, and Cheri Barry for secretarial assistance. This research was supported in part by the Medical Research Service of the Veterans Administration, by The United States Public Health Service grants NS06209 and NS07615, and by postdoctoral fellowships from Social Science Research Council and National Institutes of Health (1F32AG05007-01).

Before describing that study, we will review experimental and clinical findings regarding hemispheric specialization and its developmental course. Methodological issues encountered in studies of brain laterality will be discussed with specific focus on the dichotic-listening procedure. Important qualifications with respect to research with an elderly population will also be considered.

## Assessment of Cerebral Lateralization

### Clinical Work

It was the phenomenon of aphasia that first called attention to the differential functional specialization of the two hemispheres, which were thought at the time to be symmetrical in morphology, blood supply, and connections to lower structures in the nervous system. The discovery, shared by Dax (1865) and Broca (1865), that language disturbances follow almost exclusively from left cerebral lesions in right-handers was soon followed by the realization that aphasias resulting from right cerebral damage generally occurred in left-handers. The consequence of this discovery was the classical doctrine of cerebral dominance, which held that the hemisphere opposite the preferred hand is the one that controls language. However, the accumulation of exceptions to this rule culminated in the surveys of Goodglass and Quadfasel (1954) and Penfield and Roberts (1959), which established that control of language in left-handers was as often in the left hemisphere as in the right. In fact, however, the absence in the literature of negative reports on lesions without aphasia leaves open the possibility that left-handers might be vulnerable to aphasia from lesions of either hemisphere. The report by Gloning et al., (1969) suggests that this is indeed the case. Based on these clinical data, estimates of left cerebral dominance for language approximates 99 percent (Zangwill, 1962) for right-handers and falls between 53 percent (Goodglass and Quadfasel, 1954) and 63 percent (Roberts, 1966) for left-handers and ambilaterals.

### Experimental Work

When the Wada sodium amytal test was introduced in 1960 (Wada and Rasmussen, 1960), language dominance could be more reliably determined by noting the presence or absence of transient aphasia for up to ten minutes following surgical injection of sodium amytal into the circulation of either the right or left carotid artery. This procedure showed that 92 to 98.5 percent of right-handers became aphasic immediately following injections paralyzing the left hemisphere (Rossi and Rosadini, 1967; Milner, Branch, and Rasmussen, 1966; Perria, Rosadini, and Rossi, 1961). Although this technique is the most valid one for determining brain laterality, the technical difficulty and the risks involved limit its application to patients who are being evaluated for brain surgery.

It was not until Kimura's (1961) implementation of Broadbent's (1954) dichotic-digit technique that the necessary studies of hemispheric asymmetry in language processing could be performed with normal subjects. Recorded auditory stimuli are presented to a subject simultaneously through bilateral earphones. The subject is required to recall or recognize the stimulus heard, and the accuracy of one ear relative to the other is computed into an ear-advantage score. Studies of right-handed subjects demonstrate a right-ear (left-hemisphere) advantage for linguistic material, such as digits (Kimura, 1961), words (Bryden, 1967), nonsense syllables (Curry, 1967), consonants (Studdert-Kennedy and Shankweiler, 1970), and backward speech sounds (Kimura and Folb, 1968); and a left-ear (right-hemisphere) advantage for nonlanguage stimuli, such as melodies (Kimura, 1964), and environmental noises (Curry, 1967). Evidence that this phenomenon is indeed a reflection of brain laterality is based on its correspondence with Wada test results (Kimura, 1961) and on the opposition of the asymmetries for speech and nonspeech stimuli. One problem with dichotic-listening results is the variability in reported incidence of the right-ear advantage for verbal materials, which ranges from 75 percent to 87 percent (Satz, Achenbach, and Fennell, 1967; Blumstein, Goodglass, and Tartter, 1975).

Because of this disparity between the almost 100 percent incidence of left-cerebral dominance for language from clinical neurology and the much lower 80 percent incidence from dichotic-listening studies, the validity of the dichotic-digit technique as an index of hemispheric dominance for language has recently been challenged (Blumstein, Goodglass, and Tartter, 1975). Using a careful test-retest procedure and a sophisticated statistical correctional formula, they suggest that there exists a 15 percent incidence of right-handers with "true" left-ear superiority for dichotically-presented language material. They speculate that factors in addition to cerebral functional asymmetry of language processing, such as peripheral processes involving neurons in lower auditory centers, contribute to the ear preference in dichotic listening. A second experiment showed that about 25 percent of right-handers are consistently right-ear dominant for nonverbal (tonal) material (Oscar-Berman, Goodglass, and Donnenfeld, 1974).

**Developmental Studies of Cerebral Lateralization**

*Evidence from Childhood*

Despite recent neuroanatomical evidence that cerebral hemispheric asymmetry is present at birth (Wittelson and Pallie, 1973; Wada, Clarke, and Hamm, 1975), brain plasticity and flexibility in language functioning has been documented in childhood. In an article about the onset of aphasia as a result of hemiplegia, Basser (1962) proposes a critical-periods theory of speech development. He explains that until the age of two or three, lesions in either hemisphere could produce aphasia; however, beyond the critical period of age three, right-hemisphere lesions very rarely produce aphasia. From the third to the twelfth year, laterality is established on the left but may be changed to the right. By puberty the left hemisphere is firmly established as the dominant hemisphere and becomes fixed in this role after the eighteenth year of life. According to Lenneberg (1966), laterality cannot be altered after puberty, even with intensive conditioning procedures.

Although the pathological evidence suggests increasing left-hemisphere specialization for language from age two into puberty, the evidence from experimental studies of dichotic listening in childhood is somewhat contradictory. Though several studies suggest an increase in the right-ear advantage for dichotically-presented verbal material as a function of increasing age (Bryden and Allard, 1973; Satz et al., 1975), the bulk of the evidence during childhood does not reflect such changes (Goodglass, 1973; Peck, 1976; Hynd and Obrzut, 1977; Schulman-Galambos, 1977).

In our own laboratory, Goodglass (1973) studied children from 5.5 to 12.5 years and found age-independent equal degrees of right-ear advantage in dichotic presentation for vowels and consonants embedded in words. Peck (1976) similarly found an invariant pattern of right-ear superiority for words and left-ear superiority for melodies from age three to nine.

Although the lower end of the developmental scale has been extensively studied, little is known about the course of cerebral dominance in later years. It has been suggested, however, that observations of a decreasing incidence of left-handedness with age may reflect greater left-hemisphere specialization. Bingley's review of the handedness literature (1958) suggests that the incidence of left-handedness, approximately 8 percent among normal children entering school and 5 to 6 percent among normal adults, decreases successively with age. A more recent study by Sand and Taylor (1973) demonstrates a significant increased frequency of mixed-handedness and a significant decreased frequency of left-handedness with aging. However, this may simply be a result of changing cultural patterns in the tolerance of left-handedness, and it is not known whether this pattern extends into later maturity.

## Evidence from the Elderly

Certain observations from the study of aphasia suggest that changes in cerebral dominance may continue throughout the life span. In contrast to the noted brain plasticity and flexibility in childhood language functioning, neurological and linguistic data suggest that language functions may become more definitely and rigidly lateralized within the left cerebral hemisphere with aging. Support for these speculations comes partly from lesion studies on adults in whom, as discussed earlier, language difficulties are almost always consequential to left-hemisphere damage. Second, with aging into adulthood, recovery from aphasia may be more gradual and less complete (Smith, 1971), perhaps because of an increasing loss of potential for transfer of language to the right hemisphere. Third, with aging in the older adult range, there is greater incidence of the "fluent" type of aphasia and a concomitant development of highly organized, syntactically connected language systems (Obler et al., 1978). Aphasic speech patterns in the elderly are characterized by an increased frequency of fluent jargon speech with preserved grammatical automatisms. Brown and Jaffe (1975) observed that the same lesion that can result in a motor aphasia in a child can present as anomic or phonemic paraphasia in an adult and as a jargon aphasia in an elderly patient. However, these data regarding aphasia type do not directly address the issue of changing degree of left lateralization for language but rather the issue of intrahemispheric changes.

Clinical observation of the language of normal aged people reveals no obvious pathology beyond an occasional difficulty in recalling names. But there has been accumulating evidence that with normal aging the efficiency of functions mediated in the right hemisphere declines more than that of the left hemisphere (Albert and Kaplan, 1979). The visual motor performance subtests of the WAIS require a greater age correction than the verbal scale. This was originally construed as simply reflecting psychomotor retardation and relative impairment of new problem-solving ability with increasing age. However, observations by Ben Yishai et al. (1971) and Farver (1975) indicate that the aging subject actually makes qualitative errors, implicating right-hemisphere deficit. For example, Ben Yishai et al. (1971) note the frequency of broken configurations in the attempts to reproduce the square designs of the WAIS in both older and right-brain-damaged subjects. Farver noted the occurrence of fragmentation, or failure to appreciate part-whole relationships in several visuo-spatial tasks. For example, isolate responses were common in the Hooper Visual Organization test, stick design figures were fragmented into subunits, and object drawings featured isolated details, with neglect of the unifying outline. In contrast to these deficits, no significant age-related decline was noted in the right-left orientation, finger localization, or arithmetic, on verbal testing. The preservation of these left-hemisphere-mediated abilities emphasizes the disparity of hemispheric functioning.

## Theoretical Explanations

Inasmuch as there is no neuroanatomical evidence suggesting progressive differential degeneration of the right relative to the left hemisphere (LeMay,

1979; Pandya, 1979), the reason for asymmetrical decline in behavior with age remains a puzzle. The answer may lie in the fact that the left-hemisphere functions cited are primarily affected by focal lesions. Semmes (1968) suggests that right-hemisphere functions are diffusely represented whereas those on the left are mediated by focally organized zones. Thus, it is possible that diffuse loss of brain tissue may affect right-hemisphere functions more than left-hemisphere ones.

Kinsbourne suggests that over time the left hemisphere becomes increasingly more proficient in language processing whereas the right hemisphere tends to lose its ability to compensate for language. He states, "The normally evolving dominance of the left hemisphere may be implemented by a progressive, genetically preprogrammed displacement of right hemispheric connections from the speech output control neurons."[1] Brown and Jaffe cite evidence for an increasing differentiation of language representation in the left hemisphere throughout the life span, and suggest that this evidence implies progressive left cerebral language lateralization. In their 1975 note in *Neuropsychologia* they predict "an increasing right ear effect on dichotic listening with age" as a test of their theory. This prediction has been tested several times, but in each case methodological problems have cast doubts on the findings.

## Dichotic Listening

### Methodological Considerations

Using the dichotic-listening procedure with free recall, Inglis and Caird (1963) demonstrated that there were no performance decrements with age for digits recalled from the first channel but that performance declined progressively with age for digits recalled from the second channel. Schonfield (1969) performed a similar study, but with attention to each ear, and demonstrated that the decline occurred primarily for digits from the nondominant ear, that is, the left ear. Although Schonfield's study suggests progressive left-hemisphere specialization for verbal materials with age, his procedure failed to control for order of report. His findings may reflect the artifactual advantage of the right ear which arises from the common strategy of reporting first from that side (Kinsbourne, 1970).

Clark and Knowles (1973) repeated the paradigm, but controlled for order of report, thus giving the right- and left-ear input equal probability of being reported. They studied 112 normal females and males from ages 15 to 74. Using a dichotic-digit tape, they actually found, as Brown and Jaffe suggested, a progressive right-ear advantage with age. This advantage primarily was a result of a decrement for material presented to the left ear. It could be, however, that poorer hearing in the left ear produced such results.

Although Clark and Knowles did attempt to control for hearing differences with age, they used self-report and subjective adjustment of loudness in the two earphones. It is not known, however, whether subjective assessment for hearing is as reliable as objective measurement. The study we will report here, which is especially sensitive to hearing differences in the ears, suggests that it is not.

Dichotic-listening studies in the elderly need to control for physical and cognitive changes with age and for the hearing acuity of the two ears because of the known cognitive (Botwinick, 1967) and neurological and physiological (Jarvik, Eisdorfer, and Blum, 1973; Talland, 1968) changes associated with aging. The following variables have been studied (Eisdorfer, 1969; McFarland, 1968; Hulicka, 1967; Botwinick, 1967) as modifiers of intellectual performance with aging: cooperation, education, socioeconomic level, occupation, personality, speed, cautiousness, health-energy level, anxiety level, attention, and fear of failure. Studies using the dichotic-listening strategy to evaluate memory, however, have systematically examined some of these variables and demonstrated that overall acuity for hearing (Inglis, Sykes, and Ankus, 1968); attention (Craik, 1965; Inglis and Ankus, 1965); and motivation (Inglis and Caird, 1963) do not seem to impair performance on dichotic-listening tasks in older subjects.

*Changes in Dichotic Ear Advantage with Age*

We decided to replicate the study by Clark and Knowles with (1) greater rigor in audiological screening; (2) test/retest procedure; and (3) nonverbal, as well as verbal, materials. First, we used objective audiological screening and calibrated compensation for small differences in auditory acuity. Second, we examined the evidence of test-retest stability as an additional index of developmental change with age. As reported earlier, Blumstein et al. (1975) demonstrated that repeated testing provides an index as to the proportion of a population that is stably lateralized. Our subjects were tested twice to determine whether lateralization in the elderly is more stably located in the left hemisphere than it is in younger adults.

Finally, we looked at the degree of lateralization for melodies, which is considered a right-hemisphere function. If, as has been suggested, the minor hemisphere tends to become less functional with increasing age, dichotic musical stimuli should be less lateralized to the left ear in older than in younger subjects. On the other hand, if aging merely reduces the ability to attend to the less dominant signal, musical stimuli should become even more left-ear dominant with age.

Our subjects were 102 right-handed males between the ages of 24 and 79. They were native English-speakers with no history of alcohol abuse, neurological disorders, or learning disabilities. They were recruited from community centers and vocational services and the medical and surgical wards of the Boston Veterans Administration Hospital. All subjects underwent audiological screening; pure tone thresholds and speech discrimination scores were determined for each ear. To be included in the study, subjects had to have speech discrimination scores of 80 percent or higher and pure tone thresholds of forty-four decibels or less. Furthermore, during the testing we compensated for threshold and ear discrepancies by using an audiometer to provide equal signals at approximately forty decibels to each ear.

Subjects were administered two dichotic-listening tapes on two occasions one week apart. For the verbal condition, we used digits and expected right-ear advantages as a reflection of left-hemisphere dominance; for the nonverbal condition, we used melodies and expected left-ear advantages as a reflection of right-hemisphere dominance.

The dichotic tape consisted of 24 pairs of digit triads randomly generated so that the $S$ always heard 6 different digits in each trial. The digits 1-10 (excluding 7) were used. For example, the subject might hear "9, 1, 3" in his right ear and simultaneously hear "6, 8, 4" in his left ear. For our nonverbal condition, we used a nursery tune tape developed by Peck (1976). It consisted of 10 pairs of 5 familiar children's nursery jingles hummed by a male singer, such as "Row, Row, Row Your Boat." Each stimulus consisted of the opening phrase of the nursery tune and was 3 seconds long.

During actual testing, we controlled for order of report by tapping the subject on his right or left shoulder immediately following each trial and instructing him to report first the digits or tune heard in that ear and then to report the materials heard on the other side. Oral report was used for digits, and nonverbal report (subjects pointed to the corresponding drawing) was used to indicate the tunes heard. The two tapes were administered in random order on the first day of testing and then in reversed order on the second day. Since there was no effect of day of testing, the results we report are on data pulled from the two testings.

With respect to overall accuracy of report, scores for both digits and tunes decreased significantly as subjects got older. With respect to direction of lateralization, as we would have expected from previous studies on normal adults, there was a significant right-ear advantage for digits and a significant left-ear advantage for tunes. With respect to degree of lateralization, we would have expected age by ear interactions on analyses of variance if there were changes with age; we found no significant interactions for tunes or digits. Furthermore, there were no differences by age for incidence of test-retest stability.

These results suggest that with age, overall performance on dichotic-listening tests declines both for verbal and nonverbal materials, but there are no age-related changes in the magnitude or stability of the ear advantages for either type of material. We must, at this point, challenge Brown and Jaffe's theory (1975) that left-hemisphere specialization increases relative to right-hemisphere specialization with age. Our work also contradicts Clark and Knowles's (1973) theory that decrease in overall information-processing capacity with age affects the nondominant-ear input more than the dominant-ear input.

This contradiction of Clark and Knowles may be explained by methodological differences between the two studies, that is, our careful control for hearing differences in the two ears through objective audiological screening and compensations for differences in acuity. Further data analysis will explore this issue to see if, in fact, hearing in the left ear gets worse with age. If so, we suggest that studies of dichotic listening in the elderly carefully control this variable. In addition, these studies should be replicated with females and with visual field input. Longitudinal study of laterality, particularly of the developmental course of lateralization through adulthood, is also necessary.

### Note

1. M. Kinsbourne, Minor hemisphere language and cerebral maturation. (Boston: Veteran's Administration). Reprinted with permission.

### References

Albert, M., and Kaplan, E. Organic implications of neuropsychological deficits in the elderly. In *New Directions in Memory and Aging: Proceedings of the George Talland Memorial Conference,* edited by L.W. Poon, J.L. Fozard, L.S. Cermak, D. Ehrenberg, and L.W. Thompson. L. Earlbaum Associates, 1979.

Basser, L.S. Hemiplegia of early onset and the faculty of speech with special reference to the effect of hemispherectomy. *Brain* 85: 427-60, 1962.

Ben Yishai, Y., Diller, L., Mandelberg, J., Gordon, W., and Gerstman, L.J. Similarities and differences in Block Design performance between older normal and brain-injured persons: A task analysis. *Journal of Abnormal Social Psychology* 78: 17-25, 1971.

Bingley, T. Mental symptoms in temporal lobe epilepsy and temporal lobe gliomas with special reference to laterality of lesion and the relationship between handedness and brainedness. *Acta Psychiatra et Neurologica* 33: Supplement 120, xi. 1958.

Blumstein, S., Goodglass, H., and Tartter, V. The reliability of ear advantage in dichotic listening. *Brain and Language* 2: 221-36, 1975.

Botwinick, J. *Cognitive Processes in Maturity and Old Age.* New York: Springer, 1967.

Broadbent, D.A. Role of auditory localization in attention. *Journal of Experimental Psychology* 47 (3): 191-96, 1954.

Broca, P. *Sur* la faculte du langage articulé. *Bulletin de la Société Anthropologique de Paris* 6: 337-93, 1865.

Brown, J.W., and Jaffe, J. Hypothesis of cerebral dominance. *Neuropsychologia* 13: 107-10, 1975.

Bryden, M.P. An evaluation of some models of laterality effects in dichotic listening. *Acta Oto-Larynologica* 63: 595-604, 1967.

Bryden, M.P., and Allard, F. Dichotic listening and the development of linguistic processes. Paper presented at the International Neuropsychology Society, New Orleans, LA, February 9, 1973.

Carmon, A. Spatial and temporal factors in visual perception of patients with unilateral cerebral lesions. Paper presented at the Meeting of the American Psychological Association, Washington, D.C., 1969.

Clark, L.E., and Knowles, J.B. Age differences in dichotic listening performance. *Journal of Gerontology* 28 (2): 173-78, 1973.

Craik, F.I.M. The nature of the age decrement in performance on dichotic listening tasks. *Quarterly Journal of Experimental Psychology* 17: 227-40, 1965.

Curry, F.K.W. A comparison of left-handed and right-handed subjects on verbal and nonverbal dichotic listening tasks. *Cortex* 3(3): 343-52, 1967.

Dax, M. Lesions de la moitié gauche de l'encephale coincidant avec trouble des signs de la pensée (lu a Montpellier en 1836). *Gazette Hebdomadaire de Medecine et Chirurgie* 2: 1865.

Eisdorfer, C. Intellectual and cognitive changes in the aged. In *Behavior and Adaptation in Late Life*, edited by E.W. Busse and E. Pfeiffer pp. 237-50. Boston: Little, Brown, 1969.

Farver, P. Performance of normal older adults on a test battery designed to measure parietal lobe functions. Unpublished manuscript, 1975.

Gazzaniga, M.S. *The Bisected Brain*. New York: Appleton-Century-Crofts, 1970.

Gloning, I., Gloning, K., Haub, G., and Quatember, R. Comparison of verbal behavior in right-handed and non-right-handed patients with anatomically verified lesions of one hemisphere. *Cortex* 5: 43-52, 1969.

Goodglass, H. Developmental comparison of vowels and consonants in dichotic listening. *Journal of Speech and Hearing Research* 16(4): 774-52, 1973.

Goodglass, H., and Geschwind, N. Language disorders (aphasia). In *Handbook of Perception*, vol. 7, edited by E.C. Carterette and M. Friedman. New York: Academic Press, 1976.

Goodglass, H., and Quadfasel, F.A. Language laterality in left-handed aphasics. *Brain* 77:521-48, 1954.

Hulicka, I.M. Age changes and age differences in memory functioning. *Gerontologist* 7(2): 46-54, 1967.

Hynd, G.W., and Obrzut, J.E. Effects of grade level and sex on the magnitude of the dichotic ear advantage. *Neuropsychologia* 15: 689-92, 1977.

Inglis, J., and Ankus, M.N. Effects of age on short-term storage and serial rote learning. *British Journal of Psychology* 56: 183-95, 1965.

Inglis, J., and Caird, W.K. Age differences in successive responses to simultaneous stimulation. *Canadian Journal of Psychology* 17: 98-105, 1963.

Inglis, J., Sykes, D.H., and Ankus, M.N. Age differences in short-term memory. In *Interdisciplinary Topics in Gerontology: I,* edited by H.T. Blumenthal pp. 18-43. Basel, Switzerland: S. Karger, 1968.

Jarvik, L.F., Eisdorfer, C., and Blum, J., eds. *Intellectual Functioning in Adults: Physiological and Biological Influences,* pp. 83-93. New York: Springer, 1973.

Kimura, D. Cerebral dominance and the perception of verbal stimuli. *Canadian Journal of Psychology* 15: 166-71, 1961.

_____. Left-right differences in the perception of melodies. *Quarterly Journal of Experimental Psychology* 16: 359-60, 1964.

Kimura, D., and Folb, S. Neural processing of backwards speech sounds. *Science* 161: 395-96, 1968.

Kinsbourne, M. The cerebral basis of lateral asymmetries in attention. *Acta Psychologica* 33: 193-201, 1970.

_____. Minor hemisphere language and cerebral maturation. Paper prepared at the Center for the Study of Aging and Human Development, Duke University Medical Center, Durham, North Carolina, 1974.

LeMay, M. Personal communication, May 5, 1979.

Lenneberg, E.H. Speech development: its anatomical and physiological concomitants. In *Brain Function.* Proceedings of the Third Annual Conference of Speech, Language, and Communication, edited by E.C. Carterette, vol. 3. Berkeley: University of California Press, 1966.

McFarland, R.A. *The Sensory and Perceptual Processes in Aging,* pp. 9-52. Morgantown, WV: West Virginia University Press, 1968.

Milner, B. Interhemispheric differences in the localization of psychological processes in man. *British Medical Bulletin* 27(3): 272-77, 1971.

Milner, B., Branch, C., and Rasmussen, T. Evidence for bilateral speech representation in some non right-handers. *Transactions of the American Neurological Association* 91: 306-8, 1966.

Nebes, R. Hemispheric specialization in commissurotomized man. *Psychological Bulletin* 81(1): 1-14, 1974.

Obler, L., Albert, M., Goodglass, H., and Benson, D.F. Aging and aphasia type. *Brain and Language* 6: 318-22, 1978.

Oscar-Berman, M., Goodglass, H., and Donnenfeld, H. Dichotic ear-order effects with nonverbal stimuli. *Cortex* 10: 270-77, 1974.

Pandya, D. Personal communication, May 3, 1979.

Peck, E.A. Dichotic ear asymmetries in children aged three to nine. Ph.D. dissertation, Tufts University, 1976.

Penfield, W., and Robert, L. *Speech and Brain Mechanisms*. Princeton: Princeton University Press, 1959.

Perria, L., Rosadini, G., and Rossi, G. Determination of side of cerebral dominance with amobarbital. *Archives of Neurology* 4: 173-81, 1961.

Roberts, L. Aphasia, apraxia and agnosia in abnormal states of cerebral dominance. In *Handbook of Clinical Neurology*, Vol. 4, edited by P.J. Vinken and G.W. Brwyn. Amsterdam: North-Holland, 1966.

Rossi, G.F., and Rosadini, G. Experimental analysis of cerebral dominance in man. In *Brain Mechanisms Underlying Speech and Language*, edited by C.M. Millikan and F.L. Darley. New York: Grune and Stratton, 1967.

Sand, P.L., and Taylor, N. Handedness: evaluation of binominal distribution hypothesis in children and adults. *Perceptual and Motor Skills* 36: 1343-46, 1973.

Satz, P., Achenbach, I., and Fennell, E. Relations between assessed manual laterality and predicted speech laterality. *Neuropsychologia* 5: 295-310, 1967.

Saltz, P., Bakker, D.J., Teunissen, J., Goebel, R., and Van der Flugt, H. Developmental parameters of the ear asymmetry: a multivariate approach. *Brain and Language* 2: 171-85, 1975.

Schonfield, D. Recognition tests of dichotic listening and the age variable. Paper presented to the International Congress of Psychology, London, 1969. (Reference cited in Clark and Knowles, 1973.)

Schulman-Galambos, C. Dichotic listening performance in elementary and college students. *Neuropsychologia* 15: 577-84, 1977.

Schwartz, G.E., Davidson, R., Maer, F., and Bromfield, E. Patterns of hemispheric dominance in musical, emotional, verbal, and spatial tasks. Paper read at the Psychophysiological Research Meetings, October 27, 1973, Galveston, Texas.

Semmes, J. Hemispheric specialization: a possible clue to mechanism. *Neuropsychologia* 10: 185-91, 1968.

Smith, A. Objective indices of severity of chronic aphasia in stroke patients. *Journal of Speech and Hearing Disorders* 36: 167-207, 1971.

Sperry, R.W. Lateral specialization in the surgically separated hemispheres. In *The Neurosciences Third Study Program,* edited by F.O. Schmitt and F.G. Worden, pp. 5-19. Cambridge, MA: MIT Press, 1974.

Studdert-Kennedy, M., and Shankweiler, D. Hemispheric specialization for speech perception. *Journal of the Acoustical Society of America* 48: 579-94, 1970.

Talland, G. *Human Aging and Behavior*. New York City: Academic Press, 1968.

Wada, J., and Rasmussen, T. Intracarotid injection of sodium amytal for the lateralization of cerebral speech dominance. *Journal of Neurosurgery* 17: 266-82, 1960.

Wada, J., Clarke, R., and Hamm, A. Cerebral hemispheric asymmetry in humans. *Archives of Neurology* 32: 239-46, 1975.

Wittelson, S., and Pallie, A. Left hemisphere specialization for language in the newborn. *Brain* 96: 641-46, 1973.

Zangwill, O.L. Dyslexia in relation to cerebral dominance. In *Reading Disability*, edited by J. Money. Baltimore: The Johns Hopkins Press, 1962.

# Part II
# Clinical Issues: Diagnosis

# 8

# Neurological Aspects of Language Disorders in the Elderly: An Anatomical Overview

*Marjorie J. LeMay*

An understanding of the anatomy of the mature brain requires an overview of the morphological events occurring in the developing brain from early life. In this chapter, then, I will first review aspects of childhood brain development and aspects of cerebral regression occurring in adulthood. In order to establish a framework for viewing the life-span development for language in the brain, I will then consider anatomical asymmetries of the brain, and go on to relate these to some of the hemispheric differences underlying language lateralization.

In early life the growth of the brain is rapid and the weight of the brain reaches its peak before the age of 30 (Chernyshev, 1968; Pakkenberg and Volgt, 1964; Yakovlev, 1962). There is then a normal regression of cerebral substance beginning in the third or fourth decade. The regression is slow until about the sixth decade and accelerates in later life. There is a relatively stable relationship between the weight of the cerebellum and the brain, and the cerebellum also decreases in weight during later life (Ellis, 1920-21). Cell loss has also been described in the brain stem with advancing age (Brody, 1976).

The central parts of the brain show signs of regression early. There is evidence of progressive widening of the third ventricle from at least after the third decade of life (Borgersen, 1966; Engeset and Lonnum, 1958). Associated with the third ventricular widening is regression of the median nuclei of the thalami (Rosales, LeMay, and Yakovlev, 1968). In early life, most but not all thalami are connected by a commissure, the massa intermedia, which crosses through the third ventricle. A personal study of pneumoencephalograms of 188 patients in whom the massa intermedia could be readily measured on a lateral film showed widening of the third ventricle with aging and also showed that age per se correlates, as well as the width of the third ventricle, with the size of the massa intermedia (table 8-1). The shape of the cross section of the massa intermedia changes as the brain atrophies with advancing age and follows a definite pattern in relation to age. The configuration of the median cross-sectional area of the massa intermedia varies greatly in size and shape, but in the young (first three decades) is generally oval with a larger anteroposterior than dorsoventral diameter. In the middle ages (from fourth to seventh decades) the atrophy reduces mainly the caudal

**Table 8-1**
**Comparison of Size of MI and Third Ventricle with Age**

| Age | MI (mm²) | | 3rd Ventricle (mm) | | Number of Cases | |
|---|---|---|---|---|---|---|
| | Male | Female | Male | Female | Male | Female |
| 0-19 | 55 | 64 | 6.5 | 6.3 | 6 | 12 |
| 20-29 | 75.4 | 79 | 7 | 8 | 7 | 7 |
| 30-39 | 38.8 | 39 | 9.4 | 8 | 35 | 6 |
| 40-49 | 35.2 | 56 | 9.6 | 9 | 31 | 14 |
| 50-59 | 32.1 | 45 | 10.9 | 10 | 19 | 20 |
| 60+ | 18.0 | 28 | 12.0 | 11 | 22 | 9 |

Note: Measurements of the width of the third ventricle and calculation of the area of the massa intermedia were made on pneumoencephalograms taken at a 40-inch tube-film distance.

and superior caudal border of the massa intermedia. In older individuals with severe atrophy, the anterodorsal border of the massa intermedia is the last to disappear (figure 8-1).

Although there appears to be a fairly constant progression in width of the third ventricles during aging, there is considerable variation in width of the lateral ventricles. Air studies have shown only a slight increase in the size of the lateral ventricles until the seventh and eighth decades. Cast studies by Knudson (1958) on 183 adult brains considered to be normal showed some increases in ventricular size in those individuals over age fifty, but the casts of the ventricles in a third of the brains of individuals over age seventy had volumes in the same range as 90 percent of the twenty-to forty-year age group. This suggests that the regression of the main white matter bulk of the hemispheres is less constant with aging then that of the thalamus.

Involutionary changes with advancing age have also been noted on

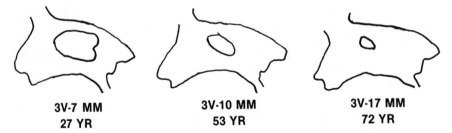

3V-7 MM
27 YR

3V-10 MM
53 YR

3V-17 MM
72 YR

**Figure 8-1.** Tracings of the Third Ventricle and Massa Intermedia from Pneumoencephalograms of Three Males, Showing the Common Appearance of the Massa Intermedia in Size, Shape, and Position with Aging and Increase in Width of the Third Ventricle

microscopic studies in the temporal region (Tomlinson, 1977; Tomlinson, Blessed, and Roth, 1968; Yakovlev, 1962), particularly in the hippocampus, uncus, and parahippocampal and fusiform gyri and about the island of Reil. Widening of the cisterns at the tips of the temporal lobes and widening of the anterior portions of the sylvian fissures can be seen with advancing age on radiographic computerized tomographic (CT) scans that correlate with the described pathological findings (figure 8-2). Table 8-2 shows CT findings on 160 patients (20 in each decade) who were not on medication at the time of the study; they showed no evidence of an intracranial mass lesion or obstructive hydrocephalus. Visualization of the anterior ends of the sylvian fissures in individuals under forty is unusual and suggests an abnormality. Figure 8-2C shows widening of the anterior ends of the sylvian

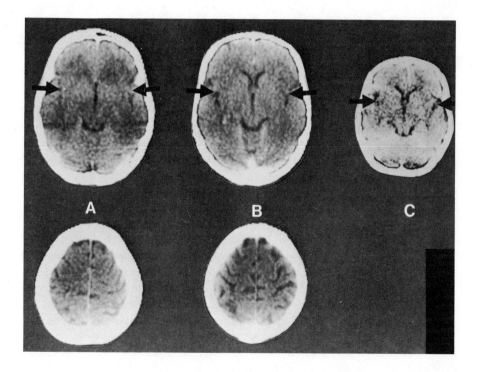

(A) Sixty-year-old female; (B) Seventy-three-year-old male; (C) Widening of the anterior ends of the sylvian fissures in a seventeen-year-old male with Down's syndrome. (Visualization of the anterior ends of the sylvian fissures in individuals less than forty years old is unusual and suggests an abnormality)

**Figure 8-2.** Computerized Tomographic (CT) Scans Showing Widening of the Anterior Ends of the Sylvian Fissures (see arrows) and Superficial Sulci in Well-Functioning Individuals with Aging

**Table 8-2**

**Widths of Anterior Ends of the Sylvian Fissures, Anterior Portions of the Inter-hemispheric Fissures and Superficial Sulci with Aging as Demonstrated on Computerized Tomographic Scans**

| Age | Anterior End of Sylvian Fissures | | | Anterior End of Interhemispheric Fissures | | | Superficial Sulci | | |
|---|---|---|---|---|---|---|---|---|---|
| | 0 trace→ | < 2 mm | ≥ 2 mm | 0 trace→ | < 2 mm | ≥ 2 mm | 0 trace→ | < 1 mm | ≥ 1 mm |
| 4-19 | 17 | 5 | 0 | 17 | 3 | 0 | 18 | 2 | 0 |
| 20-29 | 15 | 5 | 0 | 13 | 7 | 0 | 14 | 6 | 0 |
| 30-39 | 12 | 7 | 1 | 8 | 11 | 1 | 10 | 7 | 3 |
| 40-49 | 3 | 14 | 3 | 0 | 18 | 2 | 1 | 8 | 11 |
| 50-59 | 1 | 15 | 4 | 2 | 18 | 0 | 1 | 5 | 14 |
| 60-69 | 1 | 13 | 6 | 0 | 16 | 4 | 0 | 6 | 14 |
| 70-79 | 0 | 10 | 10 | 0 | 14 | 6 | 0 | 1 | 19 |
| 80 + | 0 | 9 | 11 | 0 | 12 | 8 | 0 | 3 | 17 |

Note: Measurements were made on Polaroid films which showed the brain in transaxial section reduced in size by a factor of 3.3 times.

fissures in a seventeen-year-old male with Down's syndrome. Poor development of the third frontal gyrus and narrow superior temporal gyri are common in brains of individuals with mongolism and may account for the findings in this scan. It is worth emphasizing that these are precisely the cortical regions associated with language.

An increasing widening of superficial sulci is also seen in the aging brain, particularly in the temporal and frontal regions. Tomlinson (1977), and Tomlinson et al., (1968) have noted atrophic changes to be striking in the parasagittal region. The convolutional shrinkage is sometimes described as cortical atrophy but the cortex itself is very narrow and varies in thickness in different areas of the brain, and the gyral atrophy common in aging must involve mainly the adjacent white matter. These superficial atrophic changes are readily seen on CT studies and are particularly notable frontally and in the interhemispheric fissure. On the CT scans, widening of the interhemispheric fissure is sometimes seen extending the entire length of the hemispheres but is often localized anteriorly, and the widening ends abruptly in either the pre- or immediate-post central region (figure 8-3).

With CT studies it is now much easier to study the morphological changes occurring in the brain with aging. However, caution must be used in diagnosing cerebral atrophy on CT scans because *decreases* in ventricular size and widened superficial sulci have been noted in the brains of alcoholics after they have refrained from using alcohol for a period of time (Carlen and others, 1979), and a reversible pattern has also been found in CT

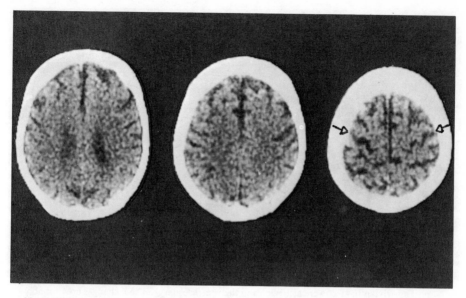

Note: Widening of the interhemispheric fissure is striking anteriorly. Arrows mark the central sulci.

**Figure 8-3.** High CT Scans of a Well-Functioning, Still-Working, Eighty-Three-Year-Old Male

studies of persons with anorexia nervosa (Heinz, Martenez, and Haenggel, 1977) and in some individuals with increased steroid levels (Bentson et al., 1978) shown in figure 8-4.

## Asymmetries of the Brain and Language

The brain has been known to show asymmetrical organizations for some functions, such as speech, for over a century (Broca, 1861) but because of the great variability in size, shape, and individual sulcal pattern of human brains it has been difficult to find consistent anatomical differences between the hemispheres. Geschwind and Levitsky (1968) reported asymmetries in the superior posterior portion of the temporal lobes in Wernicke's speech area. This finding stimulated a new search to find other morphological asymmetries and to find anatomical-clinical correlations. Radiographic studies allowed examination of intracranial structures in functioning and non-functioning individuals, and new interest in anatomical asymmetries made other asymmetries obvious (Galaburda et al., 1978; LeMay 1976; LeMay and Culebras, 1972).

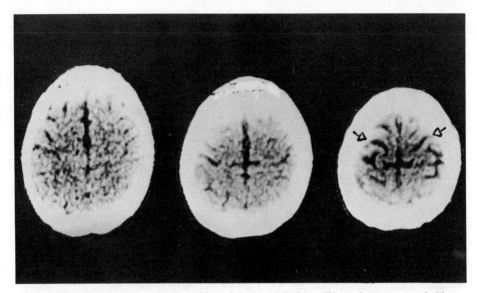

Note: The sylvian fissures were also wide and the ventricles large. These changes are probably on a metabolic basis and not a result of neuronal loss. Arrows mark the central sulci.

**Figure 8-4.** Widening of Superficial Sulci and Interhemispheric Fissure in a Twenty-Six-Year-Old Male with a Carcinoid Tumor of the Ileum and Liver Metastasis

Examination of routine carotid angiograms showed consistent difference in the course of the middle cerebral arteries in the two hemispheres. The main branches of the middle cerebral arteries course through the sylvian fissures, and the angles formed as their branches leave the posterior ends of the sylvian fissures were different in the two sides of the brain (figure 8-5). The angle formed by the left middle cerebral artery as it left the fissure was usually much smaller than on the right. Correlation of the angiographic findings with brains at postmortem and a study of the Yakovlev brain collection, now at the Armed Forces Institute of Pathology in Washington, D.C., showed the post-central suprasylvian portion of the parietal lobe on the left to be larger than on the right, which caused the left middle cerebral artery to dip downward as it left the sylvian fissure more than the right, narrowing the sylvian angle of the left artery more than that of the right (LeMay and Culebras, 1972). Examination of the external surfaces of brains showed that the posterior end of the sylvian fissure (the anatomical sylvian point) on the left extended further posterior than the right and was usually lower than on the right (figure 8-6). This pattern was also found in fetal brains and endocranial casts of some early hominoids (LeMay, 1976). Some correlation was noted between the heights of the ends of the sylvian fissures and handedness. In a small group of left-handers it was found that

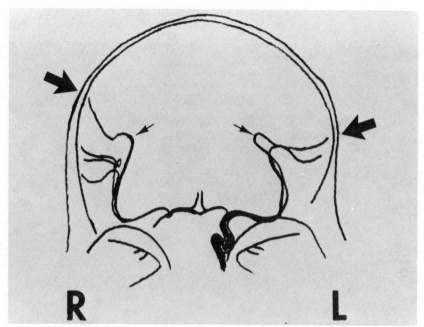

Note: The angle formed by the posterior sylvian branches of the middle cerebrals (small arrows) is more on the right than on the left.

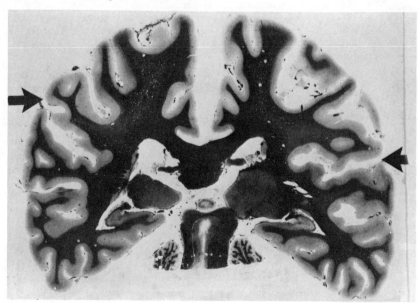

Note: The parietal operculum is larger on the left and causes lowering of the sylvian point and narrowing of the angle of the left middle cerebral artery as it leaves the depth of the sylvian fissure as shown in the top diagram.

**Figure 8-5.** Tracings of the Middle Cerebral Arteries from a Carotid Arteriogram **(top)**. Coronal Brain Section through the Posterior Ends of the Sylvian Fissures (Sylvian Points Marked by Large Arrows) **(bottom)**

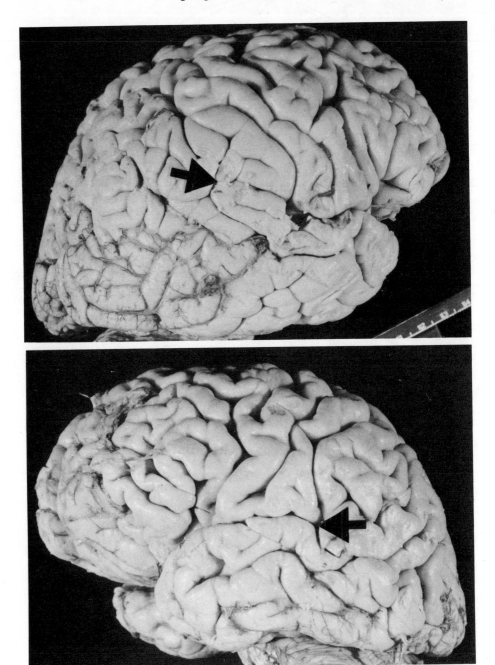

**Figure 8-6.** Lateral Surfaces of the Right (top) and Left (bottom) Hemispheres Showing the Sylvian Point to be Higher on the Right Than on the Left

the sylvian points were more often nearly equal in height, and occasionally the one on the left was even higher than on the right (LeMay and Culebras, 1972).

Study of a larger group of patients having bilateral carotid angiography confirmed the statistical difference in the heights of the anatomical sylvian points in right- and left-handers (Hochberg and LeMay, 1975). It is of great interest, particularly in relation to anatomical-clinical correlation, to look at a recent study by Ratcliff and colleagues (1978) at Montreal Neurological Institute. In their studies of patients undergoing sodium amytal tests for lateralization of speech representation they found the common vascular pattern that was described above, a narrower sylvian angle of the left middle cerebral artery in persons with left-hemisphere speech representation, but a more variable vascular pattern in patients showing an atypical cerebral dominance for speech on the amytal tests.

Other asymmetries of the brain have also been reported (Galaburda et al., 1978; LeMay, 1976). Radiographic air and CT studies show the left lateral ventricle to be larger than the right; and pneumoencephalographic studies by McRae et al. show that in right-handers the left occipital horn of the lateral ventricles were longer in 60 percent and the right occipital horn longer in 10 percent. In thirteen non-right-handers the left occipital horns were longer in 38 percent and the right longer in 31 percent.

CT studies also reveal asymmetries have some relation to handedness (LeMay, 1976). In right-handers the right frontal lobe is commonly wider than the left and the posterior portion of the left hemisphere commonly wider than the right (figure 8-7). In left-handers the hemispheric asymmetries are less striking and the left frontal and right occipital portions of the hemispheres are more often wider than they are in the brains of right-handers.

Recently a whole new field has developed for studying functional regions in the brain by the use of radioactive blood-flow patterns (Lassen, Ingvar, and Skinhj, 1978). Differences in blood flow in the two hemispheres have been noted in the main speech zone regions, for example, Broca's area in the low frontal region near the motor strip that controls the mouth, lips, and tongue; Wernicke's region in the superior posterior portion of the temporal lobe and about the posterior end of the sylvian fissure; and in the region of a supplementary motor area that lies on the median surface of the frontal lobes just anterior to the motor region of the foot.

## Hemispheric Asymmetries and Language

The injection of sodium amobarbital into the carotid arteries has been used to help determine hemispheric lateralization for speech; its use for this purpose was first reported by Wada in 1949. Its recent use at the Montreal

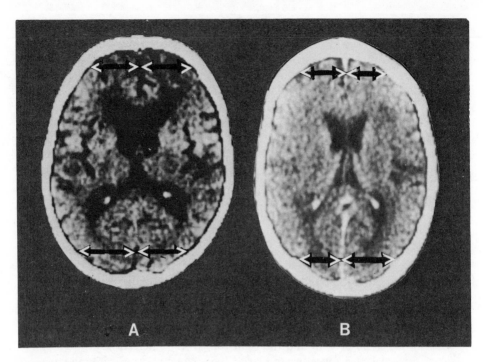

(A) Type seen commonly in right-handers. The anterior portion of the right hemisphere and posterior end of the left hemisphere are wider and protrude beyond their counterparts. (B) Reverse asymmetry from that seen in (A). More left-handers show this type of asymmetry than do right-handers.

**Figure 8-7.** Asymmetries of the Brain

Neurological Institute in patients who had no clinical evidence of early left-brain damage (Rasmussen and Milner, 1977) showed speech lateralization in right-handers to be in the left hemisphere in 96 percent and in the right hemisphere in 4 percent. Rasmussen and Milner (1977) found left speech lateralization in 70 percent of left-handers and lateralization in the others to be equally divided between right and bilateral hemispheric speech localization. Studies of patients with aphasia have also shown some relationship between language laterality of the brain and handedness. Aphasia occurs mainly in patients who have had lesions in the left hemisphere, most of whom are right-handed. Language abnormalities have been found in approximately 50 percent of left-handers who have had left hemispheric lesions (Goodglass and Quadfasel, 1954). Aphasia occurring with right hemispheric lesions is rare in right-handers. Hecaen and Sauget (1971) reported aphasia to be rare in *nonfamilial* left-handers with right-sided lesions but a similar frequency of language disturbance occurs after either left- or right-sided lesions in *familial* left-handers.

It is probable that the differences in widths of the hemispheres seen on

CT scans which show some relationship with handedness may also have some relationship with language lateralization. Hier and colleagues (1978) found an increased incidence of reversed cerebral asymmetry on the CT scans (figure 8-7B) of a group of children with developmental dyslexia who were slow to develop language. Autistic children characteristically have delayed language development. Hier and colleagues (in press) found reversed cerebral asymmetries in eight of fifteen such patients studied with CT scans and suggested that unfavorable anatomical asymmetries of the brain in children may increase the risk of developmental cognitive disorders. The type of cerebral asymmetry in an individual may influence the development, or lack of development, of language difficulties after a cerebral insult and also may influence recovery from aphasia. I have seen several patients with reversed cerebral asymmetries, such as wider left frontal and wider right posterior parietal occipital regions, who have developed aphasia with right-sided lesions, and also some patients with reversed asymmetries who showed unusually good recoveries from aphasia after large left hemispheric infarcts. This is indeed a field for further work.

**Summary**

The brain in old age is affected by the traumas of life as well as the normal regression of cerebral tissue occurring throughout the greater part of life. Atrophy, as exemplified by decreasing brain weight, enlargement of the ventricles, and gyral changes, is not consistently proportional to increasing age (Riese, 1959). Since the development of the brain is different in all individuals, the regression is also different. Individuals are exposed to different stimuli and traumas during life and their responses to them are different. It is hoped that by studying differences in the development and regression of the brains of older persons we will acquire a better understanding of cerebral functioning and learn how to help increase the maturational pleasures of life.

**References**

Bentson, J., Reza, M., Winter, J., and Wilson, G. Steroids and apparent cerebral atrophy on computed tomographic scans. *Journal of Computer Assisted Tomography* 2: 16-23, 1978.

Berg, K.J., and Lönnum, E.A. Ventricular size in relation to cranial size. *Acta Radiologica* 4: 65-78, 1966.

Borgersen, A. Width of third ventricle. Encephalographic and morbid anatomical study. *Acta Radiologica* 4: 645-61, 1966.

Broca, P. Sur le siège de la faculté du langagé articule. *Bulletin Société Anatomique de Paris* 2(6): 355, 1861.

Brody, H. Aging brain in senile dementia. Data presented at Bedford Veterans Administration Symposium, June 3-4, 1976, Bedford, Mass.

Bruijn, J.W. *Pneumoencephalography in the Diagnosis of Cerebral Atrophy.* Utrecht, The Netherlands: Drukkerij, J.J. Smits Oudergracht, 1959.

Burhenne, H.J., and Davis, W. The ventricular span in cerebral pneumography. *American Journal of Roentgenology* 90: 1176-84, 1963.

Carlen, P.L., Wortzman, G., Holgate, R.C., Wilkinson, D.A., and Rankin, J.D. Reversible cerebral atrophy in recently abstinent chronic alcoholics measured by computed tomography scans. *Science* 200: 1076-78, 1979.

Chernyshev, S.P. The weight of the human brain. (St. Petersburg, 1977) In *The Human Brain in Figures and Tables*, edited by S.M. Blinkov, and I.I. Glezer, Plenum Press, 1968.

Corsellis, J.A.N. *Mental Illness and the Aging Brain.* London: Oxford University Press, 1962.

Ellis, R.J. Norms for some structural changes in the human cerebellum from birth to old age. *Journal of Comparative Neurology* 32: 1-35, 1920-21.

Engeset, A., Lönnum, A. Third ventricles of 12 mm width or more. *Acta Radiologica* 50: 5-11, 1958.

Galaburda, A.M., LeMay, M., Kemper, T.L., and Geschwind, N. Lateral asymmetries in the brain. Structural right-left differences may represent the anatomical substrate of cerebral dominance. *Science* 199: 852-56, 1978.

Geschwind, N., Levitsky, W. Human brain: left-right asymmetries in temporal speech region. *Science* 161: 186-87, 1968.

Goodglass, H., and Quadfasel, F.A. Language laterality in left-handed aphasics. *Brain* 77: 521-48, 1954.

*Greenfield's Neuropathology.* Edited by W. Blackwood and J.A.N. Corsellis. London: Year Book Medical Publishers, 1976.

Hecaen, H., and Sauget, J. Cerebral dominance in left-handed subjects. *Cortex* 7: 19-48, 1971.

Heinz, E.R., Martenez, J., Haenggeli, H. Reversibility of cerebral atrophy in anorexia nervosa and Cushing's Syndrome. *Journal of Computer Assisted Tomography* 1: 415-18, 1977.

Hier, D.B., LeMay, M., Rosenberger, P.B., and Perlo, V.P. Developmental dyslexia. *Archives of Neurology* 35: 90-92, 1978.

Hier, D.B., LeMay, M., Rosenberger, P.B. Autism and unfavorable left-right asymmetries of the brain. *Journal of Autism*, in press.

Hochberg, F., LeMay, M. Arteriographic correlates of handedness. *Neurology* 25(3): 218-22, 1975.

Knudson, P.A. Ventriklernes Storrelsesforhold i Anatomisk Normale Hjerner fra Voksne. Copenhagen Theses. Odense, Denmark: Andelsbogtrykkeriet, 1958.

Lassen, N.A., Ingvar, D.H., Skinhj, E. Brain function and blood flow. *Scientific American* 239: 62-71, 1978.

Last, R.J., Thompsett, D.H. Casts of the cerebral ventricles. *British Journal of Surgery* 40: 525-43, 1953.

LeMay, M. Morphological cerebral asymmetries of modern man, fossil man, and nonhuman primate. *Annals of New York Academy of Science* 280: 349-66, 1976.

LeMay, M., and Culebras, A. Human brain—morphologic differences in the hemispheres demonstrable by carotid angiography. *New England Journal of Medicine* 287: 168-70, 1972.

McRae, D.L., Branch, C.L., and Milner, B. The occipital horns and cerebral dominance. *Neurology* 18: 95-98, 1968.

Pakkenberg, H.L., and Volgt, J. Brain weight of the Danes. *Acta Anat.* 56: 297-307, 1964.

Ratcliff, G., Dila, C., Taylor, L., and Milner, B. The morphological asymmetry of the hemispheres and cerebral dominance for speech: a possible relationship. Paper presented at the International Neuropsychology Symposium, June, 1978.

Rasmussen, T., and Milner, B. The role of early left-brain injury in determining lateralization of cerebral speech functions. *Annals of New York Academy of Science* 299: 355-69, 1977.

Riese, W. Weight, atrophy and repair in the very old human brain. Findings in the brain of eight patients over 90 years of age. In *1st International Congress of Neurological Sciences*, edited by L. Van Bogaert, and J. Radermeder. London: Pergamon Press, 1959.

Rosales, R.K., LeMay, M.J., and Yakovlev, P.I. The development and involution of massa intermedia with regard to age and sex. *Journal of Neuropath Exp. Neurol* 27: 166, 1968.

Tomlinson, B.E. Morphological changes and dementia in old age. In *Aging and Dementia*, edited by W.L. Smith and M. Kinsbourne. Spectrum, 1977.

Tomlinson, B.E., Blessed, G., and Roth, M. Observations on the brains of nondemented old people. *Journal of Neurological Sciences* 7: 331-56, 1968.

Wada, J. A new method for the determination of the side of cerebral speech dominance. A preliminary report on the intracarotid injection of sodium amytal in man. *Igaku to Seibutsugaker* (Japanese) 14: 221-22, 1949.

Wada, J., and Rasmussen, T. Intracarotid injection of sodium amytal for the lateralization of cerebral speech dominance. *Journal of Neurosurgery* 17: 266-82, 1960.

Yakovlev, P.I. Morphological criteria of growth and maturation of the nervous system in man. From Mental Retardation 34 Research Publications, A, R, N, M, D, 1962. Association for Research in Nervous and Mental Disease.

# 9 Changes in Cognitive Style with Aging

*Edith Kaplan*

It is known that as people age, specific changes occur in both brain and cognitive behavior. For example, in the central nervous system of the elderly there are a greater number of senile plaques and neurofibrillary tangles than in the young (Brody, Harmon, and Ordy, 1978). Examples of cognitive decline with age are particularly noted in tests of visuo-spatial processing, learning, and memory (Wechsler, 1958; Arenberg, 1973). Our knowledge of functional hemispheric asymmetries may provide a useful framework for the understanding of these age-related changes in the context of brain behavior relationships.

Studies of normal and unilaterally brain-damaged subjects have indicated that the two cerebral hemispheres are dominant for different functions, with each hemisphere specialized for a distinctive cognitive style (Levy-Agresti and Sperry, 1968; Bogen, 1969; Nebes, 1974).

The left hemisphere functions in an analytic, logical mode. It is predominant for the analysis of details, features, or component parts of a whole. It preferentially processes sequentially or temporally presented material, and thus is ideally suited for the use of language and verbal mediation. The right hemisphere functions in a holistic, gestalt mode. It is predominant for the synthesis and organization of component parts into complex wholes and the apprehension of spatial relationships. It preferentially processes simultaneously presented materials and is therefore particularly suited for visuo-spatial processing.

Though both hemispheres contribute to any given cognitive task, perceptual or otherwise, the normal young adult may have a preferential cognitive style and rely more heavily on the hemisphere associated with that mode of processing. Given the constraints of the particular stimulus, he has the capacity to *lead* with either hemisphere. In the unilaterally brain-damaged patient, when the functional contribution of the compromised hemisphere is impaired, we may assume that there is a greater reliance on the relatively intact hemisphere. Consequently the behavior of persons with unilateral brain damage may be regarded as a manifestation of the functioning of the intact hemisphere, not as a deficit performance of the damaged one.

Unlike the normal young adult, the unilaterally brain-damaged person is *obliged* to rely more heavily on the mode or cognitive style of the relatively noncompromised hemisphere. Thus greater or lesser success will be a function of the stimulus parameters or task demands.

The cognitive style or mode of processing material is best revealed in the *strategy* that is employed in problem solving. If the focus is only on the final product and the assigned quantitative score, that is, the achievement rather than the process, valuable information may be lost and in fact we may even be misled.

In 1937, Heinz Werner indicated in his paper "Process and Achievement" that a given solution may be arrived at by a variety of means. En route to a correct final solution subjects may reveal different cognitive styles or errors that are pathognomonic of different lateralized lesions. The block design subtest of the WAIS (Wechsler, 1955), which is particularly sensitive to both brain damage and aging, best illustrates this phenomenon.

Figure 9-1 shows three examples of correct final solutions arrived at within the allotted time for a full credit score, illustrating three distinctively different performances by three different populations. The young normal adults begin, as normal right-handers typically do, in the upper left and make no errors. The other two examples characterize patients with lateralized focal frontal lesions. The right-frontal patient begins with his non-hemiparetic, preferred right hand in the lower right quadrant, which for this patient is in the hemiattentional field contralateral to his noncompromised left hemisphere. Though this patient makes no errors, when other patients with this lesion make errors and self-correct for a final correct solution, the errors occur in the left hemiattentional field or the side of space contralateral to the lesioned hemisphere. Though the left-frontal patient working with his nonhemiparetic, nonpreferred left hand begins in the same upper left quadrant as the normal control subject, it is probably not for the same reason. Here, the upper left side of space is contralateral to the noncompromised right hemisphere. Note also that the perseverative error (self-corrected in time) occurs in the right hemiattentional field which is contralateral to the left lesioned hemisphere.

Figure 9-1 also shows three examples of incorrect final solutions that typify errors made by patients with different lateralized focal lesions. The first and third violate the $2 \times 2$ matrix (broken configuration), which we find to be pathognomonic of right-hemisphere pathology. Note that the left-hemisphere lesioned patient typically maintains the $2 \times 2$ configuration; the left half of space (hemiattentional field contralateral to the noncompromised right hemisphere) is correct, whereas the right side contains two errors that are not self-corrected. Errors in the hemiattentional field contralateral to the lesioned hemisphere occur even in the *absence* of a visual field defect. The difference between the right-frontal and right-parietal patient is of great interest. The strategy employed by the frontal patient reveals a very segmented approach with the focus on the most salient feature, the apex of the *chevron* (my verbal label reflects my cognitive or advancing age).

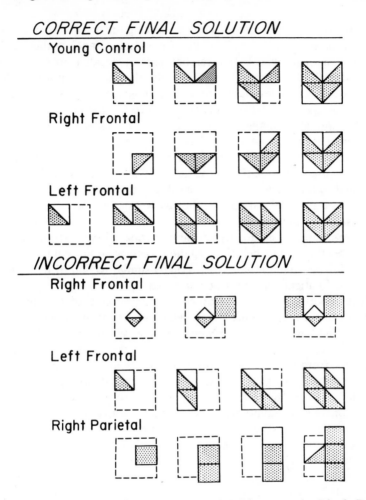

**Figure 9-1.** Flow Charts of Performance of Subjects on the Block Design Subtest of the Wechsler Adult Intelligence Scale

Though the configuration is broken, the essential property, the "V-ness" of the figure is preserved. Here the focus on the figure at the expense of the background indicates the frontal deficit of pull to saliency (the figure) and an inability to attend to more than one variable at a time, and the relative preservation of the parietal lobe function to appreciate the figural aspect. As can be seen neither the figure nor the ground are identifiable in the production of the right-parietal patient.

In the elderly, particularly those above seventy years of age, block design performance on the WAIS is remarkably similar to that of patients suffering from right-frontal lobe damage. They both tend to work from right to left and to break the configuration while preserving the essential features of the figure. This information is clinically of great importance in the evaluation of elderly patients who suffer cerebrovascular accident in the left hemisphere after the age of seventy. Presumably, they have premorbidly demonstrated what resembles right-frontal pathology, as opposed to currently evidencing bilateral involvement secondary to the current infarct.

The qualitative analysis of the strategy of the elderly permits us to dismiss some of the arguments that have been used to explain the differences that exist between verbal and performance subtests in the elderly. The lowered performance IQ relative to the sustained level of the verbal IQ has been attributed to time. The performance subtests are timed tests; the verbal essentially are not. The argument that as we age we become "slower but surer" simply is not so. We may indeed become slower, but we certainly do not become surer. The quality of the performance on block design during the allotted time, and when given all the necessary additional time, does not change. It is the quality that is so strikingly similar to that of the right-frontal lesioned patient that must be addressed.

The importance of mapping the sequence in the evolution of drawings will be demonstrated. Figure 9-2 presents the first of the three visual reproduction stimuli in the Wechsler Memory Scale (Wechsler, 1945). This figure is exposed for ten seconds, then removed, and the subject is required to reproduce it from immediate memory. The drawing sequence used by most normal young adults is as follows: the $x$ is executed first, proceeding from upper left to lower right, then from upper right to lower left; then the boxes (my cognitive style again) are added. This is clearly the most efficient sequence and contains the least number of bits of information for memory store. For example, if a subject employs verbal mediation, such as "an $x$ (cross) with two boxes (flags) facing each other at top and bottom," there are roughly four bits of information to be stored. However, if the sequence is not orderly (segmented) and lines are more or less randomly produced, instead of having two lines intersecting for $x$, there could be as many as four lines (one for each arm of $x$) and in the extreme as many as twelve lines for the boxes (a total of sixteen lines). Though such a disorganized production might occur immediately after exposure, or when instructed to copy the figure, the likelihood of a proper rendition of the stimulus after a twenty-minute filled delay is low. Not only are there too many bits of information that alone would be too taxing for memory, but more important, such a lack of organization reflects a deficit in processing and increases the chances for spatial-relationship errors, and virtually precludes effective retrieval of the design.

The types of errors produced by patients with left- and right-hemisphere lesions on the Wechsler memory design are illustrated in figure 9-3. Patients with left-hemisphere damage tend to produce the basic configuration, essentially intact; that is, they produce the $x$ but then have trouble

Source: Reporduced from the Wechsler Memory Scale. Copyright 1945, renewed 1972 by The Psychological Corporation. All rights reserved. Reproduced by special permission.

**Figure 9-2.** The First Stimulus Figure on the Visual Reproduction Subtest of the Wechsler Memory Scale

orienting the boxes (rotations). In the productions of the patients with right-hemisphere lesions, the cognitive mode of the left or noncompromised hemisphere is evident. All the features or details are present but not spatially related; the original configuration is totally lost. The last example is the production of the noble effort of a patient with significant right-hemisphere pathology, relying heavily on his left hemisphere to verbally encode. The *p* and *b* (which each appear twice) are obviously verbal approximations of the boxes in the original design.

The importance of making a distinction between process and achievement is most dramatically evident in figure 9-4. The typical normal sequential strategy described earlier was plotted for a selected group of Framingham heart study participants, namely, men and women from age fifty-five to over seventy-five, native English speakers with a high school education.[1]

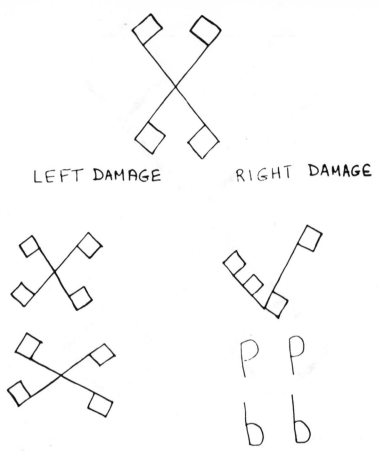

LEFT DAMAGE       RIGHT DAMAGE

**Figure 9-3.** Errors in the Production of the Wechsler Memory Scale Design by Right and Left Brain-Damaged Patients

The men and women who were high scorers on an initial cognitive screening test did not show the same pattern of change in approach. Advancing age had no impact on the sequential strategy employed by the women, but the men generally continued to produce the figure accurately but in a segmented manner. It should be emphasized that this sex difference would not have been revealed if only the final scores had been examined. By analyzing the sequence of the production of the drawn features, significant differences were observed.

The Rey-Osterrieth Complex Figure (Osterrieth, 1944), a more demanding figure, permits a finer analysis of the differences in processing styles (figure 9-5). It is presented to subjects under three conditions: (1) it must be copied; (2) immediately afterward, the figure is to be reproduced from memory; and (3) after a twenty-minute delay, it is to be reproduced once

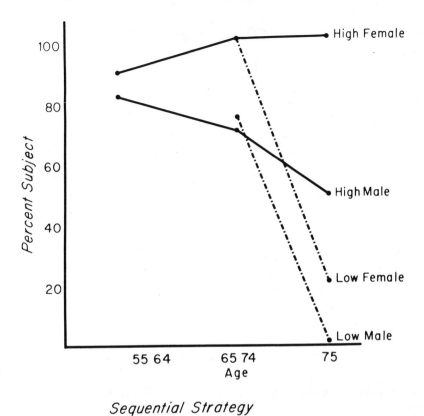

*Sequential Strategy*

**Figure 9-4.** Drawing Strategies of Male and Female Elderly

more from memory. Flow charts are kept by the examiner to chart the sequence and direction of the lines that are drawn. Normal young right-handed adults, particularly men, typically produce the base rectangle drawing from left to right, dividing the rectangle into four equal parts, drawing diagonals and then proceeding to fill in either the internal subwholes or the external features. Patients with right-hemisphere pathology proceed from right to left, that is, from the hemiattentional field contralateral to the non-compromised hemisphere; they then tend to segment lines and to proceed in a disordered fashion. However, the final product may closely approximate the model. Patients with more posterior pathology in the right hemisphere proceed in the same piecemeal manner. However, the relationship between the parts is severely violated, and the final product may bear resemblance to the model only with regard to the presence of some identifiable smaller internal details. Patients with left-hemisphere pathology again tend to work from left to right, and rather than beginning with the base rectangle, proceed to copy the outer outline with one continuous line. These patients

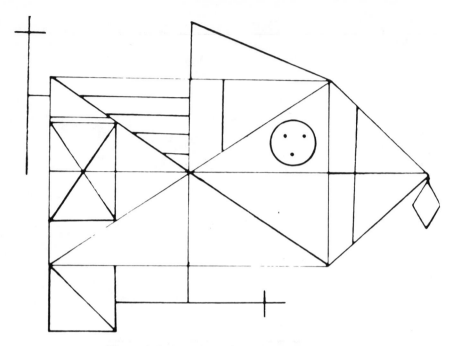

**Figure 9-5.** Rey-Osterrieth Complex Figure

make deletion errors with regard to inner details, and again errors predominate on the right side of space. With each recall internal features may be successively deleted. Patients with right-hemisphere pathology (particularly in the frontal region), like the elderly, retain the inner details, especially on the right side of space. It is interesting that their verbal encoding is so prepotent that distortions in the drawing are in the direction of the verbal label, such as railroad ties (another line is added), a little flag (stripes are added), and a TV antenna (additional lines are added). The heavier reliance on left-hemisphere strategies is very apparent.

This focus on small features that can be readily encoded verbally rather than on information that can be gleaned from the contour is most dramatically demonstrated on the Hooper Visual Organization Test (Hooper, 1958). Here line drawings of objects have been cut up and rearranged; the task is to mentally assemble them (figure 9-6). The elderly, and the patients with right-frontal pathology, tend to focus on either subwholes, that is, isolated parts from which they make their inferences about the whole. The first stimulus is reported to be a pipe, a tobacco pouch, and a watering can. On stimulus two frequent responses are a utility knife, though one interesting response is "Benjamin Franklin." A typical response for stimulus three is "handbag." It should be noted that a response to stimulus four, cat, which is in fact correct, may be inferred from the small details of eye

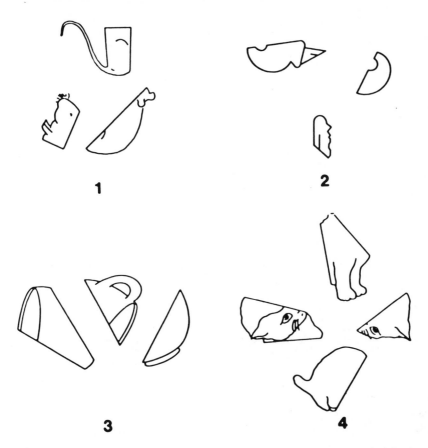

Source: H.E. Hooper, *Visual Organized Test* (Los Angeles: Western Psychological Services, 1954). Reprinted with permission.

**Figure 9-6.** Stimuli from Hooper Visual Organization Test

and whiskers. This should alert us again to the varieties of both correct and incorrect task solutions—certain stimuli lend themselves more readily to being processed on the basis of individual features, and one may be correct on those items without fulfilling the task requirement of organizing the component parts into a whole.

The perceptual organizational strategies of patients with brain damage, particularly with focal lesions in the anterior portion of the right hemisphere, and the normal elderly in the community are best illustrated on the tasks that have just been described.

Figure 9-7 shows that elderly who were low scorers on a neuropsychological screening battery evidenced profound segmentation similar to the productions of brain-damaged patients with verified lesions lateralized to the right hemisphere and focalized to the frontal system. The errors of the

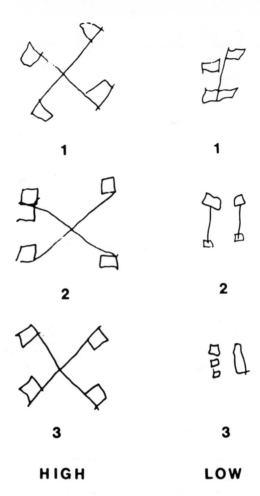

**Figure 9-7.** Wechsler Memory Scale Design Production Errors Made by
  Elderly Subjects with High and Low Scores on a Neuropsychological Screening Battery

high scorers were rare; the examples in figure 9-7 represent the poorest performance of this group. In all instances the primary configuration is preserved and errors are predominantly limited to the orientation of the
"flags," resembling the productions of patients with verified lesions of the
left hemisphere (Albert and Kaplan, forthcoming).

The implications for language are presented elsewhere in this book by
Harold Goodglass. He has demonstrated that naming may be affected because line drawings of objects are not correctly perceptually organized, and
therefore, on the basis of misperception, the wrong name is provided.

Errors of this type should not be confused with errors of misnaming, so typical in the left-hemisphere brain-damaged patient with aphasia. The anomia of the aphasic patient is a result of an inability to find the appropriate target word, not an inability to perceptually appreciate the drawing. As in the Hooper Visual Organization Test, perceptually based errors on the naming test are characteristic of patients with right-hemisphere pathology and tend to increase with advancing age. Here we have another example of how misunderstandings can arise if only achievement scores are considered. The naming score of an aphasic patient with a lesion in the left hemisphere may be identical to the score achieved by a patient with a right-hemisphere lesion *and* with the score of an elderly normal individual. The quality and source of errors that distinguish the left-lesioned patients from the right-lesioned ones are very apparent. But what of the errors that are made by right-lesioned patients and the elderly? The source of the error, the quality of the errors, made by patients with lesions in the anterior portion of the right hemisphere appear to be strikingly similar to those made by the elderly. The brain-damaged patients have structural lesions verified by CT scan, the elderly do not. What alterations in the elderly brain might there be to account for the observed similarities with brain-damaged patients? A qualitative neuropsychological approach to the study of the elderly on a comprehensive battery of tests along with comprehensive neuropathologic studies may provide the answer to this question in the future.

**Note**

1. This analysis was performed by Amy Veroff in The Normative Aging Study of The Framingham Heart Study directed by M. Albert and E. Kaplan in association with P. Wolf, A. Veroff, W. Rosen, T. Dawber, W. Kannel, and P. MacNamara.

**References**

Albert, M.S., and Kaplan, E. Organic implications of neuropsychological deficits in the elderly. In *Directions in Memory and Aging*, edited by L. Poon. Hillsdale, NJ: Erlbaum Press, forthcoming.

Arenberg, D. Cognition and aging: verbal learning memory and problem solving. In *The Psychology of Adult Development and Aging*, edited by C. Eisdorfer and M.P. Rawton, pp. 74-97. Washington, DC: American Psychological Association, 1973.

Bogen, J.E. The other side of the brain: an appositional mind. *Bulletin of Los Angeles Neurological Society* 34: 135-62, 1969.

Brody, J., Harmon, R., and Ordy, L. *Clinical, morphological and neurological and neurochemical aspects in the aging CNS*, vol. 1. New York: Raven Press, 1978.

Hooper, H.E. *The Hooper Visual Organization Test. Manual.* Los Angeles: Western Psychological Services, 1958.

Levy-Agresti, J., and Sperry, R.W. Differential perceptual capacities in major and minor hemispheres. *Proceedings of the National Academy of Sciences of the United States of America.* 61: 115, 1968.

Nebes, R.D. Hemispheric specialization in commissurotomized man. *Psychological Bulletin* 81: 1-14, 1974.

Osterrieth, P.A. Le test de copie d'une figure complexe. *Archives de Psychologie* 30: 206-356, 1944.

Wechsler, D. A standardized memory scale for clinical use. *Journal of Psychology* 19: 87-95, 1945.

_____. *Wechsler Adult Intelligence Scale.* New York: Psychological Corporation, 1955.

_____. *The Measurement and Appraisal of Adult Intelligence*, 4th ed. Baltimore: Williams and Wilkins, 1958.

Werner, H. Process and achievement: a basic problem of education and developmental psychology. *Harvard Educational Review*, 1937.

# 10 A Clinical Approach to Communication with the Elderly Patient

*R. Knight Steel*

There are some special problems in communication encountered in the day-to-day business of caring for the elderly population. To this end let me present some data and thoughts, divided into four sections. First, I feel it is essential to display some demographic facts and stress their implications. Second, I will note some of the characteristics that make the elderly patient unique or at least different from the younger patient, in the role of recipient of and giver of information. Third, I will point out something about the interview process in the doctor-patient relationship as it occurs in the field of geriatrics. Fourth, I will take a typical history form designed for teaching medical students and show how, with a few adaptations, it would be more suitable as a data-collecting instrument in the care of the elderly.

Approximately 11 percent of the population of the United States is older than sixty-five years of age, but this group accounts for at the least 25 percent of all acute hospital admissions and health-care costs nationwide (Harris, 1978). This figure is low compared to what we have found at University Hospital of the Boston University Medical Center where admissions to the Medical Service excluding a cancer unit were surveyed in March and April of 1979. During this period 45 percent of the 160 persons admitted were 65 years of age or older. Moreover, of the more than 1.2 million long-term-care beds in the United States, 90 percent are occupied by the elderly, and the number of long-term-care beds now about equals or even exceeds the number of acute-care beds.

Although the percentage of the population over sixty-five years of age will increase to only about 12 percent of the total by the beginning of the next century, some persons estimate that half or more of the services in the health-care industry will be devoted to the care of this segment of the population (Beeson, 1979). By the year 2030 when the present-day medical student is on medicare, 17 percent of the population will be older than sixty-five. I cannot predict what percentage of the health-care industry will be used for the elderly at that time.

The elderly population can be divided into two groups: the young-old, who are between sixty-five and seventy-five years of age and the old-old, who are older than seventy-five. The latter is not only the fastest growing segment of our population, but is also the group responsible for the dramatic rise in the cost of services for the geriatric population. Furthermore, among those sixty-five years of age and over the ratio of females to males rises each year. Indeed the death rate for women between the ages of sixty-five and seventy-five is just half of that for men; by the time the subjects under study become 80 years old there are two females for every male (Harris, 1978). An eighty-five-year-old woman more than likely has outlived her husband, and if she has had only male children, they may be dead as well! That is why women so outnumber men in nursing homes. Thus it is clear that communication with the elderly is now and will continue to be a most important issue for all providers of health-care services in the office, home, hospital, and long-term-care institution.

Some consideration must now be given to the characteristics of the older patient. Although the elderly as a group by most criteria are probably more variable than any other age group, let me adapt the concept of the "ideal 70-Kg man," so familiar to all medical students, and describe the "not unusual eighty-year-old woman." This "not unusual woman" is all but lacking in our medical textbooks, notwithstanding the demographic material just presented. I wonder what effect the almost total absence of such a character has on the textbook reader's ability to communicate with one! The discussion about this hypothetical individual will be divided into two parts: one directed strictly toward medical matters and one addressed to cultural considerations.

In the clinical encounter the elderly patient is frequently afflicted with not one disease but many. Although the number of items listed on a problem list has always seemed to me to be somewhat arbitrary, it cannot be denied that the number of problems possessed by the average eighty-year-old patient far exceeds the number (perhaps in a four-to-one ratio) of the average forty year old. Indeed, many an eighty year old has so many recorded that clinicians may find it difficult just to keep track of them. For diagnostic and therapeutic reasons the physician must sort out these problems, although they must not be considered individually from the standpoint of overall management.

The difficulty of separating diseases and appropriately weighing them in the formulation of a plan of management is compounded in the elderly patient because of the way diseases frequently appear in this age group. The initial symptom complex of many conditions is not nearly as dramatic as the medical textbooks would have us believe, and furthermore the presentation is often nonspecific in character. Thus for example the elderly patient with hyperthyroidism who does not have all the symptoms—tachycardia, weight loss, fine skin and hair, increased anxiety, and exophthalmos—may well have none of them, complaining only of fatigue or symptoms of congestive heart failure. Thus it can be seen that communication is not only difficult but also time consuming if the details of vague complaints are to be uncovered.

Although there are many medical characteristics of our not-unusual eighty year old, a few are worthy of special note. Since the visual and auditory senses are the pathways for the greatest amount of person-to-person communication, it should be well appreciated that both senses tend to fail with the passage of time. The decrement in hearing capability may be of such magnitude that communication is exceedingly difficult just from a technical viewpoint. Yet rarely do medical students learn to cope with this problem; if the patient is truly hard of hearing it is an unusual medical student, indeed, who is willing to compensate for this deficit over any period of time. In addition to deafness, older persons are more likely to be confused and have a diminished memory, especially for recent events. This compounds the difficulty of history taking. Leading questions may be necessary if a detailed history is to be elicited. Also, it is often necessary to take a history not only from the older patient but also from a member of the family or an acquaintance. This is rarely necessary in the care of a younger person except, of course, in the case of small children. Furthermore, because of fatigue it may be necessary to break up the initial history-taking process into two sessions. Also, time is both precious and costly; a primary-care practitioner cannot reasonably be expected to spend inordinate amounts of it with one patient.

Now let me just touch on some of the difficulties of communication that arise not from the biological characteristics of the elderly person but from the social and cultural ones. Consider the problems of communication between professionals and the more than one million individuals who reside in long-term-care facilities. I was careful to say *reside* because they do not just receive medical attention there; the facility is also their home. Yet the bedside of an old person is all too often located in a run down or sterile building and is hardly conducive to communication. The time of contact is usually extremely limited and, most important, the communicators have very little in common. After all, the resident probably remains essentially captive in that place indefinitely and is, therefore, severely restricted in social contacts. The interviewer usually has the rest of the world to return to when work is done. Subjects of concern are strikingly different. For one it is often the simple creature comforts, perhaps not easily obtained, and the power for change usually resides elsewhere. For the other it is a marriage, a mortgage, or a vacation that is the major concern, and the power for at least some change resides in one's own efforts. If commonality of experience were essential for communication there would be none at all.

Cultural heritage affects the manner in which an older person interprets a symptom or a disease. Thus, if the last experience of an individual with tuberculosis occurred at a time prior to the introduction of antituberculosis treatment it is no wonder that the threat of having the disease is felt to be horrific. In addition, a symptom may not be noted by the patient if it is felt to be a "normal" aspect of aging, because the elderly too are victims of misinformation about aging.

Persons of eighty years of age were raised in a world quite different from that of today. Many came to this country as immigrants with a strong ethnic heritage; even for those born and raised here time has produced great changes. The extraordinary speed of change in modern times is most effec-tively depicted in Toffler's *Future Shock* (1970). For our purposes we must remember that most professional communication with an older person takes place between two individuals, one elderly and one not elderly. As has been stated in the literature, "Perhaps if our interns were age 60 and expe-rienced practitioners instead of age 26 and novices" the flow of information would be improved (Steel and Williams, 1974).

Third, the interview process must be considered. There are only three sources of data in the clinical setting: history, physical examination, and laboratory, and clinical experience dictates that the majority of all correct diagnoses are made from history taking. Given the demographic character-istics of the patient population, the implications for this discussion are ob-vious. A great deal of historical information can be taken at the cost of a very few laboratory tests, and the history is often no less reliable than the laboratory tests. Also, history taking is surely less likely to harm the patient than the carrying out of many of the available diagnostic procedures. One of the reasons that history taking is not used more extensively and effec-tively may be that the cost for a laboratory workup is usually borne by a third party and payment is effectively limitless, whereas the cost of a history workup is borne, after a very modest initial payment, by the health-care professional whose time could be sold elsewhere.

The purpose of history taking is not only to collect data but also to develop the doctor-patient relationship. This point is clearly articulated in the textbook of physical diagnosis, *The Clinical Approach to the Patient* by Morgan and Engel (1969). Yet even in this generally splendid book there is little reference to some of the unique characteristics of the elderly patient. Also, there are few helpful hints on how to develop a productive doctor-patient relationship specifically with an older person, beyond the usual advice to the medical student feeling inadequate during his first clinical encounter.

Last, the form that the physician fills out during history taking must be applicable to the patient. I reviewed eleven textbooks of general physical diagnosis readily available at a major medical library, none of which was specifically geriatric in scope. My object was to survey many of the volumes that are suggested reading for the majority of medical students in the United States. I was unable to find a single reference in any of these textbooks to anything geriatric. Only a few commented in a sentence or two on how to take a history from someone hard of hearing. All assumed a hospital or office setting and not one even alluded to a nursing home or a long-term-care facility. The examples given of histories were with only one exception, of persons less than sixty-five years of age, the one exception—that of a sixty-seven-year-old man with a single complaint. Although it might be argued that the medical student requires a simple example for pedagogic purposes, I cannot help but wonder if an erroneous message is not implanted at an early stage in medical education by implying that such examples are typical of the usual state of affairs in the practice of medicine.

In this final section of the discussion I will review some of the specifics of the history form—the one, I confess, that I have used and taught. The first sentence usually begins something like, "This was the first hospital admission for this forty-year-old truck driver with a chief complaint of chest pain of twelve hours' duration." The number of admissions has great significance to most house officers who often express feelings of resentment toward persons who have been admitted more than about four times. However, it must be remembered that the fourth admission for a thirty year old carries quite a different significance than the fourth admission for an eighty-year old.

The occupation is usually included, appropriately I think, for a forty year old. Perhaps it is not as meaningful for an eighty year old. It is generally assumed that a forty year old is active, and therefore knowledge of the occupation allows the health-care professional to estimate the usual level of function for that individual. Since most eighty year olds are not employed it seems appropriate to include not only data about a work history but also data about the person's functional state. As for the "chief complaint," only a single textbook I read suggested there might be more than one. In my experience it is unusual for there to be only one concern in all but the exceptionally healthy ambulatory eighty year old.

A section on past health includes a listing of infectious diseases, which seems quite irrelevant to the care of most elderly persons. Also, the reliability of data about childhood measles, mumps, and german measles is questionable at most ages. A history of sore throats is almost always meaningless since there is never any way to determine the importance of such information in the evaluation of an 80 year old with a heart murmur thought to be rheumatic in origin. The listing of medicines being taken is absolutely essential and probably should be expanded to include information about medicines used in the previous five years. A notation about allergies is, of course, mandatory.

The review of systems, as detailed in these books, includes, as a rule, more questions about common upper respiratory infections than about diminished hearing or sight and may fail to stress problems with dentures altogether. Sleep disorders are never mentioned except in the context of paroxysmal nocturnal dyspnea or nocturia, despite the fact that they are a major concern of the elderly. Vague symptoms and signs such as fatigue and a change in activity are often overlooked. This failure might be rectified to some extent by ending all systems reviews with a general question such as, "Did I forget to ask you about anything else that might be bothering you?"

A word about the family history is important. Every text I read suggests questions about parents, siblings, and children; and almost all include grandparents in the family grouping despite their being of limited clinical significance to the management of the elderly person. Not a single book, however, suggests questions about grandchildren or great-grandchildren despite the importance of these people to the patient and to the doctor-patient relationship. Queries about nutrition are confined to low-salt or diabetic diets and include few if any questions about mastication per se. Information about possible dietary deficiencies and the difficulty of maintaining an adequate nutritional status because of financial restraints is infrequently sought.

A few books suggest recording a typical day. I have never even once seen a typical day of a person from a long-term-care facility recorded in a chart. Surely this would be instructive since most health-care professionals are unfamiliar with such settings. The majority of medical students and housestaff and, I would add, physicians in academic medicine, have never had any clinical experience in a nursing home.

In summary, then, with the consumers of health care becoming older, it is our duty as educators and health-care providers to learn more about geriatrics so that we can understand our patients as both biological and social beings. In addition, we must become familiar with the host of settings in which they live, be it a home, institution, or hospital. Furthermore, thought should be given to altering the form for recording the data gleaned from our patients, so that information more relevant to the care of the elderly will be obtained.

## References

Beeson, P. Training doctors to care for old people. *Annals of Internal Medicine* 90: 262-63, 1979.

Harris, C.S. *Fact Book on Aging: A Profile of America's Older Population.* Washington, DC: National Council on the Aging, 1978.

Morgan, W.L. and Engel, G.L. *The Clinical Approach to the Patient.* Philadelphia: W.B. Saunders, 1969.

Steel, K., and Williams, T.F. Geriatrics: the fruition of the clinician. *Archives of Internal Medicine* 134: 1125-26, 1974.

Toffler, A. *Future Shock.* New York: Random House, 1970.

# 11 Issues in Communication in Geropsychiatry

*Leon Epstein*

We live in an environment wherein communication is mediated by a range of symbols, verbal and nonverbal, whereby thought, feelings, and events, as well as tensions, anxieties, fears, and ways of coping, are communicated. Communications may be clearly and substantively expressed verbally, or we may infer as to their meaning on the basis of our constructs as to personality development or the nature of illness in aging. Communication may express subtle and inferred aspects of coping mechanisms, and may give expression to the psychological forces that influence the communication between patient and therapist.

The fundamental function of communication of any kind is the transmission of information. Frequently the individual may not be aware of what is being transmitted, and these transmissions frequently contain a host of errors of commission or omission, which can be tolerated without unduly distorting the intended message.

In general, the nature of communication in geropsychiatry scarcely differs from that for other age groups. It includes:

1. Voice (pressure of speech, tone, volume)
2. Body language (posture, gestures)
3. Visual expression (dress, adornment)
4. Touch (kissing, stroking, striking a blow)
5. Status symbols (the physician's white coat, costly clothing or jewelry)

The importance of these categories varies greatly with the individual patient. In severely disturbed patients with whom verbal communication may be almost impossible, observation of behavior is important; for example, impaired awareness may be noted via a puzzled expression, aimless wandering, or repetitive restless activity. Acutely expressed verbal ejaculations or looking over one's shoulder may indicate the presence of hallucinations. Restlessness may represent fear or dread. Sudden but fleeting laughter or crying may be indicative of superficial affect that may denote an organic brain syndrome. Impaired elderly may try to cooperate in relating an incident but their expression may lack richness, depth, illustrations, theme expansion or development, descriptive detail, sensitivity to their listener's theme, organization, or the presentation of a cohesive picture.

Communication with the elderly is greatly influenced by psychosocial and cultural factors. When meeting the elderly, we bring not only the skills learned in training, but also our personalities, experiences, and frames of reference associated with a social class. These factors may make us comfortable or uneasy and may facilitate or impair communication. We may be uneasy, for example, in a relationship with a much older person who sees us as a child figure; it may make us reluctant to discuss certain issues with him. Furthermore, language differences, and vastly different backgrounds or ways of life may also present problems for communication. Greater care is called for in cross class interviews (socioeducational status) especially if there is the added factor of a sizable age difference.

Anxiety may be aroused in the clinician by the emotional lability of older patients and their need at times to express themselves at great length. Frequently the meeting with the therapist provides a rare opportunity for the patients to express themselves and thus this loquaciousness may not be a symptom of illness but rather an avenue for expression.

There is also a variety of ways that the therapist may project, that is, communicate to the aged, the therapist's own helplessness, frustration, and even hostility. Treatment of the chronically ill elderly is scarcely the vision of the youthful therapist. As expressed by Leo Bellak, "Dr. Kildare is not a geriatrician." Even Dr. Rex Morgan's chronic cardiac elderly patient is not realistically presented; she reminds us of Molly Goldberg rather than a chronically ill older woman.

Most issues involving communication in geropsychiatry are similarly reflected in other age groups. Certain issues can be emphasized, however, that refer to the elderly specifically. Here we will give special attention to those which are all too often overlooked with the aged patient. Only passing reference, however, will be made to the other important concerns of this book, such as the aphasias and other neurological aspects of communication, and the impact of cognitive defects.

The elderly person is no exception in terms of the host of communications associated with a patient's entrance into a waiting or examining room. Many, perhaps most, are, of a nonverbal nature, such as punctuality, dress, grooming, posture, gestures, mannerisms, and autonomic signs. Any lead from these nonverbal indications must be evaluated in terms of each person's longitudinal history in order to assess its relevance to aging and to the individual. For example, slovenliness in a previously meticulous person may have a quite different meaning than it would for others who were not particularly fastidious in earlier years. Punctuality may indicate an eagerness to participate in the appointment, lateness may reflect a reluctance; autonomic signs such as sweating may reflect anxiety about the examination.

There is also the factor of nonverbal communication from the setting to the patient: the decor of the waiting room, its warmth or sterility, and the dress and conduct of the receptionist. If the setting or receptionist is unkempt, the communication perceived, correctly or incorrectly, may reflect evidence for the patient of an irrational belief of unworthiness and low status. The salutation of the receptionist may also represent a meaningful communication. A respected and creative man of sixty-six was recently greeted by a receptionist at an initial visit to a physician's office by his first name. He is turn subsequently greeted the examining physician in similar fashion. In reply to the physician's rather startled response, he stated that he had been led to believe that this was a first-name office setting! He subsequently alluded to being put down—the receptionist could address him by first name, whereas he was expected to use surname and professional title when addressing the physician, which gave the patient less status and caused some loss of the status engendered by his extensive creativity. In certain situations this could prove devastating to a depressed patient already plagued with inappropriate self-depreciation. The same applies, to be sure, in settings where much younger professional or lay personnel frequently address elderly hospitalized patients or nursing-home residents by their first names, or even "auntie" or "uncle." This is often perceived as demeaning or confirmative of an already inappropriately perceived very low self-evaluation. It may also serve to accentuate the perception of the patient as being very old. In this context, better psychological functioning is often associated with younger-age self-perception in the elderly, and, conversely, poorer functioning with older-age self-perception.

Aside from the content of what is expressed, the tone of voice, the choice of words, and the manner and rapidity of speech may communicate, for example, suspiciousness, anger, plaintive appeal, depression, or hyperactivity. Lack of spontaneity, monosyllabic responses, and failure to remember may provide clues to depression, poverty of thought, or hostility. Conversely, garrulousness and the provision of undue detail may suggest grandiosity, hypomania, or as noted previously, merely the availability of someone with whom to talk. The patient's dress, often the meticulous care in grooming and choice of accessories, may indicate the importance placed on the interpersonal aspect of the visit, or for some, may be an attempt to accentuate wellness.

There may be special situations observed in home-visit settings. For example, the presence of dishes, rubbish, and food leftovers may communicate poor locomotion rather than hoarding or habit deterioration indicative of an organic brain syndrome. Or the presence of cat or dog food and little else in the cupboard may indicate that closeness to a pet is the sole counter to isolation. A patient's concern over a pet's well-being may even supersede concern with one's own adequate nourishment. Refusing to be hospitalized because in doing so a pet may be neglected is not infrequent, and suggests the extent of the patient's isolation.

Some expressions, although also found in younger patients, may be of special relevance to the elderly. Such expressions may communicate fears associated especially with aging. Among these may be included:

1.  *Concealment of evident symptoms* may reflect a concern over frightening psychiatric symptoms, frailty, or a fear of enfeeblement, limited functioning, or death. It may also reflect the patient's desire to impress the examiner with assets and abililties because of these fears.
2.  *Accumulation of mementos*, either on one's person or in one's quarters, may serve as reminders of happier times and ward off feelings of loss, (though not to the point of trash collection as with the well-publicized Collier brothers who had collected truckloads of newspapers in their New York apartment).
3.  *Accusatory statements* may not necessarily be delusional, but may indicate a call for attention or an expression of hostility directed toward a caretaker, relative, associate, or friend.
4.  *Loquaciousness* may indicate a desire to maintain a contact with someone or may be perceived as a plea for attention.
5.  *Denial of reality* may reflect a need to maintain independence in the face of a perceived declining ability to do so.
6.  *Selfishness* may reflect a need for gratification that is not being received in more acceptable channels.
7.  *Stealing* may communicate a need for attention or affection.

Elderly patients often present delusional beliefs for the first time. One must take their beliefs seriously, listen carefully, and request additional data rather than too quickly showing disbelief. A too-early expression of disbelief might be viewed as a failure to pay attention. Others may have behaved toward them in such fashion with respect not only to their delusions, but also to their aging. Even when the delusions are no longer present it may well be the better part of valor not to insist that the patient be aware that their earlier expressions were delusional.

Communication may be fostered in rather unusual ways. An interesting study was carried out in which budgies were given to isolated, relatively immobile elderly living alone. It was found that these pets contributed markedly to the well-being of the elderly, who bought knickknacks for them and used them as discussion topics which served "to displace the monotonous awareness and discussion of past and pending medical illness" (Colson and Colson, 1979). Another researcher reported that he was able to foster communication by permitting selected patients to effect an illusion of omnipotence by venting their anger, while he appeared "suitably distressed, cautiously self-defensive, and semi-apologetic without ever admitting that the patient was correct" (Goldfarb and Sheps, 1954). Acceptance of the rage lessened fear of abandonment and the need for symptoms to obtain care and attention and increased self-esteem.

Suicidal potential may be communicated without mention of self-destruction. Durkheim pointed out that suicide may be altruistic, egoistic, or anomic. The latter two types are seen most frequently in the elderly, who because of fewer group associations receive less emotional support, and for whom disorganization ensues because guidelines and appropriateness are less clear to them. What may be communicated is a call for help because of the loss of a loved one, money, friends, possessions, and so on. Resnick and Cantor pointed out that the presence of serious health problems or the expression of recent activities that suggest the anticipation of death, such as clarifying a will or distributing cherished possessions, may be hints of potential suicide. An elderly patient who recites long lists of physical complaints with seeming little structural or functional relevance and exhibits a feeling of helplessness should alert the care taker of a serious potential for suicide.

In a cultural setting where the elderly are all too often viewed as being unattractive, argumentative, talkative, repetitive, boring, and penurious among other less desirable attributes, care should be taken not to inadvertently offer further evidence to an existing low self-esteem. This may occur when the therapist or any member of the office or hospital staff becomes impatient, assumes critical attitudes, patronizes, or underestimates capacities—all of which may serve to enhance already perceived dehumanization.

Therapists tend to pay less attention to these factors when giving care to elderly patients, especially in caring for those who are emotionally disturbed or cognitively impaired. It is all the more important to pay more attention to these concerns with the elderly, since they have become sensitive to others' reactions to them, which has led to greater anxiety and insecurity, and thus to further impairment of functions.

## References

Colson, S.A., and Colson, E. Pets as mediators in therapy in custodial institutions and the aged. In *Current Psychiatric Therapies*, edited by Masserman, vol. 18, 1979.

Goldfarb, A.I., and Sheps, J. Psychotherapy of the aged, brief therapy of interrelated psychological and somatic disorders. *Psychosomatic Medicine* 16: 209-219, 1954.

Resnick, H.L., and Cantor, J.M. Suicide and aging. *Journal of the American Geriatric Society* 18: 152-58, 1970.

# 12 Language in Normal and Dementing Elderly

*Martin L. Albert*

This chapter considers language in normal and dementing elderly from a clinical, neurobehavioral point of view. Several questions arise from clinical contact with elderly persons: (1) What are the characteristic patterns of language in healthy and brain-damaged older persons? (2) How can the clinician identify these patterns? (3) What neurological changes may explain the linguistic changes? (4) How can answers to these questions help the clinician deal with problems of communication with elderly patients?

Two underlying assumptions serve as a basis for this work. The first depends on a life-span approach to the aging nervous system. Available evidence suggests that the organization of the brain for language changes throughout the life span, and that brain-language relationships change throughout the life span (Obler and Albert, in press). Despite this evidence, many researchers study the aging nervous system by chopping human behavior into artificial segments by age. This segmented, cross-sectional research, while often useful, has provided as much misinformation as fact, and has led to a strong negative attitude toward the therapy of language disorders in later life. What is needed, then, is a series of longitudinal studies—covering the period from childhood through old age—looking at language and the brain. It is my expectation that this life-span approach will become more popular in the next decade.

The second assumption underlying our work is that language in dementia results from the interaction of several different sets of neurobehavioral events as people get older. Some of these involve improvement; others, deterioration. At least four elements must be included: (1) The continued development of language skills, which we believe is a process that continues throughout old age; (2) the senile mental deterioration of normal aging; (3) the cognitive strategies used by normal old people to overcome the effects of senile mental deterioration; and (4) the specific neurobehavioral deficits found in dementing syndromes—these include, but are not limited to, language deficits. Ordinarily researchers and clinicians look for signs of *deterioration* in the elderly. In our approach we also look for signs of strength, and even for signs of improvement. We anticipate eventually being able to develop new therapies based on these pockets of strength.

**Language in the Normal Elderly**

Perhaps the most important observation about language in healthy old people is that they have greater variability in linguistic performance than younger adults. This variability is present not only across groups but also within individuals—sometimes old people will perform one way, sometimes another way on the very same tests of language. In fact, everyone does it—but older people do it more.

What are the general medical and neurological implications of this variability? It would seem that performance by older people on specific tests of language is dependent on a complex combination of factors. One has to do with changes in language itself. Others have to do with changes in other cognitive skills, especially memory and perception. Also, changes in emotional state, such as loneliness, depression, and especially fear of making mistakes, play a role. Physical state contributes, as does social expectation. The more one expects old people to perform poorly, the more they will.

As for language changes themselves, despite the variability, older people have certain general patterns (Obler and Albert, in press; Hutchinson and Beasley, 1976). First, speech discrimination and comprehension of spoken language seem to fall off. Second, discourse—that is, spontaneous speech, responsive speech, conversation—becomes more fluent at the syntactic level and more dysfluent at the prosodic level. In other words, older people tend to use longer, more complex sentences than younger people to say the same things; this is increased fluency at the syntactic level. The actual sounds that they produce, however, the melody of language—prosody—is disturbed. A third modification in language use with aging has to do with lexicon or availability of words. Active use of lexicon (word finding or naming, for example) seems to deteriorate, whereas passive use of lexicon (word recognition, for example) is preserved and may even increase into late old age.

*Neurological Correlates of Changes
in Language with Aging*

A variety of neurophysiological and neuroanatomical studies have been carried out in aging populations that can be considered from the viewpoint of brain-language relationships. *Electroencephalographic studies* indicate that as people get older a progressive slowing of the dominant alpha activity occurs (Obrist, 1954). Of more specific interest, however, is the fact that focal dysrhythmias, slow or sharp waves, appear in the electroencephalogram of 30 to 40 percent of healthy elderly people; and the left temporal region (a region clearly related to language) is involved in 75 to 80 percent of these. It is generally taught that these electroencephalographic changes are unrelated to neurobehavioral changes. My own belief is that these electrical abnormalities are related to the language changes of normal aging.

*Regional cerebral blood flow studies* relating to language, aging, and dementia have come mainly from the cerebrovascular research groups in Sweden and Denmark (Gustafson, Hagberg, and Ingvar, 1978). Regional cerebral blood flow is reduced by about 25 percent in a variety of dementing illnesses, especially in fronto-temporal regions, the regions that might be most important for language.

Perhaps the most interesting studies for understanding brain-language relationships in aging are the *neuroanatomical studies*. Several groups have looked at changes in the normal human brain with aging, but the studies by Brody are particularly relevant (1976). He found that cortical cell loss with aging is not diffuse but selective. One of the few places in the cerebral cortex to show significant dropout of cells is the superior temporal gyrus. We know from studies of aphasics that damage to the superior temporal gyrus can produce a language disturbance that is fluent at the syntactic level and that has associated findings of impaired speech discrimination, language comprehension, and naming. These are also the cardinal features of the language disturbances of normal aging, although in normal aging they occur in much milder form.

In summary, then, as people get older their language performance becomes more variable, speech discrimination and language comprehension deteriorate, active naming skills are lost, and verbal output becomes more fluent and syntactically complex. Correlated with these behavioral changes are selective atrophic changes in fronto-temporal regions, and, in particular, in the superior temporal gyrus, a region known to be an essential component of the neural substrate for language.

## Language in Dementia

In any analysis of linguistic performance in dementing individuals, it is crucial to know what dementia is involved. A variety of classification schemes has been elaborated for the dementing illnesses. To understand how changes in the brain of the dementing person relate to language, one must specify the classification scheme that is being used.

In our research we have found it useful to apply the operational definitions of cortical versus subcortical dementia. These labels correspond to two major forms of dementia that can be distinguished on clinical, neurobehavioral grounds. Subcortical dementia is a syndrome found in patients with a variety of neurological illnesses in which prominent pathological changes are seen in subcortical nuclear structures, such as in progressive supranuclear palsy. Clinically this syndrome is manifested by emotional or personality changes, memory disorder, defective ability to manipulate acquired knowledge, and striking slowness in rate of information processing.

The subcortical dementias may be contrasted clinically with the cortical dementias, that is, those dementing illnesses in which pathological changes are prominent in cortical association areas, such as in Alzheimer's disease. In the subcortical dementias vocabulary and general facility with language are thought to be preserved. No aphasias, apraxias, or agnosias are seen. In the cortical dementias, however, aphasias, agnosias, and apraxias are present in varying combinations with the signs and symptoms of subcortical dementia.

With respect to language in dementia certain characteristics of language use are seen with dementing individuals of any sort. These include a lack of initiative in speech, perseveration, naming and word-finding difficulties, and lack of appropriateness in response. The ability to initiate speech, to maintain its normal flow, and to stop speech when desired are all taken for granted in normal people, but they may be serious problems in demented patients. These are broad categories, however, and if we consider different sorts of dementia, we may find different manifestations of these phenomena.

With the subcortical dementias, we have found both speech and language problems. Speech with subcortical lesions is characterized by a slow rate, low volume, and disturbances in rhythm, pitch, and articulation. The patient may begin a sentence at an acceptable volume, and then trail off toward the end of the sentence. One 64-year-old patient with progressive supranuclear palsy whom we saw sounded like a record played on low speed. When medicated with L-Dopa, his pace picked up and his prosody returned toward normal.

However, speech disorders are not the only disorders seen in subcortical dementias. There seem to be language problems as well. Naming abilities are impaired, both on tests of confrontation naming and on tests of word finding—even when time is taken into account. In addition, writing—in contrast with spoken language—seems to be disturbed in subcortical dementia. Agraphia, manifested by abnormal syntax and mistakes in spelling, is prominent.

One striking positive feature of language in subcortical dementia is that coherence of thought is preserved; there may be delays, anomia, circumlocutions, and perseveration, but the meaning is generally conveyed.

In patients with the Alzheimer's Disease—Senile Dementia Complex (ADSDC), meaning is often lost, even in mild or early cases. In the moderately advanced cases, disorganization of syntax, loss of words, paraphasias and neologisms, and perserveration interact with memory disorders to such a degree that coherence of thought or coherence of expression is severely impaired (Irigaray, 1973; deAjuriaguerra and Tissot, 1975). As a result, comprehension becomes difficult to evaluate. This combination of apparent defect in comprehension, and incoherent but fluent output, produces a picture that resembles that of Wernicke's aphasia.

Patients with Wernicke's aphasia resulting from acute strokes differ from the patients just described in at least one very important respect, however, along pragmatic dimensions. If we consider the intention of the speaker (not the words used but what is meant by them), we find that for patients with acute Wernicke's aphasia, although one may not be able to understand the meaning of the words they produce, one is able in many cases, even in some severe cases, to understand the intention. For the severely impaired patient with ADSDC, meaning is lost not only for the specifics of the utterance, but also for its general intention.

## Aphasia and Aging: A Life-Span Perspective

It is a common clinical observation that when a lesion produces aphasia in children, the aphasia is virtually always nonfluent. This is true whether the lesion is anterior or posterior to the fissure of Rolando. There has been a clinical suggestion that the same aphasia-producing lesions that might produce nonfluent aphasia in children produce different patterns of aphasia in older groups; specifically, more fluent aphasias. We conducted a study with 360 right-handed aphasics over age fifty (Obler et al., 1978), and found a statistically significant age difference between the Broca's and Wernicke's aphasics. Those with Broca's (or anterior, nonfluent) aphasia were significantly younger by a decade than those with Wernicke's (or posterior, fluent) aphasia. So it would seem that the clinical observation of increasing fluency of aphasia with age from childhood to adulthood may be correct. This ties in, of course, with the data presented earlier concerning increasing fluency of discourse in normal older people.

## Conclusions

The principal thesis that I am proposing was stated earlier, that the brain substrate for language changes throughout the life span and is subject to a variety of influences. Among those influences there are three major factors: (1) impact of education, (2) selective cortical atrophy of aging in the normal person, and (3) selective neuropathological changes in the different varieties of dementia. This approach to our research has obvious clinical implications as well. By understanding how brain-language relationships change throughout life, and how these changes can be influenced by education; by knowing which parts of the brain are more resilient to atrophy with aging; and by having a firm knowledge of which cognitive strategies are available to language-impaired elderly persons, a rational approach to meaningful communication with dementing elderly individuals can be developed.

## References

Brody, H. An examination of cerebral cortex and brain-stem aging. In *Neurobiology of Aging,* edited by R. Terry and S. Gershon. New York: Raven Press, 1976.

deAjuriaguerra, J., and Tissot, R. Some aspects of language in various forms of senile dementia. In *Foundations of Language Development,* edited by E. and E. Lenneberg, vol. 1. New York: Academic Press, 1975.

Gustafson, L., Hagberg, and Ingvar, D. Speech disturbances in presenile dementia related to local cerebral blood flow abnormalities in the dominant hemisphere. *Brain and Language* 5: 103-116, 1978.

Hutchinson, J., and Beasley, D. Speech and language functioning among the aging. In *Aging and Communication,* edited by H. and E. Oyer. Baltimore: University Park Press, 1976.

Irigaray, L. *Le Langage Des Déments.* The Hague: Mouton, 1973.

Obler, L.K., and Albert, M.L. Language and aging: a neurobehavioral analysis. In *Speech, Language, Hearing and the Aging Process,* edited by D. Beasley and G.A. Davis. New York: Grune and Stratton, in press.

Obler, L.K., Albert, M.L., Goodglass, H., and Benson, D.F. Aphasia type and aging. *Brain and Language* 6: 318-22, 1978.

Obrist, W. The electroencephalogram of normal aged adults. *Electroencephalography Clinical Neurophysiology* 6: 235-43, 1954.

**Part III
Clinical Issues:
Rehabilitation**

# 13 Language and Communication in the Elderly: Experimentation and Rehabilitation

*Marcel Kinsbourne*

## Who Are the Elderly?

Elderly people are of course those who were born a long time ago. But for purposes of gerontological research, elderly people are only those who are not sick or handicapped in any of the many ways that preclude them from volunteering for experimental testing or disqualify them from taking tests. These sampling criteria are so arbitrary and indefinite that one is led to wonder whether (for purposes of experimental study) there are any legitimately elderly people at all, as opposed to those who during the passage of time become decrepit on account of organic disability, or disabled by virtue of social pressure or economic deprivation. The answer might be that there are hardly any, just those few who for a miscellany of fortuitous reasons happen to be handicapped in ways not provided for by the sampling criteria. For instance, if a person suffers a sudden major stroke, he abruptly leaves the ranks of the elderly and becomes a recruit for neuropsychological study. But if instead a person suffers a multitude of little strokes, which make him or her just as aphasic, elderly status is retained because the aphasia did not come on dramatically. There is probably no way of resolving this dilemma, as the concept of aging appears to be an abstraction that cannot usefully be operationalized. What happens to people as they grow old, and the consequences for their cognitive competence, is the result of diverse and irregularly occurring damage aggravated by the ill effects of demeaning stereotypes and poverty. Aging in the sense of having been alive for a long time, having experienced much and learned or overlearned a lot, seems not to have any clearly definable systematic effect on cognition. Attempts to demonstrate that elderly people have difficulty changing mental set or adapting to novel circumstances because over time existing views and habits have become deeply ingrained, have been unsuccessful. The component of age-related cognitive deficit that is biologically based is the result of heterogeneous brain damage. When we compare samples of young and elderly people we are comparing intact people with people who may have suffered diffuse or scattered brain deficit.

## How Are They Different?

In studying aging we are dealing with people who over the years have become depleted of functioning brain elements in ways that did not cause acute or dramatically selective cognitive deficit. In essence we are studying the thinning brain.

How does a general thinning of the brain affect behavior, as compared to local inactivation of a wedge of brain? Is diffuse cerebral pathology more than the sum of all possible focal pathologies? If all the focal deficits that are known in neuropsychology were combined, would the outcome be a person who is old, senile, demented? In the limited number of instances where total cognitive collapse occurs, this appears to be the case. But in the much more interesting majority of cases, where intellectual deterioration is less than total, the pattern of age-related deficit diverges substantially from that expected on the bases of neuropsychological considerations.

Is there then some principle that will enable us to predict how a person whose brain is depleted would operate? One could begin by comparing the brain depleted by aging with the brain depleted. The important comparison is the elderly person with the mildly demented and the mildly retarded younger person. In terms of operational efficiency of the brain, these groups can be matched. How is the depleted brain in elderly people different from other depleted brains? It may be that there is no difference. Some comparisons made in this book between old people and children are instructive in suggesting that the regression hypothesis—that old people regress to a state of immature brain—has some merit. The fewer functional neurons in the very young brain and the fewer neurons in the older senile brain may, in fact, result in the same type of operational limitations.

What might those limitations be? One way of accounting for them invokes selective inhibition. In a vast expanse of brain territory, it is easier to keep things apart from each other until it is desirable for them to fuse. We hold concepts separately but concurrently in short-term store while manipulating them for the best effect. This is what we do in problem solving, we time-share. Time sharing, which features in Borod's account of a dichotic-listening experiment, (chapter 7) is at the essence of intelligent behavior. In order to solve any problem to which the answer is not immediately given, we have to restrain a predominant response bias when it happens to be incorrect, while searching for a solution that is less obvious but more correct. That restraint or inhibition is crucial to adaptive functioning. If we lose functional cerebral space, we may no longer be able to inhibit an overriding response tendency, and therefore may become unable to respond in more appropriate ways.

Let us now analyze how the elderly are different in light of that concept. What specifically do they find difficult? In contrast to focal neuropsychological syndromes, where particular operations are difficult (a conduction aphasic may have trouble with word repetition and a prosopagnosic may have trouble with face recognition), with diffuse loss it is not a specific mental operation that is difficult. Rather, doing anything is difficult that calls for active spontaneous choice of the right strategy, and operational efficiency in using it.

Storandt in her chapter discusses the various phases of information flow in memory. She points out that with regard to the passive persistence of the sensory image for a fragment of a second, there seem to be contradictory findings about age-related impairment. There seems not to be any age-related differences, with respect to rate of decay in store. She emphasizes age-related differences in active operations on the meorandum: differences in secondary memory, in manipulating, transforming, associating, and using the given data in nonstereotyped nonautomatic ways.

Storandt says some studies indicate that sensory memory is curtailed in old people, others indicate that it is prolonged. These statements are not incompatible because they apply to two different kinds of studies. The paradox reduces to the following simple, sad proposition: whatever is more difficult, elderly individuals have more trouble with. There are some experimental designs where long sensory storage is needed to get the answer right. Elderly people do not have it. There are other paradigms where short sensory storage is needed to perform well. Elderly people do not have that either. When extracting information from a fading trace is called for, the elderly have more trouble because the trace fades faster for them. But when, as in critical flicker fusion experiments, the trick is to detect discontinuity and not be deceived by an apparent continuity, the elderly get deceived. They have trouble with the task. So the different paradigms illustrate the same sad fact: where one has to perform an active operation that is hard—in other words, not automatically available—the older one is, the less efficient he is going to be.

Let us proceed to the broader subject of episodic and semantic memory. Keep in mind that remembering is not always a good thing; there is a very important adaptive reason for forgetting. Every time we are remembering something, there is something else we therefore cannot do, like watch an important ongoing event. Every time we reconstruct a previous experience, we have to turn away from a present experience. We should only do this when the time is right. If we remembered everything that happened to us, even when quite young, we would be insufferable bores, and by the time we got a little bit older, we would cease to function because we would be too involved with our memories. It is adaptive to forget, except when the circumstances require that we derive a lesson from what happened the last time things were the way they are now.

Semantic and episodic memory are two ends of a continuum. When a particular event occurs for the first time, it occurs in a certain context. It is then remembered when that context recurs. If, however, that event occurs frequently across contexts, it is remembered regardless of context. If something is going to happen many times it is adaptive to remember it, regardless of where and how it was first heard, seen, or otherwise experienced. It becomes entered into semantic memory. On the other hand, if something happens once and then does not happen again for years, there is no point in remembering it the second time because it is an improbable event, unless the situation is uncannily similar to what happed the first time, and different from everything that intervened. This information is stored in episodic memory. When people grow older and their brain becomes depleted for whatever reason, they need more context to remember context-bound information. This process actually is adaptive, because they would have experienced more things in the interim so more specifiers are called for in order for the correct experience to be reconstructed.

**Why Do They Act as They Do?**

It may be instructive to compare the way elderly people have trouble using strategies with the difficulties children experience, and to compare the operational efficiency of old people with that of children. Elderly people have difficulty choosing the right strategy. If they are cued, told how to operate, the strategy becomes available and they can use it. So the obvious therapeutic implication is to cue them. But that is impractical because we cannot accompany them as they walk through life, continuously cuing them. The problem is that mnemonic devices, imagery and the rest, do not help much in practice, because elderly people often do not generalize. Failure to generalize is part of the problem they had in the first place. They do not choose the right strategy even if they have just been taught it. Children also have trouble choosing the right strategy, but what they do is quite different. In language development when children first experience a variety of syntactic forms, they overextend a few simple strategies. They cannot yet comprehend and use more sophisticated ones. So they use those strategies they know, even when these strategies are quite inappropriate. By looking at the pattern of errors that children make in comprehension tasks, we can determine why they interpret a particular proposition in a particular incorrect way. For example, they superimpose a consecutive agent-action-object strategy on any noun-verb-noun sequence. Using strategies where they are not applicable is maladaptive. It is fortunate that most children have parents to guard them against the consequences.

When elderly people are depleted of available strategies they still have what is called metamemory, which is adaptively interesting, because it means that they know what it is they do not know. They know their limitations, unlike children. Elderly people act in certain ways that are explicable in terms of their predicament. If elderly people are cautious it may be that they should be, because their operational efficiency is such that they cannot deal as fast as they used to with quickly changing events. If elderly people are dogmatic, it may be because they know that in open discussion they would lose. An unbeatable defense against losing an argument is to be dogmatic. If elderly people are rigid, express a need for sameness, and want things not to change, it may be beacuse they would be bewildered by change. Herein lies an important moral. It is not necessarily advisable to help the elderly be less rigid, more flexible, less cautious, and so on. This type of help does not address the issue, it merely robs elderly people of adaptation. There has been a humanitarian tendency among many people in aging research, particularly sociologists, to assert that effectively old people are not old, they just seem old because we regard them as such. It is necessary, these people argue, to discard that stereotype; if we were to look at an old person in a new, unprejudiced way, we would realize he is really young. This is like saying that males are not males, females are not females, whites are blacks and blacks are white. It is ostensibly humane, but actually oppressive. If we deny the problems, we cannot do anything about them. Those people who claim that elderly people really function just as well as young people are precluding the elderly from the help that they in fact need. We are not interested in pretending that many people as they grow older stay just as effective as they were before. It is not true. We are interested in finding out what to do given the fact that they often do suffer cognitive loss.

**What Can We Do About It?**

So what can we do? Let us return to the selective inhibition idea; that if somebody fails to do something right, it is because they are doing something wrong instead. Nobody just fails, in a vacuum. When people do something that is not right, they do not perform at random; they do something more obvious but less appropriate than what they should be doing. In retraining people with organic deficit and diffuse damage, it is not sufficient just to practice the correct response, because they will still continue to do the incorrect thing, which is blocking the correct response. The way to rehabilitate is not to keep on teaching the elderly people the same old skill over again; it is to change the subject as if they had never learned it. Teach them something that purports to be a new skill. And only at the very end of learning, when they have virtually mastered the task, should we draw attention to the fact that they have reacquired an old skill.

The way we are best able to learn from the research about aging is to ignore the implication that we are addressing basic problems. If our purpose is to find out how the brain works, studying aging is a strange way of going about it, for the reasons mentioned. But if we are studying aging to find out how better to define and therefore better to alleviate problems that often trouble people who happen to be old, it is useful to have the information that research can offer. The study of aging is very much an exercise in applied science, much more than, say, neuropsychology of focal disease. We could study focal (cerebral) symptomatology constructively all our life without ever helping anybody and most neuropsychologists do just that. But it is not satisfactory to study aging in this way; we should study aging with the implicit rationale that the outcome is going to be of use to elderly people. We need to learn what strategies we can use to supplement the repertoire of those elderly people who have only a few strategies left spontaneously available to them.

# 14 Speech Input Processing, Hearing Loss, and Aural Rehabilitation with the Elderly

*Ralph R. Rupp*

*Blindness separates man from things, but deafness separates man from man.*

It has been estimated by Butler (1975) that 70 percent of an adult's waking activities are involved in the four communicative processes of listening, speaking, reading, and writing; and listening is the leading process, accounting for 45 percent of the total communicative activity. To be an effective listener in American culture requires an adequate, if not normal, hearing system. Any individual, irrespective of age, who has any degree of measurable hearing loss or deficit has a communicatively disabling sensory problem.

Ramsdell (1970) proposes that adequate hearing serves the individual in three different yet equally important functional ways: (1) an auditory monitoring of the background around the individual at an almost unconscious surveillance level, (2) an arousal facility that alerts the individual via a psychological warning system that activates when the benign background becomes auditorily threatening, and (3) an oral-aural linguistic symbol system that permits communication to occur between or among participants. Each of us employs all three hearing functions simultaneously.

For the individual with hearing loss, psychological distress may occur because of a collapse at any of these functional levels. If only partial loss exists, its effect on the impaired listener may be that the low-intensity background signals are more muted and indistinct, the alerting system may be forced to function at "overtime" levels since the individual no longer is able to distinguish easily among background sounds, and effortless communicative input is no longer possible. As the hearing loss increases, this diffuse and generalized psychological discomfort increases at all three levels in an almost linear fashion.

The overwhelming communicative challenge facing our maturing populations is that of hearing loss or hearing deficit. It is regarded by the gerontological scholar as their most prevalent health-related problem. The behavioral manifestations of reduced auditory function during the later years of life can have profound consequences. Communicative frustration and fatigue are the products of continually straining to hear and failing to understand oral communication. The individual begins to withdraw from conversation. Periods of introspection, uncomplicated by the inefficient hearing system, may be observed to be increasing in duration. Personal disengagement is speeded up by a mounting discomfort with a world that may be becoming less familiar and predictable.

These auditory input problems may become most manifest at a period when the older person is least able to cope with them successfully. It is a time of multiple health problems and needs. It may be a period of economic constraint as income fails to keep pace with the ever-escalating cost of living. Further, it is a time when the availability of close friends and relatives to lend support and advice is decreasing. It is a period when the dignity of the leadership of a family group is threatened by hearing loss. Aging individuals are beset with many challenges not of their making. Hearing loss may be one for which resolution seems the least attainable.

## Incidence

The prevalence and magnitude of hearing loss with advancing age is suggested by all surveys in the literature. The incidence of handicapping hearing loss among aging individuals has been estimated by a variety of surveys to be from 10 to 90 percent, with the institutionalized elderly demonstrating poorer audiologic findings than their noninstitutionalized peers. In addition, older men usually evidence more pronounced hearing deficits than older women. Averaged hearing levels reflect loss that progresses with age. A review of the National Health Survey reported by Rupp (1970) suggests that nearly one-half of Americans with hearing impairments are in the age bracket of sixty-five years or more.

Older persons with hearing impairments are not a homogenous group. Some move into their later years with all the enthusiasm of young adults. with their life-styles unchallenged by hearing loss. Others display behavior aimed at reducing the stress associated with their failing auditory systems. Clinically the most common method is projection, where the hearing loss is vigorously denied and the problem in its entirety is charged to the sloven and mumbling speech of others. Reactions on the part of the individual may range from embarrassment over begging too many pardons to the pronounced symptoms of the geriapathy syndrome "where the struggle to communicate in gradually relinquished and social disengagement leads to apathy and depression" (Maurer and Rupp, 1976). It is important to remember that the presence of hearing loss is so imperceptible in its early stages that many older persons are complacently unaware of the problem until it is pointed out to them.

**The Nature of Presbycusis**

Presbycusis is defined as the hearing loss in old age. Carhart (1969) and Fairbanks (1954) have synthesized the following communicative model. Each communicator, in an oversimplified grid, has five major transmission links in the individual personal system: (1) the ear or receptor segment, (2) the neural links from the ear to the brain or central integration center, (3) the central integrating system itself, (4) the neural transmission lines leading on to the (5) speech mechanism or expressor segment. For any individual, irrespective of age, communicative ease of expression and reception and integration will decrease with the presence of deficits or impairments in any one or more of these areas. The two physiological areas in this model that will cause communicative input problems for the older individual are the inner ears and their central processes leading to the brain (figure 14-1).

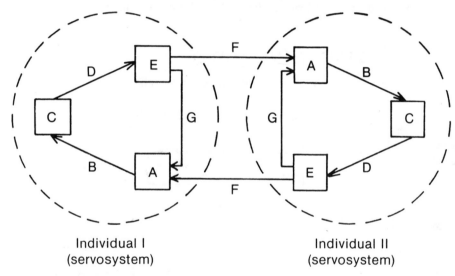

Individual I
(servosystem)

Individual II
(servosystem)

A   Ear / Receptor segment
B   Neural routing from ear to brain
C   Brain / Central integrator
D   Neural routing from brain to speech mechanism
E   Speech mechanism / Expressor segment
F   Signal movement from E: (I) to A; (II) produces a communicative interaction between subjects
G   Signal transmission from E: (I) to A; (I) produces a self-monitoring servosystem evaluation

Source: Adapted from Carhart (1969) and Fairbanks (1954).

**Figure 14-1.** A Communicative Model between Two Individuals

The term *presbycusis* reflects mixed and ambiguous etiologies. Audiologically, it is described on the audiogram as a progressive, bilateral, sensorineural pattern that generally shows it greatest elevation away from normal in the higher frequencies with similiar configurations for both ears (figures 14-2 and 14-3).

Whereas the audiogram reflects the hearing performance of the elderly individual at a certain point in her/his time-based continuity, a lifetime of influences contribute cumulatively to the threshold elevation observed on a seventy-second birthday. Such nonaging factors include: vocational and recreational noise exposure, use of ototoxic drugs, diet, head injuries, stress, ear infections, diseases, and hereditary predisposition. Investigations of hearing sensitivity in older persons from primitive rural tribes in Africa support the thesis that if all the nonaging factors contributing to the loss could be eliminated, the remaining pure-tone hearing shift away from normal might be of minimal significance (Rosen et al., 1964).

The presbycusic individual hears but does not understand easily.

# PURE TONE AUDIOGRAM

### Frequency in cycles per second (HZ)

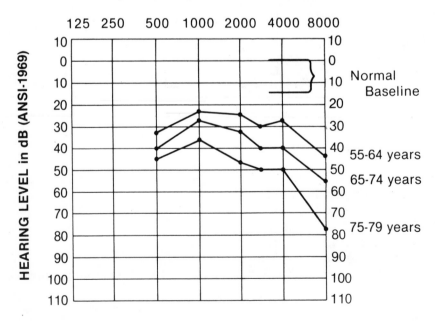

Source: Interpolated from Glorig and Roberts (1965).

**Figure 14-2.** Pure-tone, Air-Condition Threshold Sensitivity, as Central Tendency, for Women's Right Ears

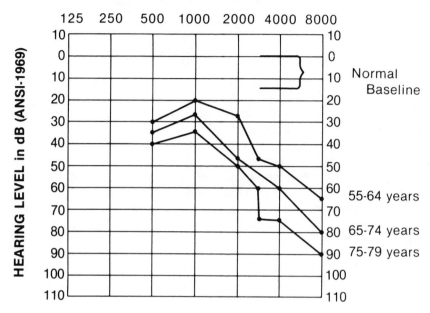

Source: Interpolated from Glorig and Roberts (1965).

**Figure 14-3.** Pure-tone, Air-Condition Threshold Sensitivity, as Central Tendency, for Men's Right Ears

Although the relationships between volitional auditory function and histologically observed structural abnormalities remain somewhat hazy, several clinical reports suggest strong interaction between performance and pathology. Schuknecht (1964) clinically classified presbycusis into four main categories. *Sensory presbycusis* is characterized by a generalized atrophy of the outer sensory hair cells in the organ of Corti and of their $VIII_n$ projections at the basal end of the cochlea. This type of prebycusis is seen in the gradually sloping audiogram with only modest reduction in understanding efficiency. *Neural or central presbycusis* is characterized by a more generalized loss of neurons in the $VIII_n$ and in the central pathways of the ascending transmission system. Both Schuknecht and Gaeth (1948) ascribe the marked understanding difficulties of certain aging individuals to a major reduction in populations of neural fibers. *Metabolic presbysucis* is reflected on the audiogram with a generalized reduction in pure-tone sensitivity across frequencies. This term was modified by Schuknecht (1972) to *strial presbycusis*. The cause of this type of presbycusis is attributed to a breakdown in the functional integrity within the stria vascularis with resultant chemical alterations in the endolymphatic fluid thus disrupting the normal functioning of the sensory hair cells even though anatomical integrity is maintained. *Mechanical presbycusis* (later termed *cochlear conductive presbycusis*) relates to transmission efficiency in the mechanics of fluid motion in the cochlea. Compliance alterations of a stiffening nature occur in the basilar membrane with resultant high-tone hearing loss (similar in configuration to both sensory and neural classes).

Support for Schuknecht's classes of presbycusis was provided by Kirikae, Sato, and Shitara (1964) who in their histopathologic observations of olders subjects, also noted atrophic conditions in the inner ear, and spiral ganglia in the central auditory pathways.

Another histopatholigic report by Hansen and Reske-Nielsen (1965) compared the temporal bones of a population of elderly subjects on whom clinical audiologic information had been obtained. Generalized arteriosclerosis was found with a reduced blood supply as a result. Johnsson and Hawkins (1972) reported on the temporal bones of 150 humans who ranged in age up to 97 years. The observed that degeneration of hair cells began in some cases as early as in utero. Since they observed that the aging process is a devascularizing one, which involves a gradual reduction in blood supply resulting from the disappearance of capillaries and the loss of arterioles, they proposed a fifth presbycusic category—*vascular presbycusis*. Support for their position is offered by Hinchcliffe (1970) who concluded that a correlate of elevated hearing levels in the ears of elderly, measured volitionally, is the extent of cerebral and labyrinthine arteriosclerosis found in postmortem studies. He suggested that this strong relationship between performance and observed pathology might support the reinstatement of the historic term *arteriosclerotic deafness*.

Five general classes of presbycusis have been reviewed from the established literature. Singly and collectively each may contribute to diminished hearing and precessing abilities in the older patient. Let us return to the effects of hearing impairment on the comprehension of language.

Feldman and Reger (1967) reported that speech discrimination skills are essentially constant through age fifty, but then this efficiency drops at about a 5 percent rate per decade. Intelligibility problems frequently are more marked than the pure-tone audiometric configurations would suggest. This finding was labeled phonemic regression by Gaeth (1948). Punch and McConnell (1969) showed that speech understanding does not show the same improvement with increased intensity levels of presentation in older subjects as compared with younger populations.

In the normal auditory system of the young, speech processing and understanding are supported by an abundance of neural networks that provide an intrinsic redundancy; this tends to offset external lack of clarity in the speech signal. Brody (1955) proposed that neuronal population is decreased by almost 50 percent in the central auditory nervous system by the time an individual reaches age seventy-five. Thus, factors that interfere with listening accumulate, leading to real comprehension disadvantages for the elderly.

Actual performance data for this physiological deficit were reported by Goldman, Fristoe, and Woodcock (1974) who studied volitional listening activities with older subjects. Reporting on a broad age span—from three to eighty years—they found that the ideal age for effective listening was from twelve to fifty years, with top performances occurring in the third decade of life. Their Auditory Skills Test Battery (ASTB) measures auditory processing abilities in four major areas:

1.  Selective attention for speech in three kinds of noise
2.  Auditory discrimination with a plotting of a "sound confusion inventory"
3.  Auditory memory with special emphasis on recognition, content, and sequencing
4.  Sound symbol relationships with assessments of sound mimicry, sound recognition, sound analysis, sound blending, association reading, and spelling

In general agreement with the developmental theory of aging (Kastenbaum, 1961, 1964), these authors found a gradual improvement in the measured auditory skills up to the golden age of auditory performance in the mid-twenties, with about an 18 percent improvement from age eight to the maximum. Following the time period of maximum performance, a gradual decrement in functional performance was found. The sixty-year-old population was approximately 10 percent poorer for these pooled performances. The eighty-year-old group showed an additional 20 percent reduction in efficiency for the pooled tasks. Totaling the cumulative reductions as a correlate of aging, the mean reduction of auditory processing efficiency for the octogenarians is approximately 30 percent.

Many of these subtle observations are manifestations of an older central processing mechanism that may not be uncovered by relatively primitive and redundant speech signals used in routine speech audiometric measurements. More demanding listening tasks, like the ones in the ASTB, can be imposed on the older listener in order to judge the relative adequacy for listening in less than ideal environments. Sticht and Gray (1969) compared understanding scores on both old and young normal hearing subjects under compression ratios up to 60 percent for phonetically-balanced word lists. They found marked performance differences between these two populations even when the older individuals showed no audiometric evidence of presbycusis. The loss of intelligibility was most marked at the higher compression ratios.

Miller (1975) compared performances of two age groups with normal hearing and normal understanding in quiet surroundings on an intelligibility task using interrupted consonant-nucleus-consonant words. He found that the older group demonstrated reduced ability, and when he combined the interrupted CNC task with an competing message to the test ear, further dramatic differences occurred.

Matzker (1959) pioneered in central auditory assessment approaches with his Binaural Fusion Test which taps the ability of the brain to integrate phonetic fragments that are split between the two ears. Palva and Jokinen (1970) used a fusion approach with an older population, and they observed a deterioration for filtered speech that occurred long before any signs of auditory aging were visible on the audiogram. These findings suggest that this test may be sensitive to early degeneration at the level of the brain stem.

Jerger and Jerger (1971) reported that the performance intensity function for phonetically balanced (PIPB) words also is reduced in the ears of older people. Speech understanding scores are expected to drop at increasing sensation levels, or to "rollover," in the ear contralateral to brain-stem disorders and in the ipsilateral ear with $VIII_n$ damage. In older subjects the deterioration was seen to occur in both ears, suggesting bilateral deficit.

Burgess and Orchik (1975) used Speaks's and Jerger's Synthetic Sentence Identification Test with a broad-aged population. They found that their subjects over age forty made an increasing number of errors as they attempted to identify these sentences buried in an ipsilaterally competing message.

Perrin (1970) found that his elderly listeners had error scores that were increasingly significant for both ears beyond the age of sixty on the Staggered Spondaic Word Test, a measurement sensitive to cortical and upper brain-stem deficits.

Investigations on the central aspects of presbycusis continue. Several trends emerge: (1) auditory aging is a process of performance reduction within both the peripheral and central auditory mechanisms, (2) presbycusis is influenced more by central than by peripheral conditions in later decades of aging, and (3) the reduction in listening ability is the result of a complex interaction of life-style, vascular resiliency, and hereditary programming.

## Diagnostic Evaluation

The older person who makes an appointment for medical or audiological evaluations for assistance in handling a hearing deficit often fits a common description. The person is between sixty-eight and seventy-two years of age, has been vaguely aware of a reduction in hearing efficiency for the last five years, and admits that the problem is gradually getting worse. The client hears when others are talking, but speech is muffled, distorted, and indistinct. Certain persons' voices are relatively easy to follow and understand, but others are difficult to follow, especially soft-voiced women and favorite grandchildren. Frequently a gradual change in social and recreational activities occurs. Participation in religious activities, movies, parties, and civic events is no longer enjoyable. Radio and television are often described in frustration as a discordant jumble of noise. Conversation in noisy environments is no longer possible. But since few elderly exactly fit the common mold, it becomes the professional practitioner's responsibility to carefully and fully evaluate the individual's hearing handicap in order to plan effectively for the management program necessary to offset the psychologically eroding effects of the hearing loss. Although less than 5 percent of older patients will be able to receive direct medical or surgical benefits for restoring hearing efficiency, a careful and thorough medical evaluation is necessary for the patient's well being.

The observations of the otologist include the history of the problem, medical diagnosis, and clearance for appropriate postmedical rehabilitational activities. These observations also include the patient's social, economic, attitudinal, vocational and avocational habits and status. Equally important are the physician's remarks to the older patient about the real need for postmedical rehabilitation.

The second source of information is the audiological assessment. When performed by the professional audiologist, this test battery identifies the crucial components of the patient's auditory processing system, which assists the physician with his or her diagnosis and contributes markedly toward proposing necessary and appropriate rehabilitational approaches for the client.

Although aural rehabilitation is essential for the continuing psychological integrity of the elderly person, it has not been noted for its success. No other age group comes to the audiology center with so many other problems. "In a psychological sense, this client also may reflect certain stresses, including preoccupation with fears of major illness or death, worries about the adequacy of funds to cover test and rehabilitational expenses, apprehensions about self-care limitations, and vanity concerning the visibility of the prosthesis" (Maurer and Rupp, 1976). All is not totally negative, however, for "if the individual needs are being fulfilled, if mental capacity is functioning adequately, and if personality characteristics are normal and adequate, then rehabilitation procedures have potential for success" (Alpiner, 1965).

The audiologist must accept the fact that the elderly client is a unique being who may need special handling and special approaches in order to reach the desired diagnostic goals. The audiologist must develop an approach of sensitive and discreet inquiry about each older client. In addition to direct inquiry, there is another effective approach—formal questionnaires provide a means of assessing personal attitudes about hearing impairments. Several such inventories are in the literature. A common goal is to assess the status of the person in terms of personal feelings about the hearing loss and its effect on listening ability. An example of such a questionnaire is that of Ewertsen and Nielsen (1973) in which their Social Hearing Handicap Index covers some twenty-one areas analyzing day-to-day listening situations and their associated difficulty.

The information from the medical findings, the diagnostic audiological findings, and informal and formal interrogations are then combined to attempt to answer the following question. How crucial are the communicative input problems associated with the hearing loss in relation to the personal goals of the subject? In other words, what are the individual's listening needs? If the client wants to hear better and if he or she has the determination to try a therapeutic program, then the audiologist will outline one.

The therapeutic plan will include a hearing-aid evaluation. Positive attitudes about amplification are not high among older persons in the United States. In countries where hearing aids are dispensed to hearing-handicapped individuals after comprehensive otological and audiological assessments and where clients have undergone extensive rehabilitational follow-up with state assistance, the acceptance rate for amplification with the elderly is about the same as for younger age groups. Ewertsen (1974) reported that in Denmark older clients use their hearing aids at the same high rate as younger populations because of the strong financial and educational support programs.

Traditional and minimally successful hearing-aid delivery systems in the United States are being challenged by professional audiologists. In support of innovative dispensing of aids, the American Speech-Language-Hearing Association (1979) now permits the audiologist to sell hearing aids and to retain ethical standards. Medicaid benefits now provide coverage in many states for hearing tests, purchase of hearing aids, and subsequent aural rehabilitation when administered by qualified audiologists. An increasing number of private and group insurance carriers are now including audiological services and purchase of hearing aids under the benefits system when the individual's hearing loss cannot be medically corrected. For example, the auto companies' contracts with their workers, dependents, and retired beneficiaries now cover the costs of the audiological assessment and the hearing aid following medical clearance by a certified otologist. Over the last several years, legislation has been repeatedly introduced at the federal level to add the purchase of amplification to the benefits list under Medicare coverage following very conservative restrictions. Such an expansion of coverage is needed.

Assuming there are financial resources available to cover the costs of a recommended hearing aid, several variables play a part in a hearing-aid evaluation with an older person that are crucial to the subsequent successful wearing of the instrument. These variables must be studied carefully by the audiologist in order to make a strong provisional estimate as to the ultimate daily usefulness of the subject's recommended hearing aid. Perhaps the most analytic formula for weighing these important variables comes from the article by Rupp, Higgins, and Maurer (1977) where they proposed the clinical use of their Feasibility Scale for Predicting Hearing Aid Use (FSPHAU) with Older Individuals. The scale and its implementation formula are based on an in-depth study of prognostic factors relating to the potential hearing-aid user and the measureable benefits derived from the instrument under observation as worn by the subject. The factors are as follows:

1. Motivation of the patient and mode of referral to professional services
2. Self-assessment of the subject's communicative difficulties prior to wearing a hearing aid
3. Verbalization by the individual as to the cause of communicative input difficulties
4. Magnitude of the hearing loss and understanding difficulties, expressed in audiological decibel hearing loss values and percentage correctly understood, both before and after amplification
5. Informal verbalization during the hearing-aid evaluation with reference to size, feel, and fit of the ear mold, to quality of the sound of speech through the aid, and to size and weight of the instrument
6. Audiological estimate of patient's general adaptability and flexibility with specific reference to general alertness and interest beyond that of the self
7. Age of the patient as a general indicator of adjustability to a hearing aid
8. Manual finger, hand, and arm dexterity and mobility of the patient in order to assess the subject's ability to manage the very small off-on switches, volume controls, secondary adjustment controls, and the small button-sized batteries
9. Visual ability of the patient (with glasses on) to assess the potential abilities for speech-reading and to determine if the individual will be able to take charge of the manipulations of the hearing aid
10. Financial resources of the client for the purchase of the instrument and subsequent battery and repair costs
11. A significant other person who can assist the client in the total rehabilitative process; someone who will be able and willing to perform as an extension of the client in terms of understanding the limitations of the hearing loss, the realities of the amplification potential, the maintenance process and trouble-shooting activities when the aid malperforms, and the therapeutic process involved in making the client a better listener.

As the score sheet reflects (see figure 14-4), factors #1 and #2 carry the greatest weight. The primary purpose of the FSPHAU is to make an early objective prognosis about the eventual wearing of a hearing aid by the indi-

| PROGNOSTIC FACTORS/DESCRIPTIONS (continuum, high to low) | ASSESSMENT 5-High: 0-Low | WEIGHT | WEIGHTED SCORE (Possible) Actual | |
|---|---|---|---|---|
| 1. Motivation and referral (self . . . . family) | 5 4 3 2 1 0 | x 4 | (20)_____ | 1. |
| 2. Self-assessment of listening difficulties (realistic . . . . . . denial) | 5 4 3 2 1 0 | x 2 | (10)_____ | 2. |
| 3. Verbalization as to "fault" of communication difficulties (self caused . . . projection) | 5 4 3 2 1 0 | x 1 | ( 5)_____ | 3. |
| 4. Magnitude of loss: amplification results. | | | | 4. |
|   A. Shift in spondaic threshold: ____ | 5 4 3 2 1 0 | x 1 | (5)_____ | |
|   B. Discrimination in quiet:_____ at_____dBB HTL | 5 4 3 2 1 0 | x 1 | (5)_____ | |
|   C. Discrimination in noise:_____ at_____dB HTL | 5 4 3 2 1 0 | x 1 | (5)_____ | |
| 5. Informal verbalizations during Hearing Aid Evaluation Re: quality of sound, mold, size (acceptable . . . awful) | 5 4 3 2 1 0 | x 1 | ( 5)_____ | 5. |
| 6. Flexibility and adaptability versus senility (relates outwardly . . . self) | 5 4 3 2 1 0 | x 2 | (10)_____ | 6. |
| 7. Age: 95 90 85 80 75 70 65 ⪦ (0   0   1   2   3   4   5) | 5 4 3 2 1 0 | x 1.5 | (7.5)_____ | 7. |
| 8. Manual hand, finger dexterity, and general mobility (good . . . . limited) | 5 4 3 2 1 0 | x 1.5 | (7.5)_____ | 8. |
| 9. Visual ability (adequate with glasses . . . limited) | 5 4 3 2 1 0 | x 1 | ( 5)_____ | 9. |
| 10. Financial resources (adequate . . . very limited) | 5 4 3 2 1 0 | x 1.5 | (7.5)_____ | 10. |
| 11. Significant other person to assist individual (available . . . none) | 5 4 3 2 1 0 | x 1.5 | (7.5)_____ | 11. |
| 12. Other factors, please cite | ? | ? | ? | 12. |

Client _____     FSPHAU:   Very limited    0 to 40%

Age _____             Limited       41 to 60%

Date _____             Equivocal    61 to 75%     %

Audiologist _____          Positive      76 to 100%    Total Score

Source: R.R. Rupp, The significant other person: An essential factor for success with the elderly hearing aid user, *Hearing Aid Journal* 30, no. 12 (October 1977). Reprinted with permission.

**Figure 14-4.** The Feasibility Scale for Predicting Hearing-Aid Use (FSP-HAU) with Older Subjects

vidual under observation. As the score ranges found at the bottom of figure 14-4 suggest, there are four general classifications of total scores in the FSPHAU. Those subjects who place in the positive class will probably become excellent hearing-aid users. Those in the equivocal class may become well organized and oriented hearing-aid wearers, but the counseling and training period will need to be much more intensive and realistic. For subjects in this provisional classification, the prognosis regarding eventual adjustment to the hearing aid must be more guarded. For the patients in the limited or very limited classes, the realistic recommendation on the part of the audiologist will probably be to advise against the use of amplification as a route for improved listening skills. There are some exceptions. If an individual in either of these two classes can enlist the volunteer or paid services of a friend or relative who will assume fully the role of the significant other person, then an experimental training program and trial wearing program with the suggested amplification can be recommended. The scale was created to help the client, family, and audiologist establish a beginning point for the follow-up activities needed to bring the subject into the category of successful hearing-aid wearer. For the limited number of elderly clients who cannot be trained and assisted into being hearing-aid users, the scale identifies a population that will need alternative programs to help them improve their receptive language base.

Assuming that the older client is a realistic candidate for amplification, an important decision should be made on the appropriateness of a monaural or binaural hearing aid. Opinions vary as to the number of benefits to be derived from monaural versus binaural amplification for the elderly. Perhaps the most conservative position is that a single aid offers fewer disadvantages than do two instruments. Factors such as cost, convenience, and less possibility of rejection seem to favor the idea of one aid for the elderly wearer. On the other hand, some clients have been so pleased with the results from their first hearing aid that they returned to the audiologic centers and requested an expanded trial process with two hearing aids. The majority of this latter population were people heavily committed to extensive communicative interaction in their still-busy social and professional lives—for example, they were still acting as consultants to their corporations or were still very involved in service organizations and wanted to hear to their best advantage. Two well-recommended hearing aids stimulating both ears of the older listener generally will give better performance for understanding in situations where there are low levels of background noise. It is the responsibility of the audiologist during the training period to consider the listening demands of the client, his preference about the number of aids, and the general adjustment to the first and second instrument. There are no exact rules on monaural versus binaural amplification since each listener is unique.

The second major therapeutic approach is to increase the contribution of visual communication skills for heightened listening ability with the elderly. The process of aging takes its toll on both visual acuity and visual perception (Birren, 1959) as it reduces auditory performance. The attempt to actually teach lipreading may not be practical for older listeners. McGhie, Chapman, and Lawson (1965) found that short-term memory decreased more quickly for visual stimuli than for auditory information. Perhaps the strongest support for an informal speech-reading orientation program is that it tends to help the hearing-impaired listener focus attention more directly on the other speaker. If an honest goal of the rehabilitational audiologist is to foster an attitude of attentive visual observation as the client auditorily listens to another individual, then heightened input may occur because the listener is actively and volitionally attending visually as well as auditorily.

In summary, five areas of investigation have been proposed for hearing-loss management in the elderly: (1) medical observation and diagnosis by the otologist, (2) evaluative data from the audiological assessment, (3) formal and informal assessments of the listening needs of the subject, (4) prognosticating with regard to the feasibility and practicality for successful use of a hearing aid by the client, and (5) realistic appraisal of speech-reading skills.

**The Aural Rehabilitational Process**

This aural rehabilitational process begins when the elderly client decides to try to do something about his or her hearing loss. Following this important step, the medical and audiological evaluations are performed, decisions are made cooperatively between client and audiologist about the feasibility of amplification, and the process is a continuing one from that time forward. The intensive phase is the time period immediately following the acquisition of the recommended hearing aid. During this time period, which may vary from a few weeks to several months, the client, the significant other person (if possible), and the audiologist work together. Their goals are to:

1. maximize the benefits of the amplification
2. learn how to adjust the hearing aid for best performance in ideal and challenging environments
3. develop a realistic attitude about the potential gains from the amplification
4. reorganize the listening set in order to focus on the incoming auditory and visual signals
5. practice polishing listening skills in order to sharpen auditory discrimination for those speech sounds which may have been dulled and distorted by the hearing loss

6. develop a complete understanding of the subject's hearing limitations in order to set realistic listening goals
7. develop skills in managing the environments where possible in order to "set the stage" for the best listening backgrounds
8. learn to objectively inform friends and relatives about the limitations of the hearing loss as assisted by the hearing aid
9. develop a brief repertoire of suggestions to these associates when they ask if there are things they can do to help with communication.

The assignments given to the older listener during this intensive phase are demanding, challenging, and sometimes fatiguing. It is for this reason that personal motivation on the part of the client received the greatest weighting on the feasibility scale. The well-motivated older person who still wants to be in the mainstream will follow through with this intensive process.

In a community where there were several residential facilities for older individuals, we had considerable success in group training programs. The clinical staff audiologist and a team of graduate clinicians organized an eight-week program and met the senior students at their residence (Harless and Rupp, 1974). Peer interaction and sharing of experiences proved to be a far more effective way of making a theoretical point than having the staff inform the clients. Following this intensive stage, the clients "graduated" to the nonintensive time period where they and the significant other persons were on their own in implementing the training they have received.

A series of surveillance appointments with both medical and audiological resources were set up so that periodic professional observation could be assured. Further, the clients were strongly encouraged to return to the audiological facility prior to the periodic appointment times if problems or challenges developed. With the elderly, we must maintain a flexibility of availability in order to keep them performing at the desired level of listening performance.

When the hearing-impaired individual has followed through with rehabilitational process and has built an effective listening program, and when the important people in the environments have learned a cooperative approach to conversing with him or her, the result is improved interpersonal communication. Heavenrich (1964) labels this positive interaction *auditory reach*. As long as the backgrounds are relatively quiet, the older hearing-impaired listener will be able to reach across auditorily and will be an effective listener. She states, "Regardless of effort or degree of motivation, the auditorially handicapped person can 'hear' only within the limits of his (or her) auditory reach . . . When others move in to meet the handicapped individual at the boundaries within which he is arbitrarily confined, intelligent cooperation functions to extend the limits, permit him to participate within the group, fill the gaps in his knowledge, and for the particular situation, remove the handicap." In summary, it takes three factors for a hearing-impaired person to reach across, auditorily, in a communicative interaction: (1) a well-motivated and well-trained listener, (2) a cooperative and compassionate cocommunicator, and (3) an idealized, quiet-as-possible environment in which to listen. When all three factors are present, auditory reach is achieved. Conversely, when any factor or factors are altered negatively, auditory reach is reduced and the handicap is again present. Heavenrich cautions that hearing loss per se does not handicap the listener; it is the condition of not knowing what is going on in the personal world that is the truly demoralizing and isolating facet.

The role of the significant other person was identified as factor #11 in the feasibility scale. For many older individuals, the participation of a second and important person in the total program of assessment and remediation is necessary to move it along successfully. This other person may be a daughter, son, younger sibling, good friend, or paid companion. The essential goal of this person is to participate intellectually and psychologically in all facets of the program. As an integral component in the process, the other person receives all the counseling, advice, and guidance that is given to the client. The other person becomes the "shadow" of the client and participates as fully as possible in the entire process. "In short, this significant helping person should be as knowledgeable about the individual's hearing, hearing loss, hearing aid, therapeutic approaches and goals as is the individual himself" (Rupp, 1977). This other person can function as a team member in a reinforcing and supporting manner with the elderly client. He or she can perform as a sounding board for the client, review important findings and recommendations to the client, and assist in expediting the necessary steps in the total program. The end goal of this team approach will be to have two people with close personal ties who have a firm knowledge of the individual's hearing difficulty, who have worked together through the rehabilitational process, and who are able to explain the program to other crucial individuals in the client's life. (Figure 14-5 shows the varied and multiple interactions that the patient and teammate will make during the intensive remediational programs.)

An important factor in Heavenrich's concept of auditory reach was the "intelligent cooperation" of others who interact, communicatively, with the older hearing-impaired person. There are five very simple yet effective methods that cocommunicators can use to help the older hearing-impaired subject maintain that important contact with his important world. They include:

1. Speaking more slowly to the older person. This allows the central processing segment to keep up and prevents overloading the system.
2. Speaking as clearly as possible to the senior person. The creation of an ideal auditory signal reduces the distortion that is caused by the slope of the hearing loss and provides the best and clearest signal.

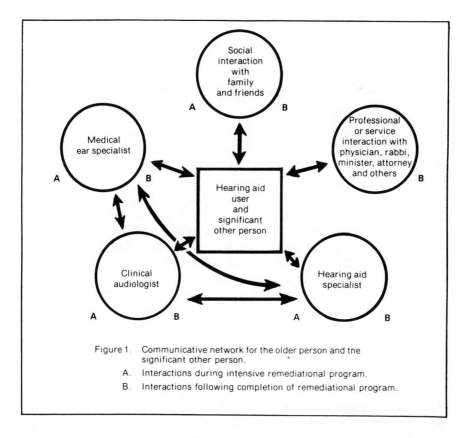

Figure 1.   Communicative network for the older person and the significant other person.

   A.   Interactions during intensive remediational program.

   B.   Interactions following completion of remediational program.

Source: R.R. Rupp, The significant other person: An essential factor for success with the elderly hearing aid user, *Hearing Aid Journal* 30, no. 12 (October 1977). Reprinted with permission.

**Figure 14-5.** Interactive Roles of the Significant Other Person on Behalf of the Older Hearing-Aid User

3.  Speaking slightly louder than usual. This approach counteracts the actual decrease in intensity of the spoken signal created by the hearing loss. If the subject finds that you are speaking too loudly, the individual may either reduce the volume of the hearing aid or inform you that a slightly lower volume will still be effective.

4.  Speaking to the individual from an ideal distance of three to six feet and facing the listener so that both auditory and visual signals reach the client. This gives the listener visual clues, directs the spoken signal toward the listener, and helps focus the attention of the listener on the speaker.

5. Speaking to the other person with the background as quiet as possible. Noise is the number-one deterrent to effective listening for any hearing-impaired person and is even more disabling to the elderly hearing-impaired individual. If conversational communication is the goal, the radio, television set, stereo, and barking pets should be quieted.

For the family members and close friends who communicate frequently with the older listener, there are many additional techniques that can be developed to modify the environment in order to enhance the listening potential of the hearing-impaired person. The extent to which the important other can help to set the stage for better listening is limited only by their ingenuity and creativity, and compassion for the older listener. For example, one should not stand in front of a picture window when talking to the person, for the strong light should be on the speaker's face and not in the eyes of the hearing-impaired listener. When going out to a restaurant, one should make reservations in advance so that a small table for four or fewer can be reserved in the quietest location, away from kitchen noises and intercom systems. The furniture in the listener's living room should be arranged in a cluster so that friends and relatives can be seated near to and facing the listener. And finally, friends should keep hands away from their face, and pipes, cigarettes, and pencils out of their mouth when they are talking. There is an endless list of things that can be done to help create the ideal environment.

To summarize, the auditory remediational plan is essentially a twofold one. First, it consists of a carefully developed assessment and training program for the individual, including the use of a hearing aid if possible. Second, it includes a broadly faceted environmental monitoring and modification program to create an idealized listening world for the elderly person with impaired hearing. As part of the monitoring program, the cooperating others will do their part in enhancing the communicative interaction.

**Conclusion**

Deafness separates man from man. The primary communicative goal for the hearing-impaired elderly client—and similarly for the younger hearing-handicapped individual—is to maintain communicative contact with the important persons in his or her environments. To remain in the intellectual company of people through communicataive interaction is a primary goal for each of us. For the older person with an irreversible hearing loss, reaching this goal takes courage, motivation, and the support of others in the environment. It can be the common goal of us all to help elderly hearing-impaired people keep tuned in, auditorily, to what is going on around them.

## References

Alpiner, J.G. Diagnostic and rehabilitative aspects of geriatric behavior. *ASHA* 7: 455-59, 1965.

American Speech-Language-Hearing Association. *ASHA* 21(3): 188, 1979. (Legislative Council Report, LC 25-78, Ethical Practice Board).

Birren, J.E. Sensation, perception, and modification of behavior in relation to the process of aging. In *The Process of Aging in the Nervous System*, edited by J.E. Birren, H.A. Imus, and W.F. Windle. Springfield, IL: Charles C. Thomas, 1959.

Brody, H. Organization of the cerebral cortex: III. A study of aging in the human cerebral cortex. *Journal of Comparative Neurology* 102: 511-56, 1955.

Burgess, J.W., and Orchik, D.J. Synthetic sentence identification (SSI) performance as a function of the age of the subject. Paper presented at the American Speech and Hearing Association Convention, Washington, D.C., 1975.

Butler, K. Auditory perceptual skills: their measurement and remediation with preschool and school-age children. Program of the 1975 annual meeting, American Speech and Hearing Association, Washington, D.C., 1975.

Carhart, R. *Human Communication and Its Disorders—An Overview*. Bethesda, Maryland: National Institutes of Health, U.S. Department of Health, Education, and Welfare, 1969.

Ewertsen, H.W. Use of hearing aids (always, often, rarely, never). *Scandinavian Audiology* 3: 173-76, 1974.

Ewertsen, H.W., and Nielsen, B.H. Social hearing handicap index. Social handicap and relation to hearing impairment. *Audiology* 12: 180, 1973.

Fairbanks, G. Systematic research in experimental phonetics: 1. A theory of the speech mechanism as a servosystem. *Journal of Speech and Hearing Disorders* 19(2): 133-39, 1954.

Feldman, R.M., and Reger, S.N. Relations among hearing, reaction time, and age. *Journal of Speech and Hearing Research* 10: 479-95, 1967.

Gaeth, J. A study of phonemic regression associated with hearing loss. Ph.D. dissertation, Northwestern University, 1948.

Glorig, A., and Roberts, J. Hearing levels of adults by age and sex: United States 1960-1962. *Vital and Health Statistics*, U.S. Department of Health, Education, and Welfare. Series 2, number 2, table 2, p. 28, 1965.

Goldman, R., Fristoe, M., and Woodcock, R. *The Auditory Skills Test Battery*. Circle Pines, Minnesota: American Guidance Corporation, 1974.

Hansen, C.C., and Reske-Nielsen, E. Pathological studies in presbycusis. *Archives Otolaryngology* 82: 115-32, 1965.

Harless, E., and Rupp, R. Aural rehabilitation of the elderly. *Journal of Speech and Hearing Disorders* 37(2): 79-84, 1974.

Heavenrich, A. A view from within: a consideration of how hearing loss is mediated into behavior. Master's thesis, Wayne State University, 1964.

Hinchcliffe, R. Future research topics. In *Sensorineural Hearing Loss*, edited by G.E.W. Wolstenholme and J. Knight, p. 336. London: J. and A. Churchill, 1970.

Ismail, A.H., Corrigan, D.L., MacLeod, D.F., Anderson, V.L., Kasten, R.N., and Elliott, P.W. Biophysiological and audiological variables in adults. *Archives Otolaryngology* 97: 447-51, 1973.

Jerger, J., and Jerger, S. Diagnostic significance of PB word functions. *Archives Otolaryngology* 93: 573-80, 1971.

Johnsson, L.G., and Hawkins, J.E. Sensory and neural degeneration with aging, as seen in microdissections of human inner ear. *Annals of Otology, Rhinology, and Laryngology* 81: 179-93, 1972.

Kastenbaum, R. The dimensions of future time perspective, an experimental analysis. *Journal of General Psychology* 65: 203-215, 1961.

_____. *New Thoughts on Old Age.* New York: Springer, 1964.

Kirikae, I., Sato, R., and Shitara, T. A study of hearing in advanced age. *Laryngoscope* 74: 205-220, 1964.

Matzker, J. Two new methods for the assessment of central auditory function in cases of brain disease. *Annals of Otology, Rhinology, and Laryngology* 68: 1185-97, 1959.

Maurer, J., and Rupp, R. Hearing problems and aging. *Audiology, An Audio Journal for Continuing Education* 1(9), 1976. (Grune and Stratton)

McGhie, A., Chapman, J., and Lawson, J. Changes in immediate memory with age. *British Journal of Psychology* 56: 69-75, 1965.

Miller, W.E. A comparison of geriatric and young adults in their ability to discriminate interrupted monosyllabic words in the presence of interrupted contralateral and ipsilateral competing speech. Paper presented at the American Speech and Hearing Association Convention, Washington, D.C., 1975.

Palva, A., and Jokinen, K. Presbycusis V: filtered speech test. *Acta Oto-Laryngologica* 7: 232-41, 1970.

Perrin, W.F. The effect of age on three audiometric tests for central auditory lesions. Ph.D. dissertation, University of Michigan, 1970.

Punch, J.L., and McConnell, F. The speech discrimination function of elderly adults. *Journal of Auditory Research* 9: 159-66, 1969.

Ramsdell, D. The psychology of the hard-of-hearing and the deafened adult. In *Hearing and Deafness*, edited by H. Davis and S.R. Silverman. New York: Holt, Rinehart, and Winston, 1970.

Rosen, S., Plester, D., El-Mofty, A., and Rosen, A. High frequency audiometry in presbycusis: a comparative study of the Mabaan tribe in the

Sudan with urban populations. *Archives of Otolaryngology* 79: 1-32, 1964.

Rupp, R.R. Understanding the problems of presbycusis. *Geriatrics* 25: 100-107, 1970.

_____. The significant other person: an essential factor for success with the elderly hearing aid user. *Hearing Aid Journal* 30(12): 9, 38-40, 1977.

_____. The community challenge—hearing loss in the elderly: a charge to the rest of us. *Hearing Instruments* 30(4): 16-17, 34, 1979.

Rupp, R., Higgins, H., and Maurer, J. A feasibility scale for predicting hearing aid use (FSPHAU) with older individuals. *Journal of the Academy of Rehabilitative Audiology* 10(1): 81-104, 1977.

Schuknecht, H.F. Further observations on the pathology of presbycusis. *Archives Otolaryngology* 80: 369-82, 1964.

_____. *Pathology of the Ear*. Cambridge: Harvard University Press, 1972.

Sticht, T.G., and Gray, B.B. The intelligibility of time compressed words as a function of age and hearing loss. *Journal of Speech and Hearing Research* 12: 443-48, 1969.

# 15 Working with the Aging Aphasic Patient: Some Clinical Implications

*Audrey L. Holland*

I have recently completed norming a test for measuring functional communication of aphasic adults (Holland, in press). This test is called Communicative Abilities in Daily Living (CADL). It has been normed in relation to age by comparing the performance of 130 aphasic patients and 130 normal people in four age brackets: under 45, 46 to 55, 56 to 65, and over 65. Some features of CADL's norming are pertinent to this discussion of clinical aspects of working with the aging.

Figure 15-1 shows aphasic and normal performance for each age group in this study. In norming the CADL test, an attempt was made to produce an age distribution that approximated the age characteristics of aphasic adults. Hence the columns of figure 15-1 differ in width proportionately to the number of subjects in each group. Columns to the left at each age interval represent normal people (that is, people who had no history or evidence of brain damage at the time of testing); columns to the right are the aphasic subjects. The last two column arrays also feature the variable of institutionalization, which was included because earlier work on validating CADL had indicated that institutionalization itself appeared to have a detrimental effect on functional communication for aphasic patients, and it seemed important to develop some normative data that would be useful for evaluating the older patients who are most likely to be institutionalized. It can be seen in the figure that older aphasic subjects in general perform worse than younger ones; this factor is complicated by great variability in the aphasic sample. The normal sample is of major interest here, however. The slight drop apparent between the normal subjects under age 46 and those over 65 on this test of unsophisticated communication ability is a statistically significant phenomenon. These statements concerning the overall age effects derive from a one-way analysis of variance used to analyze CADL performance as a function of age.

Performance by the forty normal and forty aphasic subjects 65 years of age or older was further assessed (using $X^2$ analysis) by comparing the subjects 75 and over with those under 75 in each group. In the aphasic group there were significantly more older subjects who performed better than the aphasic group mean. More important, the normal group had more members 75 or older with scores below the mean.

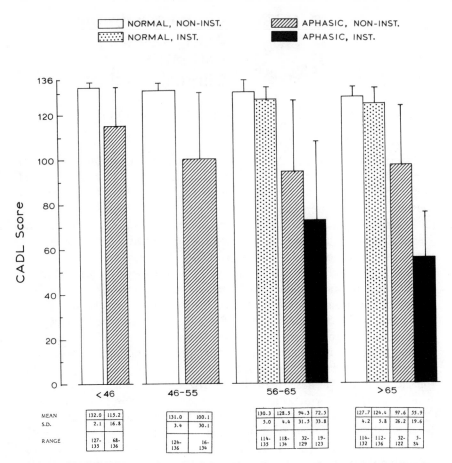

**Figure 15-1.** Aphasic and Normal Performances on Communicative Abilities in Daily Living Test

Together these data suggest some minimal, but real restrictions in the give-and-take of ordinary communication as measured by CADL, imposed by the process of aging itself, independent of documentable brain damage.

Table 15-1 shows the numbers and percentages of types of aphasia in patients who took this test at each of the age levels. Since the frequency of type of aphasia is not clearly known, this study made no attempt to control for it, but instead allowed the large sample of predominantly post-stroke patients to furnish information relevant to that question. In essence, this represents what happens when one controls for age and lets aphasia type "fall out" as a result of that control. It shows that Broca's aphasics dominate the youngest group, with anomics the next most frequent, and globals and mixed patients the fewest. No Wernicke's aphasics appeared in

**Table 15-1**
**Types of Aphasic Patients Participating in Communicative Abilities in Daily Living Test, by Age**

| Type of Aphasia | 46 | | 46-55 | | 56-65 | | 65 | | Total Sample | |
|---|---|---|---|---|---|---|---|---|---|---|
| | Number | Percent | Number | Percent | Number | Percent | Number | Percent | Number | Percent |
| *Anterior* | | | | | | | | | | |
| Broca's | 14 | 70 | 13 | 43 | 10 | 25 | 10 | 25 | 47 | 36 |
| Global | 1 | 5 | 3 | 10 | 8 | 20 | 8 | 20 | 20 | 15 |
| Mixed | 1 | 20 | 6 | 20 | 12 | 30 | 7 | 17.5 | 26 | 20 |
| *Posterior* | | | | | | | | | | |
| Wernicke's | — | — | 1 | 3.5 | 5 | 12.5 | 11 | 27.5 | 17 | 13 |
| Transcortical sensory | — | — | — | — | 1 | 2.5 | 1 | 2.5 | 2 | 2 |
| Anomic | 4 | 20 | 6 | 20 | 2 | 5 | 2 | 5 | 14 | 11 |
| Conduction | — | — | 1 | 3.5 | 2 | 5 | 1 | 2.5 | 4 | 3 |
| *Total* | 20 | | 30 | | 40 | | 40 | | 130 | |

this group. The youngest Wernicke's aphasics first appear in the second youngest group (ages 46 to 55) and increase in frequency as age increases. In fact, all the types of aphasia encountered in this study occurred only in the upper two age intervals, but with decreasing proportions of the milder deficits. A one-way analysis of variance was used to analyze the relationship of age to type of aphasia. It revealed that Wernicke's aphasics not only were significantly older (mean age 67.05) than Broca's aphasics (mean age 54.23), but also were significantly older than the anomics. Global aphasics also were significantly older than the anomics. In essence, these data suggest increasing difficulties with comprehension in older aphasics. This is a matter of some interest since it concerns the relationship between language deficit and cognitive function at the far end of the life span. Further, these data suggest that if focal deficit is imposed on an aging brain, there is more potential for serious consequences than when the aphasic patient is younger. The clinical implications include possible reassessment of both treatment and outcome. This reassessment also requires of the clinician a greater sensitivity to a host of other aging factors, such as presbycusis or cognitive change, to name the most obvious ones that might be interactive in the case of the older aphasic. Finally, these data reaffirm the need for great care in the differential diagnosis of aphasia in older persons, particularly as it relates to cortical dementia and atrophy.

Figure 15-2 shows only the upper two age levels, those for which normative data related to the variable of institutionalization were gathered. Roughly equal numbers of males and females and exactly equal numbers of normals and aphasics were tested, in and out of institutions. This figure was originally prepared to help disambiguate a three-way analysis of variance, comparing institutionalization, aphasia, and sex for which a significant group $x$ institution $x$ sex interaction was found. Its most important features for this discussion are: (1) the small but consistent drop in performance for normals who are relegated to institutional living (2) the subtle, but almost general superiority of women over men, not only in the upper ages, but actually in all groups but one in this study, and (3) the single exception — the very poor performance of institutionalized female aphasics. Sociological phenomena may account for this last finding. The Veterans Administration's chronic-care facilities have made it easier to institutionalize males than females in this society. In addition, our society appears to be more likely to keep and care for its chronically ill females at home. Finally, at postretirement ages women's life experiences have more adequately prepared them to care for themselves at home. This figure is included here to emphasize that cultural and sociological aspects of aging in America cannot easily be excluded when discussing clinical aspects of aging and language.

So far I have raised three concerns: normal aging effects on language, aphasia in an aging population, and cultural and sociological concerns in

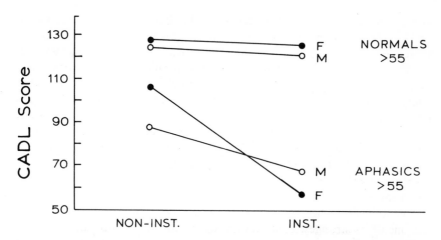

**Figure 15-2.** Scores of the Upper Two Age Levels, Comparing Institution-alization, on the Communicative Abilities in Daily Living Test

aging. All have clinical implications which will be expanded in the remainder of this chapter.

### Aging and Normal Language

CADL was developed to test most basic functional communication skills. It shows subtle but consistent age-related effects. Tests measuring more sophisticated aspects of language and language interactions, then, should also show age effects. The first clinical implication, then, is that age-related norms for more standard clinical measures are needed, if the purpose of testing elderly is to aid in description, diagnosis, and prognosis. More important are the possible treatment implications that follow if the language of the normally aging is subtly different from the language of their younger counterparts. Such a result might suggest a lower ceiling for expected recovery from aphasia for an older person than for a younger aphasic with similar symptomatology. Basso, Capitani, and Vignolo (1979) and Sarno (chapter 16) have suggested that age by itself is not a deterrent to recovery. The problem is that age by itself apparently marches on very infrequently in the so-called normally aging, and even much less frequently in the aging aphasic population—and clinicians must be aware of it.

In gathering data on the normal subjects for CADL, I found several interesting subtleties in the performance of the normal sample. For example, the older people were far less reticent than the younger ones in saying precisely what they though of the instrument itself. One eighty-four year old who scored well above her age group mean prefaced her answers with comments such as "Well, this is the dumbest thing I ever had to do, but . . . " If she had been an aphasic who was this judgmental, undoubtedly her score would have been lower than the aphasia alone would account for.

The effects of presbycusis and visual difficulties were both noted in data on the normal groups. Visual misperceptions apparently not related to acuity were also noted, such as describing a picture of a car with a flat tire as a car stuck in a snow drift. Some brittleness in changing set and some garrulousness also occurred in the data on normally aging subjects. These features indeed negatively affect functional communication and should be accounted for by lowered scores. The point is that the presence of such problems is not limited only to people who are not aphasic; they represent treatment hurdles for the aphasic as well. The clinical predilection to assume aphasia to be imposed on an otherwise totally healthy individual gets one of its strongest contraindications in the aging population.

**Aging and Type of Aphasia**

The presence of more serious aphasias generally in the older aphasic sample is of great clinical importance. Clinicians are least prepared to manage patients whose aphasias place them at either end of the severity scale. Useful techniques, by and large, are mostly geared toward moderately impaired aphasic patients. Mild problems are not the concern here—severe problems are. It is in this regard that the development of new treatment techniques, such as Helm's (1978) procedures for global aphasics, must continue to be encouraged. A major part of treatment for the severely impaired is counseling. Thus, honing these skills and developing insight into gerontological problems are clinical necessities.

The relationship between aging and Wernicke's aphasia suggest the need to develop sharper methods for working with auditory comprehension and controlling verbal output. But this relationship has clinical implications that are even more challenging; it substantiates the work of Obler et al., (1978) and brings into clearer urgency the matter of differentiating aphasia from cortical dementia and its language patterns. Benson's (1979) cautions about defining aphasia in the presence of the complex memory losses of the closed-head injured perhaps can be compared to defining aphasia in the elderly stroke patient. If clear focal brain damage and suddenness of onset can be documented in the history of the aging language-impaired patient, then differential diagnosis and appropriate rehabilitation planning remain relatively simple. Beyond that, and in the more typical case, there appear to be more questions than answers for the aphasiologist. Among them are: (1) Is it fair to consider aphasia in an aging person if there is history of a previous stroke? (2) What if the history is obscure? (3) What is the effect of long-standing atherosclerosis on the symptoms made apparent by a single major stroke? (4) What aspects of speech and language clearly differentiate the fluent speech of the Wernicke's patient from the equally fluent speech of the cortically demented patient? (5) What is the role of the language pathologist in the treatment of cortical dementia?

## Social and Cultural Implications

Being old in a society geared toward youth presents problems. Being in an institution generally has depressing effects on language use. Being in an institution is more likely if one is old. Observations such as these serve to remind clinicians that treating aphasia without considering the social context is probably not much better than not treating it at all. Understanding the family dynamics of aging, the appropriate materials for treatment, and even the role of talk in the life of an elderly person are necessary for clinicians. The focus of this section of the paper, then, switches away from the elderly themselves and onto the almost invariably younger persons who work with the elderly.

Studies of medical students (Geiger, 1978), psychologists, psychiatrists, and social workers (Garfinkel, 1975), and occupational therapists (Mills, 1972) all suggest that working with the elderly has low professional status for these health workers. It is not likely that people who work with the elderly language-impaired are differently inclined. This is one major sociological phenomenon regarding aging over which perhaps some professional control can be exerted.

Most of us are apprehensive about aging because we have had no direct personal experience with it (it is easier to understand adolescence because we have been there). We are afraid of at least some aspects of it; and, finally, we recognize its inevitability. As with other attitudes, change does not occur as a result of being preached to. Thus, it is important in training health professionals to increase their contact with the normally aging. An appropriate model might be one in which a better understanding of children is fostered by direct observation and contact with normal children. Formal course work in gerontology is as important for training clinicians who intend to work with the elderly as is course work in child development for for clinicians who intend to work with children. Just as professionals are trained to talk to children, to become familiar with what is and is not relevent to them, so professionals should be trained to talk with the elderly. For example, having been raised by a mother who today would be among the elderly, I was carefully taught never to call people a generation ahead of me by first name. That was a custom of the day. And to this day I flinch when I hear people my age and younger addressing people of my mother's era by first name without having received their permission to do so. I cannot help but think that subtle features such as this have a negative effect on mutual interchange and interact with clinical outcome to some degree. This, incidentally, is as applicable to the researcher as it is to the clinician.

Learning the world of the elderly patient in more individual and direct ways also increases respect for that world. A particularly useful device in this regard is a time-event line, derived from the work of Kimmel (1974) and described in more detail by Davis and Holland (in press), in which significant historical events are marked for each few years. Against this historical line the important life events of the elderly patient are plotted. This simple activity simultaneously sharpens the clinician's understanding of an elderly patient's world view and what shaped it and increases understanding of what the patient perceives as important personal events. It also promotes topics of conversation and provides great amounts of relevant language materials for the treatment process.

There is a final point to be made. Clinical intervention with the elderly aphasic patient all too often imposes the younger clinician's world view and understandings, rather than focusing on the patient's often quite different one. But treatment itself is also frequently the imposition. The elderly patient is, I believe, more frequently "treated" against his or her wishes than any other group of patients. Possibly this is because the clinician confuses the elderly patient with the child who "needs" it. This should be considered a clinical error of gross magnitude. It dehumanizes, and wastes time that could be better spent in attending to patients who wish treatment or in listening to the elderly patient in question. Dignity, and the patient's perception of what constitutes it, is a most important aspect of being old, and should be preserved in whatever way possible.

## References

Basso, A., Capitani, E., and Vignolo, L. Influence of rehabilitation on language skills in aphasic patients. *Archives of Neurology* 36 (4): 190-96, 1979.

Beasley, D.S., and Davis, G.A., eds. *Speech, Language and Hearing and the Aging Process.* New York: Grune and Stratton, in press.

Benson, D.F. *Aphasia, Alexia and Agraphia.* New York: Churchill-Livingstone, 1979.

Davis, G.A., and Holland, A.L. Age in understanding and treating aphasia. In D. Beasley and G.A. Davis, in press.

Garfinkel, R. The reluctant therapist. *The Gerontologist* 15: 136-37, 1975.

Geiger, D.L. How future professionals view the elderly: a comparative analysis of social work, law and medical students' perceptions. *The Gerontologist* 18: 591-94, 1978.

Helm, N. Visual action therapy for the global aphasic patient. Paper presented to the Academy of Aphasia, Chicago, 1978.

Holland, A. *A test for Measuring Aphasic Patients' Communicative Abilities in Daily Living.* Baltimore: University Park Press, in press.

Kimmel, D.C. *Adulthood and Aging.* New York: Wiley, 1974.

Mills, J. Attitudes of undergraduate students concerning geriatric patients. *American Journal of Occupational Therapy* 26: 220-23, 1972.

Obler, L.K., Albert, M.L., Goodglass, H., and Benson, D.F. Aging and aphasia type. *Brain and Language* 6: 318-22, 1978.

# 16 Language Rehabilitation Outcome in the Elderly Aphasic Patient

*Martha Taylor Sarno*

Although age has been considered an important variable in the outcome of language rehabilitation in aphasia (Vignolo 1964; Sands, Sarno, and Shankweiler, 1969; Darley, 1972; Sarno, 1976), no study has addressed itself specifically to the influence of chronological age per se in the elderly post-stroke aphasic population. Since the available evidence concerning the effect of age of recovery is not clear-cut (Basso, Capitani, and Vignolo, 1979; Sarno, 1976; Yarnell, Monroe, and Sobel, 1976) and the majority of aphasic patients fall into the older age group (Schuell, Jenkins, and Jimenez-Pabon, 1964; Sarno, 1970) we considered this an important and timely topic for investigation.

Age, paradoxically, has been reported as both a decisive and a weak factor in studies of recovery from aphasia. Sarno and Levita (1971), Culton (1969, 1971), Rose, Boby, and Capildeo (1976), and Messerli, Tissot, and Rodriguez (1976) did not find age to be a significant correlate of improvement. In a study of thirty-one treated aphasic patients who ranged in age from 46 to 80 with a median of 65 years no reliable differences in recovery were detected as a function of age (Sarno, Silverman, and Levita, 1970). Nor did the recent study by Kertesz and McCabe (1977) report a correlation for age and recovery from aphasia in the first three months after a stroke (mean age 58.4). Basso et al., (1979) also did not find that age affected improvement in 281 patients (mean age 50.2) of whom 85 percent had aphasia secondary to stroke.

In contrast, other investigators have found that prognosis in aphasia is related to age. In Vignolo's (1964) retrospective investigation improvement was much less frequent in older patients. More than 70 percent of the young patients in his study improved, and 40 percent reached a functional though defective communication level, whereas only two of nine patients (22.2 percent) over the age of sixty showed improvement. Vignolo noted, however, that there was improvement in two patients over sixty years of age

The author wishes to thank Toni Buonaguro for her assistance in collecting and analyzing the data; Eric Levita, John Sarno, and Karen Riedel for their constructive comments; and Rita Sternberg for typing the manuscript.

whom he first examined within two months after onset. One of the patients who was seventy years old recovered completely within four months, showing that prognosis in aphasia in patients over sixty years of age need not necessarily be pessimistic.

Sands el al. (1969) reported on the recovery course of thirty post-stroke treated aphasic patients who were initially assessed at about 7.5 months post-stroke and retested 13 months later. Their average age was 56.5 years. The contribution of age to improvement was assessed by examining the least- and most-improved patients in the group. When the sixth of the group that improved most was compared with the sixth that improved least, age emerged as a potent variable. The group that recovered least had an average age of sixty-one and those who recovered most averaged forty-seven years of age. The results suggested that aphasic patients of less than fifty years of age have a better prognosis for recovery than those over the age of sixty.

This study is limited to the influence of age in the post-stroke aphasic patient over the age of fifty—that is, a group of aphasic patients most representative of the majority of aphasic patients who seek rehabilitation services.

## Methodology

### Subjects

The study population consisted of sixty-three aphasic patients treated in the Speech Pathology Service of the Institute of Rehabilitation Medicine. Patients were selected for study who were over age fifty and sustained vascular lesions of the left hemisphere confirmed in most cases by neuroradiologic studies. All were Caucasian, right-handed adults, native speakers of English with normal hearing thresholds across the speech frequencies.

Patients were excluded from the study if they had a history of alcoholism, preexisting speech disorder, psychiatric disease, previous cerebrovascular accident, or known transient ischemic attack, or had already received aphasia therapy. Those with aphasia secondary to head trauma, arteriovenous malformation or ruptured aneurysm, neoplasm, equivocal handedness, or evidence of right-hemisphere pathology were also excluded. No patient was included who acquired English after the age of twelve. Patients who were not alert, attentive, or who otherwise seemed unable to cope with the testing process because of illness, fatigue, severity of cognitive or aphasic deficits or symptoms associated with senile dementia were excluded. The rationales for controlling these variables have been pointed out frequently in the literature (Vignolo, 1964; Darley, 1972; Sarno, 1975, 1976).

There were 41 males and 22 females. Their ages ranged 51 to 77 years (mean age: 61.4; median 60). Education ranged from 8 to 20 years (mean 14.4 years, median 16 years).

*Classification*

Patients were assigned to three diagnostic groups according to the classification scheme of Benson (1967), Geschwind (1971), and Goodglass and Kaplan (1972): fluent (F), (n = 16); nonfluent (NF), (n = 18); and global (G), (n = 29). All of the patients selected for study fell unequivocally into one of the diagnostic categories. No patient was classified as transcortical, isolation, or conduction aphasia. Table 16-1 shows the age, sex, education, and employment characteristics of the patients according to aphasia type. In terms of these variables the three groups were essentially equivalent.

Aphasia type was determined by a consensus of clinical impressions combined with an analysis of linguistic deficits obtained on tests of language performance (such as relationship of speech proficiency to auditory comprehension). Judgments of fluency were made according to the guidelines elaborated by Goodglass and Kaplan (1972); that is, a judgment of speech production during extended conversation and free narrative was the basis for assigning a patient to the fluent or nonfluent group.

Fluency is best rated in terms of the longest occasional uninterrupted string of words produced, and is considered an important and reliable diagnostic criterion (Goodglass, Quadfasel, and Timberlake, 1964; Wagenaar, Snow, and Prins, 1975). The fluency dimension allows for a grouping among aphasic syndromes into two types, fluent and nonfluent.

Fluent Aphasia is usually associated with a lesion in the vicinity of the posterior portion of the first temporal gyrus of the left hemisphere (Goodglass and Kaplan, 1972), and is characterized by impaired auditory comprehension in the presence of well-articulated speech. The melody and rate of speech in the fluent aphasic are generally normal in all respects. Word and sound substitutions may be of such magnitude and frequency that the patient's speech is virtually a meaningless jargon.

Nonfluent Aphasia is characterized by awkward articulation, limited vocabulary, hesitant, slow output of speech, restricted use of grammatical forms, and a relative preservation of auditory comprehension. The syndrome is associated with anterior lesions usually involving the third frontal convolution of the left hemisphere. The severe category, referred to as global aphasia, is characterized by an "evenness" of dysfunction across all modalities and a severely limited residual use of all communication modes for everyday oral-aural interactions (Sarno et al. 1970; Yarnell et al. 1976; Kertesz and McCabe, 1977).

**Table 16-1**
**Characteristics of Total Subjects According to Aphasia Type**

| Group | Age Median | Age Range | Sex Male | Sex Female | Education Median | Education Range | Employment Active | Employment Inactive | Severity Index[a] Median | Severity Index[a] Range |
|---|---|---|---|---|---|---|---|---|---|---|
| Global ($N=29$) | 61.0 | 52-77 | 19 | 10 | 14.0 | 8-19 | 22 | 7 | 15.4% | 1.8-28.0% |
| Fluent ($N=16$) | 60.5 | 51-73 | 10 | 6 | 15.5 | 12-20 | 13 | 3 | 33.2% | 20.5-72.0% |
| Nonfluent ($N=18$) | 59.5 | 51-72 | 12 | 6 | 13.5 | 10-20 | 13 | 5 | 40.1% | 16.6-79.0% |
| Total ($N=63$) | 60.0 | 51-77 | 41 | 22 | 14.0 | 8-20 | 48 | 15 | 26.2% | 1.8-79.0% |

[a]Functional communication profile/overall intake score.

A consensus of clinical impressions of the speech pathology staff and language test scores provided the basis for designating global aphasia. Of the 29 patients so designated, 27 had intake overall Functional Communication Profile (FCP) scores of 25 percent or less. The remaining two patients scored 26.2 percent and 28.9 percent.

Using FCP overall scores as an index of severity, the spread of severity for the total group was wide, ranging from 1.8 percent to 79.9 percent. The absence of scores at the milder end of the severity continuum was anticipated since aphasic patients with minimal residuals are less apt to seek speech-therapy services. In the fluent group FCP overall scores ranged from 20.5 to 72.8 percent (median 33.2; mean 37.8). The nonfluent group had overall FCP scores ranging from 25.7 to 79.9 percent (median 40.1; mean 46.8). In the global group FCP overall scores ranged from 1.8 to 28.9 percent (median 15.4; mean 14.7).

*Testing*

The Functional Communication Profile (FCP) (Taylor, 1965; Sarno, 1969) and the Neurosensory Center Comprehensive Examination for Aphasia (NCCEA) (Spreen and Benton, 1969) were administered to each patient. FCP ratings were "blind," that is, the rater filled in a rating sheet at each retest session. For the purposes of this study the FCP overall score, the FCP speaking score, and the FCP understanding score, as well as the word fluency (WF) and the token test subtests of the NCCEA, were analyzed.

The FCP is a rating scale for aphasics that considers forty-five everyday communication behaviors. Ratings of each behavior are made on a nine-point scale, based on observations of the patient during an informal conversation. An item is given a rating of eight or normal (100 percent) when it is estimated that the patient performs the behavior as well as he or she did premorbidly. The rationale, reliability, and validity of this instrument have been elaborated elsewhere (Taylor, 1965; Sarno, 1969).

The NCCEA consists of twenty tests of language performance covering a broad range of communication modalities designed to yield a quantitative profile of specific deficits associated with brain damage. It has the advantage of having been standardized on large samples of normal and aphasic subjects, allowing for interpretations according to percentile ranks derived from aphasic and normal populations. The scoring is quantitative and objective and requires no clinical inferences (DeRenzi and Vignolo, 1962; Benton, 1967).

We elected to analyze the scores obtained on the NCCEA word fluency and token test as subtests, since these are believed to be sensitive detectors of subtle speech deficits and performance in speaking and auditory comprehension (Lomas and Kertesz, 1978). On the word fluency test the patient is instructed to give within one minute as many words as possible beginning with a specified letter. The token test consists of thirty-nine verbal commands of increasing complexity that require the patient to manipulate twenty plastic tokens of two shapes, two sizes, and five colors. "Show me a circle" is an example of one of the simplest commands. "Put the white square behind the yellow circle" is a more difficult one. The token test has been well studied for its sensitivity and discrimination powers in the measurement of auditory comprehension and for its reliability (DeRenzi and Vignolo, 1962; Orgass and Poeck, 1966; Hartje et al., 1973: Gallagher, 1979).

Initial test results (mean, 6 weeks after stroke; range, 4-13) compared with follow-up test results (mean, 24 weeks after stroke; range 16-24) provided the basis for evidence of impairment. A minimum three-month interval was required before follow-up testing.

All patients were receiving speech therapy in a comprehensive rehabilitation medical setting during the entire study period. The intensity of speech therapy ranged from three to five individual and group therapy sessions weekly. Speech pathologists administered speech therapy without knowing which patients were being studied. The specific therapeutic goals were essentially determined by the individual speech pathologist and generally followed a stimulation-pedagogical approach (Sarno, 1974, 1975).

**Results**

The primary result of this study was the lack of any age effect on recovery in post-stroke aphasic patients over fifty years of age on all measures except functional speaking. There was no age difference between the most-improved (MI) and least-improved (LI) groups and no difference in recovery outcome between the ten oldest (OP) and the ten youngest (YP) patients.

*Ten Oldest and Ten Youngest Patients*

Table 16-2 shows the characteristics of the ten oldest and ten youngest patients. The OP ranged in age from 69 to 77 (median 72) whereas the YP ranged from 51 to 54 years of age (median 53.5). The OP group consisted of 5 global, 3 fluent, and 2 nonfluent patients and the YP group 3 global, 4 fluent, and 3 nonfluent patients. At the time of stroke, half of the older patients were employed and half were retired, whereas all of the young patients were employed.

On overall severity (FCP/O) the OP group made a change of 9.8 percent (range —3.5 to 26 percent), whereas the YP made a median FCP/O

**Table 16-2**
**Characteristics of Ten Oldest and Ten Youngest Patients**

|  | Ten Oldest | Ten Youngest |
|---|---|---|
| *Age* | | |
| Median | 72.0 | 53.5 |
| Range | 69-77 | 51-54 |
| *Education* | | |
| Median | 16 | 16 |
| Range | 8-20 | 10-20 |
| *Type* | | |
| Global (n) | 5 | 3 |
| Fluent (n) | 3 | 4 |
| Nonfluent (n) | 2 | 3 |
| *Sex* | | |
| Male | 6 | 7 |
| Female | 4 | 3 |
| *Employment* | | |
| Active (n) | 5 | 10 |
| Inactive (n) | 5 | 0 |

change score of 16.6 percent (range —1.4 to 28.8 percent). This difference was not significant at the .05 level. Mann-Whitney values for comparisons between the OP and YP groups are shown in table 16-3.

In functional speech (FCP/S) the older patients made a median change score of 9.0 percent (range 0 to 33). The median change score for the younger patients was 18 percent (range 9 to 36 percent). The improvement difference on this measure was significant at the .05 level (Mann-Whitney $U$ value of 19.5).

**Table 16-3**
**Comparison of Ten Oldest and Ten Youngest Patients with Respect to Change Scores**

| | Mann-Whitney Values[1] |
|---|---|
| FCP/overall | 24  $(U)$ |
| FCP/speaking | 19.5 $(U)$[a] |
| Word fluency | 29  $(U)$ |
| FCP/understanding | 41.5 $(U)$ |
| Token Test | 44  $(U)$ |

[1]Method for determining Mann-Whitney values taken from Siegel, S. *Nonparametric Statistics for the Behavioral Sciences.* New York: McGraw-Hill, 1956.
[a]Significant at .05 level.

On the word fluency task median change scores were 0 (range —9 to 21) for the oldest and 6.0 (range 0 to 23) for the youngest group.

In functional understanding (FCP/U) the median change score for the OP was 10.5 percent (range —1 to 21 percent) and for the young group 13.5 percent (range —3 to 27 percent).

Token test change scores ranged from —7 to 66 for the oldest patients and —6 to 121 for the youngest. Token test median change scores were 23.5 and 28.5 respectively.

*Ten Most-Improved and Ten Least-Improved Patients*

The characteristics of the most-improved and least-improved patients are shown in table 16-4. The MI group consisted of two global, five fluent, and three nonfluent patients. At intake the range of FCP overall scores for the MI group was from 4.1 percent to 61.6 percent. The LI group consisted of six global, one fluent, and three nonfluent patients. At intake their FCP overall scores ranged from 11.6 percent to 79.9 percent.

Comparison of changes on overall severity as measured by the FCP/O scores between the LI and MI groups are shown in table 16-5. The analyses show a median FCP/O change score for the LI group of 1.8 percent (range

**Table 16-4**
**Characteristics of Ten Most-Improved and Ten Least-Improved Patients**

|  | Ten Most Improved | Ten Least Improved |
|---|---|---|
| *Age* |  |  |
| Median | 58.0 | 62.0 |
| Range | 51-72 | 54-72 |
| *Education* |  |  |
| Median | 12 | 14 |
| Range | 12-19 | 10-19 |
| *Type* |  |  |
| Global (n) | 2 | 6 |
| Fluent (n) | 5 | 1 |
| Nonfluent (n) | 3 | 3 |
| *Sex* |  |  |
| Male (n) | 5 | 8 |
| Female (n) | 5 | 2 |
| *Employment* |  |  |
| Active (n) | 9 | 8 |
| Inactive (n) | 1 | 2 |

**Table 16-5**
**Ten Most-Improved and Ten Least-Improved Change Scores**

|  | Ten Most Improved | | Ten Least Improved | |
| --- | --- | --- | --- | --- |
| Subtests | Median | Range | Median | Range |
| FCP/overall | 27.0 | 23.8-38.1 | 1.8 | −9.4-4.1 |
| FCP/speaking | 33.5 | 29-41 | 0 | −15-0 |
| Word fluency | 16.5 | 12-23 | 0 | −9-0 |
| FCP/understanding | 28.5 | 26-40 | −2.5 | −18-1 |
| Token test | 88.0 | 66-121 | −6.5 | −25-0 |

—9.4 to 4.1 percent) and a median FCP/O change score for the MI group of 27.0 percent (range 23.8 to 38.1 percent).

Neither education, sex, or employment status were significant correlates of recovery at the .05 level as measured by FCP/O change scores (Mann-Whitney $U$value = 44.5, $X^2$ = 3.52 and 0, respectively).

Change scores on FCP/S showed some relationship to age for the LI and MI groups. The median change score was 0 percent (range —15 to 0 percent) for the least-improved group and 33.5 percent (range 29 to 41 percent) for the most-improved group.

On the word fluency task the LI group had a median change score of 0 (range —9 to 0), and the MI group median change score was 16.5 (range 12 to 23).

The median change score on FCP/U ratings for the LI group was —2.5 percent (range —18 to 1 percent). Median change scores for the MI group was 28.5 percent (range 26 to 40 percent). Age did not emerge as a significant variable on the functional understanding measure.

The median change score on the token test for the least-improved patients was —6.5 (range of —25 to 0), for the most improved 88.0 (range of 66 to 121).

*Change of Aphasia Type and Age*

In the course of the study, seven patients changed from one aphasia classification to another. Five global aphasic patients evolved into non-fluent types. Their ages were 53, 56, 61, 64, and 66, lending support to the idea that the younger patient need not necessarily carry the better prognosis. One 51-year-old global aphasic patient emerged as a fluent aphasic patient and a 58-year-old patient who was classified as severely nonfluent at six weeks (FCP overall 25.5 percent) was reclassified at twelve weeks after stroke (FCP 46 percent) as a fluent aphasic. Furthermore, our analyses showed no relationship between age and type of aphasia (fluent/global, nonfluent/global, and fluent/nonfluent comparisons yielded Mann-Whitney values of $z = .83$, $z = .50$ and $U = 133$, respectively. None of these were significant at the .05 level).

A descriptive table of the characteristics of the most and least impaired patients in the total group is shown in table 16-6.

**Discussion**

This study did not confirm the idea that chronological age per se has a negative influence on recovery in the post-stroke aphasic patient over age fifty. This finding has immediate application to the selection of patients for treatment and suggests that chronological age alone should not exclude the elderly patient from speech rehabilitation services. The results assume particular relevance in view of current reports that the older population in the United States is increasing at a rapid rate. Although older aphasic patients generally have no vocational future, the recovery of communication function has great relevance to the quality of the remainder of their lives. This is not always discernible to the observer or measurable by traditional yardsticks. The loss or impairment of the ability to communicate is a devastating experience at any age.

**Table 16-6**
**Characteristics of Total Group**
(*Based on FCP/overall change score*)

|  | *Median and Above* | *Below Median* |
|---|---|---|
| *Age* | | |
| Median | 59.0 | 61.0 |
| Range | 51-76 | 52-77 |
| *Education* | | |
| Median | 14 | 15 |
| Range | 10-20 | 8-20 |
| *Type* | | |
| Global *(N)* | 14 | 16 |
| Fluent *(N)* | 8 | 7 |
| Nonfluent *(N)* | 10 | 8 |
| *Sex* | | |
| Male *(N)* | 19 | 21 |
| Female *(N)* | 13 | 10 |
| *Employment* | | |
| Active *(N)* | 25 | 24 |
| Inactive *(N)* | 7 | 7 |

In their early study on the question of age and recovery from aphasia, Weisenberg and McBride (1935) elected to exclude aphasic patients over age sixty "to prevent a picture complicated by senile changes." Recently, Basso et al., (1979) reported a "rather weak inverse relationship between age and improvement," whereas Sarno (1970) suggested a possible relationship between age and severity. The wide discrepancy in the literature with respect to the influence of age on recovery from aphasia may be related to differences in sampling and the choice of analytic procedures. The strength of the present study rests in the careful selection of patients which provided a relatively homogenious group with respect to etiology, education, time since onset, and other socioeconomic variables. In this regard, the $N$ would have been substantially larger if the group had not been sharply limited with respect to time since onset. However, the importance of this parameter mandated strict adherence to a limited time span and testing schedule. Furthermore, by using a method of analysis that compares extremes for age and improvement, we intended to highlight differences at the extremes and avoid diluting the findings by averaging all scores.

As indicated, the FCP speaking-change scores were the only ones to yield a statistically significant difference between the youngest and oldest groups. We make no attempt to explain this but simply draw attention to it as a deviation from the major conclusion. The overall score more nearly reflects the functional communication effectiveness of the aphasic patient, so this is where attention should be focused. The sum of communication skills in a complete system of information processing reflected in the FCP overall rating of severity is probably the single most meaningful score since it is based on the aphasic's actual use of language in an everyday, naturalistic setting. This is in opposition to performance on specifically structured tasks which may or may not truly reflect an individual's spontaneous use of residual and compensatory skills.

If chronological age is not a factor in recovery, what should we be looking at in the equation? Weisenberg and McBride (1935) assumed the existence of "senile changes" in patients over sixty but as is well known, there is great variability in the onset of such changes. Nevertheless, it is no doubt true that the presence and severity of associated intellectual deficits only significantly modify the course of recovery from aphasia. These include such things as impairments of memory, judgment, span of attention, and activation level. Similarly, deficits in high-level perception probably further detract from recovery, particularly in reading and writing. The extent of the etiologic lesion, of course, must play a role in the degree of recovery, both with respect to language pathology and associated intellectual functions.

Another variable, again unrelated to chronological age, is the emotional state of the patient. Enduring and severe depression, either endogenous or reactive, cannot help but retard recovery, and accounting for depression should be part of any evaluation of progress. The patient's life situation often has a powerful influence on his or her emotional state.

Although this study confirmed a long-held clinical impression that chronological age per se does not influence recovery in the elderly post-stroke aphasic patient, the results cannot be considered final. Further studies are needed that incorporate younger patients and extend over a longer period. Clinically, we shall continue our present practice of providing speech therapy for all aphasic patients regardless of age, secure in the knowledge that there is at least some objective evidence that the practice is warranted.

## References

Basso, A., Capitani, E., and Vignolo, L. Influence of rehabilitation on language skills in aphasic patients. *Archives of Neurology* 36: 190-96, 1979.

Benson, D.F. Fluency in aphasia: correlation with radioactive scan localization. *Cortex* 8: 373-94, 1967.

Benton, A.L. Problems of test construction in the field of aphasia. *Cortex* 3: 32-58, 1967.

Culton, G. Spontaneous recovery from aphasia. *Journal of Speech and Hearing Research* 12: 825-32, 1969.

_____. Reaction to age as a factor in chronic aphasia in stroke patients. *Journal of Speech and Hearing Disorders* 36: 563-64, 1971.

Darley, F. The efficacy of language rehabilitation in aphasia. *Journal of Speech and Hearing Disorders* 37: 3-21, 1972.

DeRenzi, E., and Vignolo, L. The token test: a sensitive test to detect receptive disturbance in aphasics. *Brain* 85: 665-78, 1962.

Gallagher, A. Temporal reliability of aphasic performance on the token test. *Brain and Language* 7: 34-41, 1979.

Geschwind, N. Current concepts: aphasia. *New England Journal of Medicine* 284: 654-56, 1971.

Goodglass, H., and Kaplan, E. *Boston Diagnostic Aphasia Examination.* Philadelphia: Lea and Febiger, 1972.

Goodglass, H., Quadfasel, F.A., and Timberlake, W.H. Phrase length and the type and severity of aphasia. *Cortex* 1: 133-53, 1964.

Hartje, W., Kerschensteiner, M., Poeck, K., and Orgass, B. A cross-validation study on the token test. *Neuropsychologia* 7: 119-21, 1973.

Kertesz, A., and McCabe, P. Recovery patterns and prognosis in aphasia. *Brain* 100: 1-18, 1977.

Lomas, J., and Kertesz, A. Patterns of spontaneous recovery in aphasic groups; a study of adult stroke patients. *Brain and Language* 5: 398-401, 1978.

Messerli, P., Tissot, A., and Rodriguez, J. Recovery from aphasia: some factors of prognosis. In *Recovery from Aphasia—Neurolinguistics*, vol. 4, edited by Y. Lebrun and R. Hoops, pp. 124-35. Amsterdam: Swets and Zeitlinger, 1976.

Obler, L., Albert, M., Goodglass, H., and Benson, D.F. Aphasia type and aging. *Brain and Language* 6: 318-22, 1978.

Orgass, B., and Poeck, K. Clinical validation of a new test for aphasia: an experimental study on the token test. *Cortex* 2: 222-43, 1966.

Rose, C., Boby, V., and Capildeo, R. A retrospective survey of speech disorders following stroke, with particular reference to the value of speech therapy. In *Recovery from Aphasia—Neurolinguistics*, vol. 4, edited by Y. Lebrun and R. Hoops, pp. 189-197. Amsterdam: Swets and Zeitlinger, 1976.

Sands, E., Sarno, M.T., and Shankweiler, D. Long term assessment of language function in aphasia due to stroke. *Archives of Physical Medicine and Rehabilitation* 50: 203-207, 1969.

Sarno, M.T. *The Functional Communication Profile: Manual of Directions*. Monograph 42. New York: Institute of Rehabilitation Medicine, New York University Medical Center, 1969.

_____. A survey of 100 aphasic medicare patients in a speech pathology program. *Journal of the American Geriatric Society* 18: 471-80, 1970.

_____. Aphasia rehabilitation. In *Communication Disorders: Remedial Principles and Practices*, edited by S. Dickson, pp. 399-440. Illinois: Scott, Foresman, 1974.

_____. Disorders of communication in stroke. In *Stroke and Its Rehabilitation*, edited by S. Licht, pp. 380-408. Baltimore: Williams and Wilkins, 1975.

_____. The status of research in recovery from aphasia. In *Recovery in Aphasics—Neurolinguistics*, vol. 4, edited by Y. Lebrun and R. Hoops, pp. 13-30. Amsterdam: Swets and Zeitlinger, 1976.

Sarno, M.T., and Levita, E. Natural course of recovery in severe aphasia. *Archives of Physical Medicine and Rehabilitation* 52: 175-79, 1971.

Sarno, M.T., Silverman, M., and Levita, E. Psychosocial factors and recovery in geriatric patients with severe aphasia. *Journal of the American Geriatric Society* 18: 405-409, 1970.

Sarno, M.T., Silverman, M., and Sands, E. Speech therapy and language recovery in severe aphasia. *Journal of Speech and Hearing Research* 13: 607-623, 1970.

Schuell, H., Jenkins, J., and Jimenez-Pabon, E. *Aphasia in Adults*. New York: Harper and Row, 1964.

Spreen, O., and Benton, A.L. *Neurosensory Center Comprehensive Examination for Aphasia: Manual of Directions*. Victoria, B.C.: Neuropsychology Laboratory, University of Victoria, 1969.

Taylor, M.L. A measurement of functional communication in aphasia.

*Archives of Physical Medicine and Rehabilitation* 46: 101-107, 1965.

Vignolo, L. Evolution of aphasia and language rehabilitation: a retrospective study. *Cortex* 1: 344-67, 1964.

Wagenaar, E., Snow, C., and Prins, R. Spontaneous speech of aphasic patients: a psycholinguistic analysis. *Brain and Language* 2: 291-303, 1975.

Weisenberg, T., and McBride, K. Aphasia: a clinical and psychological study. New York: Hafner, 1964 (1st ed., Commonwealth Fund, 1935).

Yarnell, P., Monroe, P., and Sobel, L. Aphasia outcome in stroke: a clinical neuroradiological correlation. *Stroke* 7: 514-22, 1976.

# 17 Language and Communication in the Elderly: An Overview

*Norman Geschwind*

I would like to point out, not the extent of what we know about language and communication in the elderly, since much of that has been covered in other chapters of this book, but rather the extent of our ignorance. We must realize that when we talk about changes in communication and language in the elderly we are speaking primarily about changes in nervous tissue: that nervous tissue may be peripheral, for example, in the hair cells of the cochlea, or it may be in the central nervous system. Neurological disorder is not rare. It is probably the most common cause of hospitalization in the United States. It is a major cause of chronic hospitalization. The largest group of such chronic neurological patients are in mental hospitals. The largest number of neurological patients in the mental hospitals are, of course, people who are over sixty-five. In talking about language in the elderly we are therefore talking about a vast number of people with neurological alterations.

Despite the existence of this vast number of people with neurological alterations, our ignorance about the changes going on in the nervous system with age is still boundless. For example, in what way do the brains of the Adenauers, the George Bernard Shaws, and others who preserve remarkable intellectual activity until very late differ from those of other people? We do not know. We cannot, in fact, discuss normal aging because we lack clear criteria. Some of the questions are clear. Consider the eighty-year-old person who is still running a business successfully, is managing personal affairs, and, in fact, is performing in a superior fashion. How does his or her brain differ from what it was at age sixty-five? However, even the changes in the brain of such a person should not necessarily be regarded as normal. For example, the brain may have lost some of its reserve capacity. Such a change is in the strict sense of the term a result of disease, since a disease is by definition any bodily change, regardless of origin, that diminishes function. Inevitability should not be confused with normalcy, at least in the medical sense.

The major reason for being concerned about these changes is that we are interested in how they might be prevented. Unfortunately, we have only limited information on changes in the nervous system in aging. The nervous system is a vast structure. It will be many years before we know in even elementary detail what change occurs in each distinguishable region with aging. Furthermore, certain types of investigation give us little information. The brain wave and the CT scan may show no changes with aging for many people, but these measures simply lack the kind of detailed neurological information that we require. Conceivably, more advanced electrical techniques, such as evoked potential studies (electrical responses of the brain to particular stimuli) may give us further data, but these studies remain to be done.

A recent study by Herzog (1979) illustrates the problem. In association with Kemper he has shown that the amygdala changes with aging. Yet ten years ago this structure was rarely, if ever, mentioned in studies on aging.

Since human beings are difficult to study experimentally, we might expect that there would have been a considerable amount of work on aging in nonhuman animals. Yet studies of this kind are rare. We know, for example, that when nerves in the central nervous system are destroyed in young animals, adjacent intact nerve fibers may sprout. Yet only recently have studies been done on the changes in sprouting in older animals. As expected, sprouting occurs less with age. Other types of biochemical changes in response to stimulation or after injury, however, have yet to be investigated in older animals. We have data about certain changes in aging. We know that whereas many functions decline, others seem to increase. The production of antidiuretic hormones increases with age, in contrast to most other hormones. All of these hormones have effects on the brain. We have no idea what this differential pattern means. Kaplan has pointed out in chapter 9 some of the changes that occur in psychological testing with increasing age. The major significance of her elegant work is in demonstrating to us that we are only just learning how to describe these psychological changes. My own guess is that she is describing part of a larger alteration, and that the greatest change in age is in attentional systems. These systems underlie the ability to deal with very large numbers of simultaneous stimuli and to make coherent responses. It is the change in these systems that leads to the older person's problem with noise and other extraneous stimuli.

I have been discussing until now what for want of a better term is called "normal" aging, that is, the declines in ability among those who continue to function successfully. We must, however, contrast this group of "normal" with those suffering from *dementia*, that is, declines in abililty that prevent normal functioning. We must understand clearly that one cannot speak of dementia as a uniform entity, since there are many types of dementias differing from each other in their clinical features. Albert in chapter 12 has emphasized the important distinction between cortical and subcortical dementias. We should remember, however, that even within these two major groups there are many differentiable conditions. For example, aphasia is a common feature of Alzheimer's disease, but is probably never seen in Huntington's chorea. Thus one cannot simply contrast the demented and those without dementia, since the demented do not constitute a homogeneous group. Unfortunately, many textbooks of both psychiatry and neurology discuss an entity called the *chronic brain syndrome*. Since there are many different conditions, this usage is unfortunate and can only serve to obscure diagnosis and confuse research.

There are some further points to make about the dementias. Probably the most common diagnosis made in the aged undergoing intellectual decline is "cerebral arteriosclerosis." This diagnosis embodies the theory that dementia is commonly the result of chronic lack of blood flow in the brain. This view is rejected by most experts, and chronic vascular insufficiency is not regarded as a cause of steady intellectual decline (Corsellis, 1975). Multiple strokes can lead to dementia, but this is rarely a diagnostic problem. Occasional hypertensives do suffer what appears to be a gradual decline in intellectual function, but this is still probably a small group compared to the vast number of cases of degenerative disease (such as the death of nerve cells), the causes of which are, with rare exceptions, still unknown.

Although the diagnosis of chronic brain syndrome is inaccurate and that of cerebral arteriosclerosis is usually erroneous, we should not assume that our level of accuracy of diagnosis is high. Many neurologists make the diagnosis of Alzheimer's disease in nearly all cases of dementia, and although this is the most common cause of dementia in the old, it is far from the only one. It is often incorrect. Indeed, it is my guess that we do not yet know all the causes of dementia in the old. A complete description of the pathology of dementia means specification, not only of the nature of the damage, but also of its location. At one time many textbooks said that Alzheimer's disease involved the brain diffusely. Yet it is clear that both clinically and pathologically the disease is selective. It involves many areas, but others, such as the primary motor and visual cortexes, are usually spared, either absolutely or relatively (Geschwind, 1978).

The issue of depression is a very important one in the aging population, since the differential diagnosis between dementia and depression is an ever-recurring problem and sometimes cannot be made on clinical grounds. No one has had enough experience to formulate reliable rules. The problem is that we try to predict whether a patient's intellectual difficulties will disappear, either with antidepressant drugs, psychotherapy, electric-shock therapy (which is, in some cases of depression masquerading as dementia, the only effective treatment), or simply by waiting. In some instances careful interviewing may lead to a great flow of depressive affect, but this is not always the case. The presence of memory deficit without aphasic disorder is often seen in the depressive cases (but can also be seen in many cases of Alzheimer's disease), but rare cases of depressive pseudodementia do produce aphasic speech, so this criterion is not absolute. The only reliable rule I know is that demented patients who are actively euphoric do not respond to any form of antidepressant treatment.

Another point to stress is that a depression presenting as dementia is almost never seen in young depressives (for example, at age forty) and is usually seen only in those over sixty-five. It is curious that at this age the patient may complain about cognitive difficulty and may even be unaware of the presence of depression.

Let me further point out that although psychological testing is indispensable, it cannot be relied on as the only criterion for differentiating between a true dementia and a pseudodepressive dementia. I have seen patients who responded dramatically to antidepressant treatment who had been labeled *organic* on psychological testing and patients with gross neurological disease labeled *functional*. Psychological testing must be done and the results must be weighed along with all the other evidence. In some cases only a trial of treatment can decide the issue, and in some cases electric-shock therapy must be used.

Let me make a brief comment on sex differences. We already know that the male and female brains are different in birds and rats and I believe they will be found to be different in humans. Let me stress that *difference* is not equivalent to superiority and inferiority. A true Darwinian view makes it clear that members of a population may differ in talents, and the presence of considerable variation is beneficial for the survival of the population. We know that disease incidence differs in men and women. Heart disease is more common in men, but Alzheimer's disease is more frequent in women. I think that the study of sex differences in the aging population will become increasingly important.

Let me comment briefly on hearing difficulties in the aged, a topic that Rupp covers thoroughly and elegantly in chapter 14. In younger deaf patients (for example, at age forty) it is rarely a problem of deciding whether the patient is aphasic rather than deaf. Furthermore, preceding deafness in the aphasic patient rarely alters the clinical picture significantly. On the other hand, the presence of deafness in some older dementing patients may lead to speech that sounds paraphasic. This disorder may disappear when the deafness is corrected (although the true features of the dementia persist). Although rare, this phenomenon can be dramatic. Obviously, correction of deafness may make it far easier to manage such a patient.

An old German psychiatric observation was that the aged deaf were more likely to become paranoid than those with normal hearing. The English psychiatrist Martin Roth confirmed this a few years ago by showing a higher incidence of hearing loss in older paranoid patients than in their normal age-mates. The detection and correction of deafness therefore have special importance as a possible means of preventing or correcting psychiatric disability in the aged patient.

I would like to make one further point about communicating with the deaf. I have been repeatedly surprised by the failure of physicians to realize they can communicate with pencil and paper, a simple and highly effective method that is often totally overlooked. It often saves a remarkable amount of shouting, misunderstanding, and embarrassment.

Let me bring up another point about communicating with the patient who cannot speak. I have found that patients who are aphasic in speech are always aphasic in writing. However, not all patients who are mute are aphasic. I have now seen several patients who had been diagnosed as aphasic who were actually suffering from pseudobulbar dysarthria. These patients could write fully normal language. The failure to use this means of communication when it is available is most unfortunate.

Let me now turn to my final comment prompted by Sarno's elegant discussion of prognosis. The main point to keep in mind is that statistical averages for groups mean little, and our prognostic judgments must depend on the individual case. Some colleagues of mine saw a composer in his late seventies suffering from an aphasic disorder for over a year who had been told by some of his physicians that his prognosis was poor. He was told that some people continue to improve even after a couple of years. This patient, with no change in his treatment program did, in fact, improve considerably. He recently had a new piece of music performed publicly. This illustrates clearly that judgments of prognosis must be guarded and that at any age there are patients who do very well.

## References

Corsellis, J.A.N. The pathology of dementia. *British Journal of Psychiatry* 125: 110-118, 1975.

Geschwind, N. Organic problems in the aged. *Journal of Geriatric Psychiatry* 11: 161-66, 1978.

Herzog, A., and Kemper, T. Amygdaloid changes in aging and dementia. *Neurology* 29: 586, 1979.

McHugh, P., and Folstein, M.F. Psychopathology of dementia: implications for neuropathology. In *Congenital and Acquired Cognitive Disorders,* edited by R. Katzman, pp. 17-30. New York: Raven Press, 1979.

# Index

# About the Contributors

**Joan C. Borod** received the B.A. from Smith College and the Ph.D. in clinical psychology from Case Western Reserve University. She did postdoctoral work at the Aphasia Research Center, Boston University School of Medicine, through fellowships from the National Institutes of Health and the Social Science Research Council, and currently works as clinical neuropsychologist and research associate at the Boston Veterans Administration Medical Center. In addition she has a private practice in psychotherapy in Cambridge, Massachusetts. She has published in the areas of sex differences, emotional expression, and hemispheric specialization.

**Elisabeth O. Clark** was graduated from Newcomb College and received the M.A. in psychology from New York University, where she is presently a doctoral candidate. She has worked as a research psychologist at the Geriatric Study and Treatment Program of the New York University Medical Center, Department of Psychiatry, and is currently director of a family study of Alzheimer-type dementia at Brentwood Veterans Administration Medical Center and the Clinical Project on Aging, Department of Psychiatry, University of California, Los Angeles. Ms. Clark has coauthored a paper on the nature of memory loss following Valium injection and a chapter on brain damage and memory deficit included in the *Handbook of Behavioral Neurobiology*.

**Leon Epstein** completed his undergraduate education at Vanderbilt. University and received the Ph.D. in psychology from Peabody College. He received the M.D. from the University of Tennessee and completed psychiatric residency training at Saint Elizabeth's Hospital, Washington, D.C. He was director of research for the California Department of Mental Hygiene for five years and is currently professor and vice-chairman of the Department of Psychiatry, School of Medicine, and associate director of the Langley Porter Psychiatric Institute, University of California, San Francisco.

**Norman Geschwind** was graduated from Harvard College and from Harvard Medical School. He received neurological training at the National Hospital, Queen Square, London, and at Boston City Hospital. Dr. Geschwind has held academic positions at the Boston University Medical School and the Boston Veterans Administration Medical Center, and is currently James Jackson Putnam Professor of Neurology at Harvard Medical School. He has published many papers dealing with the higher functions of the nervous system, with a special emphasis on anatomical foundations.

**Harold Goodglass** received the B.A. from City College of New York, the M.A. in clinical psychology from New York University, and the Ph.D in clinical psychology from the University of Cincinnati. Dr. Goodglass is director of the Boston University Aphasia Research Center, professor of neurology (neuropsychology) at Boston University, and director of psychology research at the Boston Veterans Administration Medical Center. His major interest is in brain/language relationships, and he has published more than seventy articles and two books in this area. His published works include *Boston Diagnostic Aphasia Test* (coauthored with Edith Kaplan) and *Psycholinguistics and Aphasia* (coedited with Sheila Blumstein).

**Audrey L. Holland** is professor of speech and research assistant professor of psychiatry at the University of Pittsburgh, from which she received the Ph.D. degree. Dr. Holland has taught at Emerson College and worked as a behavioral scientist at the American Institute for Research. Her major clinical and research interests are in the areas of aphasia and speech/language problems of the aging.

**John M. Hutchinson** is an associate professor of speech pathology and director of graduate studies in the Department of Speech Pathology and Audiology at Idaho State University. He received the B.A. degree from the University of Redlands and the M.S. and Ph.D. degrees from Purdue University. He has published more than thirty journal articles and book chapters and is coauthor of *Communication Disorders of the Aged: A Guide for Health Professionals.*

**Mary Jensen** received the bachelor's degree in French from the University of Idaho. She received the master's degree in speech pathology from Idaho State University and worked as a speech therapist with mentally and physically handicapped children in Blackfoot, Idaho. She is currently employed by the Firth, Idaho school district as a speech therapist and teacher of English as a second language to migrant children.

**Edith Kaplan** received the B.A. from Brooklyn College and the M.S. and Ph.D. from Clark University. She is clinical neuropsychologist at the Boston Veterans Administration Medical Center, associate professor of neurology (neuropsychology) at the Boston University School of Medicine, and affiliate professor of psychology at Clark University. Dr. Kaplan is coauthor of *Assessment of Aphasia and Related Disorders* and has written numerous articles on brain/behavior relationships. Her current research focuses on organic implications of neuropsychological deficits in the elderly and the impact of focal lesions on higher cortical functions.

**Marcel Kinsbourne** was educated at Oxford University, where he obtained his medical degree and higher doctorate in medicine (neuropsychology). He trained in pediatrics and in neurology and has held positions in child neurology at Duke University. Dr. Kinsbourne is professor of pediatrics and psychology at the University of Toronto. His research into biobehavioral issues has resulted in about 170 scientific articles and several books, including *Aging and Dementia,* which he coedited. His current research involves relating cognitive life-span developmental findings and drug and diet effects to their brain basis.

**Marjorie J. LeMay** is presently associate professor of radiology at Massachusetts General Hospital, Harvard University Medical School, and radiologist to the University Health Service. She is also assistant clinical professor of neurology (neuroradiology) at the Boston University Medical Center. Dr. Le May received the M.D. from the University of Kansas Medical School. She trained in radiology and worked for some time at Presbyterian Hospital, Columbia University College of Physicians and Surgeons. She was a visiting scientist in the Department of Radiotherapeutics at Cambridge University, England. Since then she has been at teaching hospitals in Boston with the exception of the year she spent as visiting professor and acting chairman of the Department of Radiology at the American University of Beirut. Her interests and publications have been in the field of neuroradiology and particularly in morphological variations of the brain.

**Ralph R. Rupp** received the B.A. and M.A. degrees from the University of Michigan and the Ph.D. degree from Wayne State University. He was formerly a speech and hearing consultant in the Detroit public schools, executive director of the Detroit Hearing and Speech Center, and associate in audiology at the Henry Ford Hospital. He is coauthor (with James Maurer) of *Hearing and Aging: Tactics for Intervention* and is the senior editor of *Speech Protocols in Audiology.* His current interests are in gerontological audiology and in assessment of auditory processing deficits in school-age children.

**Martha Taylor Sarno** is an associate professor of rehabilitation medicine at the Institute of Rehabilitation Medicine of the New York University School of Medicine. She received the Gold Key Award for Distinguished Contributions in Rehabilitation Medicine from the American Congress of Rehabilitation Medicine and was made a Fellow in the American Speech and Hearing Association. Her numerous publications include *Aphasia: Selected Readings, Stroke,* and *Acquired Aphasia.* Her current research focuses on aging and recovery from aphasia after stroke, on delineating the various types of global aphasia, and on long-term follow-up of head trauma.

**K. Warner Schaie** is director of the Research Institute at the Andrus Gerontology Center and professor of psychology at the University of Southern California. He taught previously at the University of Nebraska and West Virginia University, where he chaired the Department of Psychology. He has authored or edited five books and contributed more than a hundred articles to the psychological and gerontological professional literature.

**R. Knight Steel** received the B.A. from Yale University and the M.D. from Columbia University College of Physicians and Surgeons. His current positions are associate professor of medicine and chief of the Geriatrics Section, Division of Medicine, Boston University Medical Center, and director of the Gerontology Center, Boston University. He is recipient of the Geriatric Medicine Academic Award from the National Institute on Aging.

**Martha Storandt** received the Ph.D. in psychology from Washington University, St. Louis, Missouri. For two years she was a clinical psychologist with the Veterans Administration in St. Louis, serving medical and psychiatric geriatric patients. Since that time she has been a faculty member of the Aging and Development Program, Psychology Department, Washington University, and is now associate professor. Her research interests are in the areas of cognition and memory and clinical programs as they relate to older adults. She is coauthor of *Memory, Related Functions and Age* and coeditor of *The Clinical Psychology of Aging.* She presently serves as editor of the Psychological Sciences Section of the *Journal of Gerontology.*

# About the Editors

**Loraine K. Obler** received the bachelor's degree in studies in religion, the master's of arts degrees in linguistics and in Near Eastern languages and literatures, and the Ph.D. in linguistics from the University of Michigan. Dr. Obler worked as a research associate and then as director of the Aranne Laboratory of Human Neuropsychology of the Hadassah Hospital of the Hebrew University in Jerusalem, where she carried out the research on which her earlier book with Martin Albert, *The Bilingual Brain: Neuropsychological and Neurolinguistic Aspects of Bilingualism,* is based. She is now a research associate in psycholinguistics and assistant professor of neurology (neurolinguistics) in the Aphasia Research Center of the Department of Neurology at the Boston Veterans Administration Medical Center and Boston University Medical School. Her current work is on language in aging in both healthy and dementing elderly, monolinguals, and bilinguals.

**Martin L. Albert** is currently professor of neurology and clinical director of the Aphasia Research Center at Boston University Medical School and chief of the Clinical Neurology Section at the Boston Veterans Administration Medical Center. He received the M.D. degree from Tufts Medical School and the doctorate in psychology (neuropsychology) from the University of Paris. He has served as chief physician in the Department of Neurology, Hadassah Hospital of the Hebrew University, Jerusalem; director of the Aranne Laboratory of Human Psychophysiology, Hebrew University Medical School, Jerusalem; and director of the Neurobehavioral Clinic, Boston University Medical Center. He is coauthor of *Human Neuropsychology* (with Henry Hecaen); *The Bilingual Brain: Neuropsychological and Neurolinguistic Aspects of Bilingualism* (with Loraine Obler); and *Clinical Aspects of Aphasia* (with Harold Goodglass, Nancy Helm, Alan Rubens, and Michael Alexander).